Reinventing the Family

Reinventing the Family

The

Emerging

Story

of

Lesbian

and

Gay Parents

Laura Benkov, Ph.D.

Crown Publishers, Inc.
New York

Excerpted from "Good Mirrors Are Not Cheap" by Audre Lorde in CHOSEN POEMS OLD AND NEW. Reprinted with the permission of W.W. Norton & Company, Inc. Copyright © 1970 by Audre Lorde.

"Poem For My Sons" by Minnie Bruce Pratt in CRIME AGAINST NATURE by Minnie Bruce Pratt. Reprinted with the permission of Firebrand Books, Ithaca, New York. Copyright © 1990 by Minnie Bruce Pratt.

The lines for "Eastern War Time" are reprinted from AN ATLAS OF THE DIFFICULT WORLD, poems 1988–1991, by Adrienne Rich, by permission of the author and W.W. Norton & Company, Inc. Copyright © 1991 by Adrienne Rich.

Reprinted from a ON LIES, SECRETS, AND SILENCE, Selected Prose, 1966–1978, by Adrienne Rich, by permission of the author and W.W. Norton & Company, Inc. Copyright © 1979 by W.W. Norton & Company, Inc.

Reprinted from OF WOMAN BORN, Motherhood As Experience and Institution, by Adrienne Rich, by permission of the author and W.W Norton & Company, Inc. Copyright © 1986, 1976 by W.W. Norton & Company, Inc.

Excerpt from "Gay and Conservative," by Margaret O'Brien Steinfels, 12/12/93. Copyright © 1993 by The New York Times Company. Reprinted by permission.

Reprinted by permission of the publishers from THE ALCHEMY OF RACE AND RIGHTS by Patricia Williams, Cambridge, Mass.: Harvard University Press, copyright © 1991 by the President and Fellows of Harvard College.

Published by Crown Publishers, Inc., 201 East 50th Street, New York, New York 10022. Member of the Crown Publishing Group.
Random House, Inc.   New York, Toronto, London, Sydney, Auckland

CROWN is a trademark of Crown Publishers, Inc.

Manufactured in the United States of America

Library of Congress Cataloging-in-Publication Data

Benkov, Laura.
    Reinventing the family : the emerging story of lesbian and gay
parents / Laura Benkov.
        p.   cm.
    Includes bibliographical references.
        1. Gay parents—United States.   2. Custody of children—   United States.   I. Title.
HQ76.3.U5B46   1994
306.85—dc20   94-4822
                                                                          CIP

ISBN 0-517-58743-2
10   9   8   7   6   5   4   3   2   1
First Edition

For my mother, Beatrice Benkov

Contents

Author's Note

While some people I interviewed chose to be identifiable, others wanted to maintain their privacy. Accordingly, some names have been changed. When describing situations that were publicly documented elsewhere (for instance, in court records, newspapers, or literary works), I have used real names, both first and last. Other than that, for the most part first names only are used, sometimes fictional and sometimes real.

*Justice is indivisible. Injustice anywhere
is a threat to justice everywhere.*

Martin Luther King, Jr.

Reinventing the Family

· 1 ·

Journey

Three-year-old Danielle, just home from preschool, is playing with her best friend, Sophie. Their paraphernalia is spread across the living room—a curly-haired doll, a pillow for a "crib," blankets, a "stove" made out of blocks, pots and pans pilfered from the kitchen cabinet, a borrowed pocketbook. They've assembled all the makings for a good game of house, but before they can play they have a conflict to resolve. "I'll be the mommy and you be the daddy," Sophie tells Danielle.

"No, I don't want to be the daddy—and you were the mommy last time," Danielle protests.

"But you always get to be the mommy," Sophie retorts plaintively.

Danielle's mother, Dana, peers over her book, curious about how they'll resolve this struggle. After a few minutes, with no progress in sight, she matter-of-factly suggests, "Why don't you both be mommies?" to which her daughter, exasperated, responds, "You can't have two mommies!" Dana is nonplussed. "But Danielle, you have two mommies!"

The three-year-old is brought up short. "Oh yeah," she says, "I forgot."

About five years later, Dana recalls this scene as the instant in which the power of mainstream culture revealed itself to her. "It showed me that even at three, culture is so strong that it denies your own reality, so strong that you deny what's right in front of your face."

Long before there were children like Danielle, there was Danielle's idea, an age-old notion: you can't have two mommies. You can't have two daddies either, for that matter. You can't be lesbian or gay and also be a good parent. But before there were children like Danielle, someone, somewhere, heard a different voice inside her head. "You can," it whispered, "you can."

To me, the emergence of this voice is a moment of majestic proportions—the moment from which invention springs. As a child I imagined evolution like time-lapse photography. I conjured up images of the history of the world and strung them together in an epic film: the instant the earth came into being, an explosion of matter in an infinity of darkness; fish transforming into reptiles and crawling onto dry land for the first time; apes metamorphosing into humans, their grunts becoming words; cave dwellers moving into structures built with their own hands. I was captivated by the unfathomable in each of these moments: how could something that previously had no existence grow out of all that came before it?

Invention, like evolution, is movement through time. Derived from the Latin *invenire*, it means literally "to come upon, to find." Interestingly, this term has been expanded to refer to the activity of coming upon something in the mind and bringing it forth into the world, thereby creating that which previously did not exist. In this way, invention transforms the very cultural context from which it springs.

I have always been fascinated by the "click"—the moment when the unimaginable becomes possible, simply because the mind opens up to it. I began the project that has led to this book in the midst of my own private "click." In 1979, at age nineteen, I fell in love with a woman. As first love sometimes does, it made me know with unprecedented clarity whom I was and how I wanted to live my life. Being a young adult from a politically progressive family and coming of age in New York City during the height of the feminist movement, I easily embraced my lesbian identity with vigor and pride, even when those around me did not.

Nonetheless, from the moment of our first kiss I was exquisitely aware of the painful and seemingly irresolvable contradiction that had become my life. I was one of those women who with unwavering passion had always wanted to be a mother. In fact, that vision was the only part of my being that I knew to be continuous since the dawn of my consciousness. The desire was but heightened by falling in love. Making a family with my lover felt like the most natural thing in the world, yet it was unimaginable.

I knew no lesbian mothers, and the ones I had heard about had children from previous marriages. Though I didn't know it at the time, there were in fact many lesbians becoming parents. My lover and I must have passed some of them on the street as we walked arm-in-arm, imagining we were the only two lesbians in the world thinking about having children.

Our conversation was driven by my passion and held back by her ambivalence. But somehow I came to know that, whether or not it was possible with her, motherhood was indeed possible for me. Looking back, I see clearly that my realization grew out of one thing only—my urgent move toward self-integration. Even after I realized that I could be a lesbian mother, I still didn't know there were other women choosing that same path. No one in my world was affirming my vision. But it didn't matter—the vision affirmed itself.

Over the years, conflicts between my lover and myself about this issue began to resemble those of any couple, straight, gay, or lesbian who disagree on whether or not to have children. I viewed raising children as unquestionably one of the most valuable life experiences imaginable; she saw primarily the drawbacks of such responsibility and the sacrifices demanded in time and energy.

Although our conversations echoed those of my heterosexual friends, there was at the same time a quality unique to us as lesbians. Often—especially in the beginning—a shameful, homophobic tone crept into the discussion. "Is it possible?" became "Is it fair?" "The world is so homophobic," she said. "What will happen to a child of lesbians?" I reasoned that, as with other prejudices and as we had done, we would help the child develop resilience in the face of bigotry—that although it would take some work, neither the child nor we would bow under. She responded, "You're stronger than I in that way." Those words ushered in a bewildering sense of guilt. It rose in my throat and silenced me.

"You're stronger than I" translated easily to "You're stronger than a child will be." And then, with no one to suggest otherwise, I saw myself inflicting pain on a not-yet-conceived but nonetheless already treasured child—inflicting pain by the very act of bringing her into the world. This, of course, was totally unacceptable to me. Framed this way, the fact that as a lesbian I so longed to nurture a child was in and of itself evidence that I was far too selfish to do so. My central passions—two ways of loving—could not coexist inside this frame. Each seemed destined to destroy the other. But that didn't happen.

The moment of my believing we were the only lesbian couple struggling with these issues was very short-lived. Its power lay not in its duration but rather in its intensity. There is both exhilaration and terror in feeling that unique—that alone in your own uncharted trajectory. In part my guilt and confused silence arose simply from that circumstance. It was not until I moved beyond the isolated discussion with my lover into a larger conversation that I began to make enough sense of that silence to transcend it.

I moved from conversations with my lover to discussions with others—lesbians and gay men who had had children in traditional marriages, and those who were choosing to have children after coming out. As I enlarged my view, I began to see myriad connections between the most private levels of emotional experience and the most public, social interchanges.

My conflict between desire and shame in becoming a lesbian mother reflected but one of many sharp divisions society makes: lesbians and gay men are on one side, and children and families are on the other. My struggle reflected that division, not as a fixed entity but, rather, as an idea in flux. It was no coincidence that I was thinking about lesbian and gay parenting at a moment when both the meaning of "family" and the position of lesbians and gay men in our culture were changing dramatically.

The Meaning of Family

The family as a contested domain in our society is aptly illustrated by an event reported in the *Boston Phoenix* in 1992. Australian Toyota dealers ran an ad aimed at gay audiences, featuring "two thirtyish men, a pair of dalmations, and a picnic basket beside a Toyota Seca Ultima. Its headline: The Family Car. The text says 'When we talk to you about a family car we mean a car that is big enough for a couple and their friends to stretch out in comfort.' " In response, the American Family Association, an archconservative group, called for a Toyota boycott and organized a letter-writing campaign to pressure the company to refrain from advertising that undermines "traditional family values."

I imagine this incident would be perplexing to someone just learning the English language and trying to derive the meaning of *family* from this context. Furthermore, the situation raises this specter: what if the advertisement had included a couple of children? The rigid view that sees lesbians and gay men in opposition to children and families reflects both homophobia and the idealization of a particular family structure—the so-called traditional or nuclear family, consisting of a married heterosexual couple and their biological offspring. Though this structure accounts for a minority of American households, as a culture we cling to the idea that it is the quintessential—some even say the only morally acceptable—family. We tend to think of this family as a natural, perhaps God-given, phenomenon, though a careful look at other places and other times reveals it to be but one of many possible human arrangements.

In actuality, we live in a culture where family structures are far more diverse than our notions about family suggest. In our society many children grow up in families that veer from the traditional model, in a variety of ways, some more obvious than others. Out-of-wedlock pregnancies, divorce, or the death of a parent create single-parent and blended stepfamilies. Current practices address infertility through insemination, surrogacy, or adoption—arrangements which tease apart biological and social parenting roles.

Many people don't set out to diverge from the traditional family, but increasingly more consciously choose alternative family structures, as when unmarried people become parents on their own or in cooperation with others.

Lesbians and gay men become parents on a continuum within this range of family forms. The fact is that lesbians and gay men have always been part of family life and have always had a role in children's lives. We are sons, daughters, brothers, and sisters. We have forged family bonds with each other, whether or not those bonds are acknowledged by the state. Homosexuals with children from previous heterosexual relationships and those choosing to have children after coming out exist in the shadow of the traditional family. At the same time they challenge that model at its core, raising fundamental questions about the relation between gender and parenting, the significance of biological versus social connections, and the role of the state in family life.

Though the traditional family is dwindling in reality, it remains a tremendously powerful force as an institution and ideology. Many people bristle at the thought of diversity in family models, instead seeing nontraditional arrangements as evidence of the "destruction" of the family—both the cause and consequence of societal breakdown.

I have serious trouble with rhetoric that idealizes traditional "family values." When people frame the nuclear family as morally superior, they focus on the shape of families (how many parents? of what gender combination?) rather than on the quality of relationships both within and beyond the family. At the same time, idealizing the traditional family obscures the violence and gender inequity often hidden behind closed doors. Perhaps most important, the emphasis on "family values" diverts attention from societal problems such as poverty and racism by locating all difficulties in "the breakdown of the family."

The rhetoric of "family values" is problematic on another level as well. Not only does it falsely elevate a particular family structure over all others, but it places the concept of the family on the highest moral ground—as though participation in family life were both a necessary and a sufficient determinant of one's humanity.

Lesbians and gay men challenge "family values" rhetoric by expanding the definition of family—emphasizing relational aspects like love and commitment over any particular family structure. We challenge the myth that places lesbians and gay men on the side opposing children and families. And in reclaiming our relations to family life, we assert our humanity in the face of dehumanizing forces. Remapping the territory that constitutes the family is, thus, a critical part of the work we need to do. But in doing this work, it is important we not buy into the fetishism of family—the idea that participation in family life, above all else, defines one's morality and that family relationships are paramount. At a time when so many people live in dire circumstances, we have a responsibility not just to our own but to all humanity.

Homophobia—Lesbians and Gay Men versus Children

Homophobia is intertwined with idealization of the traditional family—they are interdependent though distinct influences in our lives.

The gay rights movement emerged at the end of the 1960s. A strong backlash, denigrating and decrying the very existence of lesbians and gay men, followed close behind. And the symbolic pitting of lesbians and gay men against children has been a key part of that backlash ever since.

Beginning in the 1970s, when more and more gay parents came out publicly, many lost custody and visitation rights solely on the basis of their sexual orientation. In the late 1970s, Anita Bryant launched the Save Our Children campaign to repeal the Dade County, Florida, gay rights law, which led to a Florida statute prohibiting lesbians and gay men from adopting children. Meanwhile, in California, voters narrowly defeated Senator John Briggs's initiative aimed at keeping gay men and lesbians from teaching in the public schools.

During the 1980s, as increasing numbers of lesbians and gay men were becoming parents, Massachusetts and New Hampshire enacted laws to prevent foster care and/or adoption by homosexuals.

Amid the "family values" rhetoric of his 1992 presidential campaign, George Bush ushered in the current decade, declaring that "homosexuals raising children is not normal." As this book goes to press heated battles surround the question of whether books and school curriculum dealing with lesbian and gay issues should be available to children. Once again, the homophobia of the religious right is a virulent force in many cities and states.

Homophobia ranges from the extreme to the subtle. But when it comes to relationships between homosexuals and children, even those who take an antidiscrimination stance often draw the line. Those who attack lesbians and gay men frequently evoke vivid images of monsters who threaten children and family life. These attacks rest on and perpetuate false, narrowly defined images of all parties involved: lesbians, gay men, heterosexuals, and children. According to them, all children are heterosexual, sex is the defining mode of gay—but not straight—life, and gay men are pedophiles out to recruit the next generation.

To the contrary, not all children are straight; and because of their isolation, lesbian and gay youth are three times more likely than their peers to commit suicide. The estimated 4 to 10 million children with lesbian and gay parents are hurt, not helped, by the myths that homophobia perpetuates. As far as sexual abuse goes, perpetrators are predominantly heterosexual men. Though homophobes cast themselves as children's protectors, in reality many children are casualties of their rhetoric.

Silences, Myths, Realities

Both personal and social change require breaking through silences and deconstructing myths. This point was brought home to me time and again during the course of writing this book.

As a graduate student in clinical psychology, I decided to write my dissertation on lesbians who chose to have children. My doctoral program was fairly traditional. The sparse curriculum on homosexuality stressed pathology. Though determined to pursue my work, I was fearful. I stood trembling in the door of my adviser's office as I told him that I wanted to do my dissertation on lesbian mothers. I remember glancing over my shoulder, afraid someone would hear me. Later, I thought about that fear: what was the point of the work, if not eventually to be heard?

From that whispered intention came my first steps. I began my research in New York City in 1983, before the "lesbian baby boom" had taken off. Like all graduate students, I started with a literature review—as it turned out, a very brief literature review. Virtually no one had written about lesbian and gay parents prior to 1979. The only studies I found were done in response to the increasing number of custody battles emerging during the 1970s. For the most part, these studies compared children of divorced lesbians and children of heterosexual mothers, sometimes also divorced, sometimes not. They asked whether children of homosexuals were more likely to have emotional problems, be confused about gender identity or sex roles, or grow up to be gay. Researchers found no differences with respect to these issues.

The psychological literature did not say very much about the lives of lesbian and gay parents or their children. Instead, it described what they were not; lesbian and gay parents had moved from total invisibility in the psychological literature to a presence that was still an absence. Homophobic questions shaped the inquiries, and heterosexual parents constituted the norm against which lesbian and gay parents were measured.

These studies were enormously important in the fight for fair standards in lesbian and gay custody disputes. They dispelled key myths one by one, and allowed many lesbian and gay parents to maintain relationships with their children. Nonetheless, I was distressed that lesbian and gay stories had not been told on their own terms. In the stacks of psychology journals, I searched to no avail for images of myself and of the women I would soon interview. I was not naïve; I hadn't really expected to find myself represented in these journals. Yet as I surveyed the vast quantity of writing, the noticeable absence made me feel as if I were in a horror film, passing a mirror and seeing no reflection.

Simultaneously dismayed by the existing studies and appreciative of what they had accomplished, I realized that I was beginning my work from a particular historical vantage point. I had the luxury to look beyond such frameworks, because those studies already existed. Lesbian and gay parents still lose custody in court, but in contrast to the early 1970s, there is now a body of respected literature that can be brought to their defense.

Perhaps I am emblematic of the evolution of lesbian and gay voices. As one currently popular gay rights slogan goes "Homophobia? Get over it." As with all marginalized groups, the progress of lesbians and gay men depends in part on being able to answer to and dismantle stereotypes. But this is a process that rather quickly becomes quite tiresome. It's unacceptable to define oneself strictly in contrast to myths. I was fortunate in beginning my work from a position of both wanting to move beyond such limits and of having the opportunity to do so. When I began my work, I needed to know how lesbian parents saw their lives: the issues they struggled with and the resolutions they found. I set out to create a mirror that would reflect their realities. As a lesbian wanting to be a mother myself, I most hungered for their descriptions.

At first I thought little about what these lesbian motherhood stories would mean to the heterosexual world. But that changed when, shortly after I began my research, I sent my pilot interviews to a member of my dissertation committee. Married and a new father, he found himself connecting with one woman's description of her child's first year. "It was really amazing," he said. "I'd be reading along, feeling so identified with her, then it would hit me that this woman is a lesbian!"

I asked him what he meant. "Well, you know," he said, "I hadn't expected it to be so normal. I'd thought as a lesbian she'd relate to the child in a narcissistic way, as an extension of herself," he explained, echoing the pathologizing characterization of homosexuality prevalent in the psychoanalytic community of which he was a part. Knowing no lesbians, he had nonetheless quite developed ideas about them.

My first reaction was regret that I hadn't screened him before asking him to be on my committee. But later I realized how unfortunate that would have been, as I saw those lesbian voices transform his understanding.

At that point, I grasped how wide the gulf is separating true lesbian and gay experiences and what many well-meaning people believe about homosexuals. I also learned how difficult and yet crucial it is to speak across that gulf. Though not always, homophobia is sometimes more a matter of ignorance than of hatred—or more accurately, a matter of ignorance into which the language of hatred seeps. It is not surprising that this occurs. Homophobia is ubiquitous, while much of lesbian and gay life is still blocked from view. We often think we know a great deal about things we have no experience of. Bigotry thrives on that tendency—it is what enables reality to be drowned out by myth.

I began this work with a narrow focus that gradually expanded over the years. Initially, I most wanted to hear from women similar to me. What kinds of families do lesbians create? What obstacles do they face? What lessons do they learn along the way? As I listened to the stories of lesbians who chose to have children, I grew more interested in the broader phenomenon of lesbian and gay parenting. There was a history I needed to understand. Those who had children before coming out had laid the groundwork for the "lesbian baby boom" we were now in the midst of. Many of them had borne the brunt of the most vehement initial homophobic attacks on lesbian and gay parents. As my work progressed, so too did the lesbian and gay parenting boom. Gay men choosing to be fathers were few and far between when I began my research, but soon they were contributing a fascinating comparison between the old and new ways that gender shapes parenting. Perhaps most important, my research expanded to include the children raised by lesbians and gay men. Throughout the work, they often were the ones who asked the most pointed questions and helped me see things anew.

Individual and Social Change

These days I often meet young lesbians and gay men who assume they'll have children when they're ready. I am taken aback by their certainty, amazed that they have never experienced the sense of impossibility that so clouded my path little more than a decade earlier. Back then, isolated in my wish to be a lesbian mother, I had no inkling that the lesbian baby boom was just around the corner. Now I am struck by how easy it is, in the heat of the struggle to invent one's life, to be blind to our interdependency. Though I didn't know it at first, I was clearly a product of my time. My own journey was predicated on changes wrought by those who came before me, and it would in turn become part of other people's futures.

I see the relationship between individual consciousness and culture as similar to the process of painting. An artist uses tools that are manufactured by people, out of materials derived from nature. These tools include a canvas, brushes, and paint. As an artist approaches her canvas, she brings an individual consciousness that has been formed in particular social and historical contexts, and she uses symbols derived from those contexts. Thus culture is within the painting, and in fact makes it possible. Simultaneously, the artist's approach is uniquely her own. She creates a painting that is both part of her world and part of herself. The painting, which is now both a material object and an extension of her consciousness, is available for others to view. Its image is taken up in other people's minds and creates a new set of possibilities. For instance, a person viewing the painting might be moved to see a particular situation anew and, in turn, create something of her own. Thus, culture creates and transforms our lives, just as we create and transform culture.

When lesbians and gay men create families, these families are part of the world and influence it as much as they are influenced by it. This kind of relationship between individual and social change is strikingly clear in the legal arena. While during the 1970s the primary legal issues with respect to lesbian and gay parenting were custody disputes involving heterosexual divorces, now the courts must grapple with more complex questions: Is a sperm donor a father? What are the rights of nonbiological lesbian and gay parents in the event of a split-up or death? One of the most important issues highlighted by lesbian and gay parenting is the role of the state in regulating our most intimate relationships. Families are shaped in part by legal parameters, but new types of families challenge those parameters.

The process of invention interweaves social and personal change. As lesbians and gay men create new family forms, they work within the set of limits and possibilities of the cultural context. In this process, they also feed back into the culture, transforming the set of constraints and possibilities therein.

The Book's Structure

In this book I examine the tensions between dominant notions of the family and the realities of families headed by lesbian and gay parents. Chapters 2 and 3 explore the experiences of parents coming out of heterosexual marriages. These gay men and lesbians reconceptualized themselves and their sense of family, tearing apart the automatic pairing of heterosexuality and parenthood. Their custody battles produced a legal discourse in which homophobia was articulated for the first time and then contested. By the 1980s, AIDS began to figure prominently in many custody disputes. Chapters 2 and 3 examine these developments, focusing both on individual experiences and on legal developments.

Questions about lesbians and gay men as parents, as taken up by the state in relation to adoption and foster care, form the basis of the next chapter. Chapter 4 explores the battles surrounding legislation banning gay adoption and/or foster care in Florida, Massachusetts, and New Hampshire, and also describes the role homophobia plays in the experiences of prospective lesbian and gay parents.

Lesbians and gay men create families in the context of the complex, changing social circumstances that surround parenting in our culture today, including quickly evolving developments in reproductive technology and an adoption system rife with class and race issues. Homophobia and the ideology of the traditional family affect access to reproductive technology and adoption. The role of the state and social institutions such as the medical system in regulating family life is clearly manifest in this arena. At the same time, these ways of forming families raise other complex issues. Do children need both fathers and mothers? How significant are one's genetic roots? How does one think about the creation of a transracial or transcultural family through adoption?

Lesbians and gay men create families that do not fit the legal parameters of the family. Hence there is conflict between people's self-definitions of their families and the states' definitions. For example, lesbian and gay couples cannot adopt as couples, but must instead do single-parent adoptions. In the case of biological conception, many lesbians conceive with the help of a known donor whom the family may not consider the father, but who is seen as the father by the courts. Beyond this conflict of definitions, the realm of family creation is fascinating because lesbians and gay men are inventing new forms, such as four-parent families. Chapters 5 through 7 explore these issues as they play out in people's ways of structuring their families.

Chapter 5 looks at how lesbians and gay men who have chosen biological conception structure their family relationships. It focuses particularly on how ideas surrounding the traditional family model are both absorbed and challenged by lesbians and gay men creating new family forms.

Chapter 6 looks at notions of gendered parenting roles, the significance of biological versus social connections, and how a lack of societal recognition affects the way homosexuals establish and feel about parenting roles. Are there two mommies or daddies? Is one more real than the other? How is the work of parenting divided in the absence of gender differences? In the realm of gender, lesbian and gay parents both mimic society's dominant notions and challenge them.

Chapter 7 looks at how language influences the construction of family life. It explores the process of naming children and of determining role names such as "mama" or "mommy." Particular uses of language grow out of and also affect the relationship between gay families and their surrounding communities.

Chapter 8 explores how families interact with both their immediate and larger communities, focusing on how parents and children deal with coming out. I also look at the controversial issue of presenting lesbian and gay lifestyles in the school curriculum—an issue which has sparked debate in many communities.

Chapter 9 turns to the legal issues that lesbian and gay parenting raises: What happens in the event of the death of a biological or legal parent, given that nonbiological, nonadoptive parents have no legal standing as parents? Similarly, given the legal assymetries created by the dominant notion of the family, what happens to children when lesbian and gay parents split up? This section explores the often tragic consequences of conflicting definitions of the family, and looks at the new legal definition that is needed in order to protect children from traumatic loss.

Our society's foundation, its very bedrock, has been shaken by the realization of lesbian and gay parenthood. When lesbians and gay men reveal their connections with children, as part of families of their own, a cultural earthquake ensues. We are in the midst of many such quakes. This book is a chronicle of the faultlines, tremors, aftershocks, and landscapes we reconstruct.

· 2 ·

Toward an Unknown Place

Parents Come Out

I can only pray:

That you'll never ask for weather, earth,
angels, women, or other lives to obey you;

that you'll remember me, who crossed, recrossed
you,

as a woman making slowly toward
an unknown place where you could be with me,
like a woman on foot, in a long stepping out.
Minnie Bruce Pratt
"Poem For My Sons"

She sat motionless at the bottom of the stairwell listening to the rhythmic breathing of her children sleeping above. Their soft and steady sighs were punctuated by an occasional cricket, the only reminder that there was a world outside this house. The night was so still that it seemed something must be about to happen—some sudden crack of thunder, a blinding flash of light. Or could this go on forever? The peace around her only served to underscore the turmoil inside. She sat this way for hours, listening.

Above her they slept, each embracing the night just as he approached the days—the seven-year-old tossing and turning until his covers were strewn halfway across the room, the five-year-old melting into his sheets as though they were his nighttime skin. She would always remember them this way.

Their sleeping bodies pressed against her mind as she sat in the stairwell reviewing her options. Options—the irony of the word made her grimace. She had begun to hear the whispers of voices long buried inside her. They called to her more and more clearly. She wanted to let them take her to the place where she belonged. But she couldn't imagine that she would be allowed to take the children with her to this land where women embraced each other— this land where it seemed there were no mothers.

When she thought about her life without them, and their lives without her, she saw only gaping wounds—wounds beyond all healing. She recoiled from this vision and tried to imagine staying—simply rising from the stairwell and turning off the voices as she flicked the light switch on the living room wall.

But then she saw herself years from now desperately trying to revive these long-lost voices. You couldn't do it, of course. That's why you have to take hold of the life inside you while you can.

A Mother Comes Out—Fayetteville, North Carolina, 1975

How had she come to be in this place, sitting at the bottom of a stairwell suspended between two nightmare visions of her future: exile from the children she had borne, suckled, and loved immeasurably; or exile from her self?

Minnie Bruce Pratt was born in Selma, Alabama, in 1946. She grew up in Centreville, a poor town in the last county at the southern end of the Appalachian mountains. She was an only child, raised to be a good Southern woman. Growing up in an emotionally arid home, she sought company in books. She huddled in the attic, avidly consuming tales of other lives, other worlds. She never thought of herself as someone who was going to get married; she thought of herself as someone who would work. Her father was an alcoholic and her mother, a social worker, was the economic mainstay of the family. Despite rhetoric to the contrary, Minnie Bruce knew early on that if you were a woman you had to be ready to work because you couldn't necessarily count on a man.

She had never thought of herself as a lesbian. In fact, throughout her teen years in a Southern town during the sixties, neither the word nor the concept existed for her, though she had always had close female friends. "You can look back and say 'look, look.' My first girlfriend when I was five years old—we used to get into roaring fights," Minnie Bruce recalls. "My last girlfriend in high school—we were drummers together in the band—she's a lesbian now. I had a sense of us being strange and different together in a completely unarticulated way." As often happens in adolescence, the intensity of those childhood loves gave way to convention. Yet Minnie Bruce did not slip into heterosexuality. She made a choice. "I know exactly when I decided that I had to accommodate myself to boys. My friend went through a very difficult time in her life, and had a breakdown and was sent away to a mental institution. She was very poor. I turned away from her at that point. I said 'I'm not going to have anything to do with her. I'm going to make myself pleasing to boys.' So I became heterosexual. I began to make an effort."

In the fall of 1964, Minnie Bruce went off to the University of Alabama, where she was soon introduced by her freshman composition teacher to the editor of the campus literary magazine. He was the first person who ever talked to her about poetry. "It was an era when if you were a good girl you didn't have sex without being married. I had sexual feelings. He asked me to marry him."

Her future husband was going to be a poet, and Minnie Bruce was going to support the family. That was their plan when they got married. He was the poet. She was a poet, "sort of, not really." The fact that she had started to write poetry, and had won a prize or two, did not deter their professors from confidently telling him, "you're going to be the poet," and then turning to Minnie Bruce to say, "you're going to be the academic."

They were married in December, and by November of the following year she was pregnant. She was a senior and twenty-one years old.

Right after she found out that she was pregnant, Minnie Bruce received other news: she'd been granted a Fulbright scholarship. If she accepted the grant, she would deliver two weeks before her arrival in England. She would be alone with an infant because her husband couldn't leave the country; the Vietnam War was raging, and he was about to be reclassified 1A. "In a kind of desperation I went to the only woman dean in the university. I think I wanted her to tell me I could do it, or to just help me try to figure it out. She was very cold and discouraging, saying something along the lines of 'obviously you can't do this.' "

Minnie Bruce declined the Fulbright. Instead she took a job as a temporary bookkeeper for a construction firm in order to pay for her pregnancy. It was a moment of self-submersion that almost went unnoticed; it seemed simply to be part of the natural order of life. She was, after all, about to become a mother.

She delivered her first son in 1968, and began graduate school in North Carolina about a month after he was born. She tried to get married-student housing but couldn't because she was a woman. Instead of a financial test, married women were screened out whereas married men, even those whose wives worked, were accepted. That was her introduction to overt sexual discrimination.

Inexperienced and young when the baby was born, Minnie Bruce and her husband learned about parenting as they went along. They shared child care, arranging their schedules so that each was home three days a week. He was a difficult baby; he had colic, which made him scream and cry for days on end. It was physically exhausting, but they seemed to be managing. Then, when the baby was nine months old, Minnie Bruce got pregnant again.

She attended classes throughout her pregnancy, an uncommon occurrence at the time. When the men at the university joked about being caught in the elevator with her, she felt lonely and uncomfortable, but she had no words to explain these feelings to herself. She had not yet discovered feminism. In fact, she used to cross to the other side of the street to avoid the table containing feminist literature because it frightened her so.

One winter evening, a student in her Shakespeare seminar walked her to the parking lot. She was the person who staffed the infamous literature table. "I just wanted to tell you that I know this is really hard," she said. "Lots of women would give up and go back to being a housewife. I think what you're doing is great. I hope you'll be able to keep going." That night, Minnie Bruce drove home with tears streaming down her face. "Nobody had acknowledged any of it—all they had done was make jokes. Nobody had said 'This is really hard.' It was just like 'That's what you do—accept being pregnant and having a nine-month-old and being in graduate school.' Nobody said anything. She was the only one."

Gradually, Minnie Bruce became a feminist. She began to recognize that there was a culture—an intellectual challenge—that excited her more than her English studies. Feminism reached down to the submerged core of her being, touching the child huddled with books in the attic, the young girl who loved her female friends—the self she had long ago turned away from. She saw a glimmer of another way to live; once surfaced, this vision could not be submerged yet again. She was at home with the children and was supposed to be writing her dissertation, but instead she fell in love with another woman and came out.

So that is how she came to be sitting in the stairwell, knowing that to move into the future, she had first to traverse a fork in the road that seemed to require nothing less than tearing apart her very soul.

The question that kept her chained to the stairwell, unable to move forward, was this: could she be true to the self she was just coming to know and at the same time be a good mother to the children sleeping upstairs? If the answer were to be found in her heart alone, it would be easy. What better way to mother than as a full, loving person, living an authentic life? Having made her way past the deadening maze of "shoulds" and "oughts" to her deepest truths, she knew her authenticity could only strengthen her ability to nurture her children, to light in whatever way a parent can their paths so that they, too, could find the ways to their own truths. To be a lesbian and a mother—yes, of course, it was possible.

Yet she also knew that the answer was not to be found in her heart alone. It would be forged, as the question itself was, by the time and place she and her family were suspended in—a time and place in which it seemed lesbian mothers did not, could not, exist. Mothers, American as apple pie, were model women. They were deferential, nurturing, and generous to the point of selflessness. Lesbians were aberrant, unwomanly creatures—selfish, disturbed, immoral criminals. Just as surely as children needed to be nurtured by mothers, they needed to be protected from lesbians. These ideas lived not only in the hearts and minds of many citizens but also formed the foundation of American life.

Women like Minnie Bruce were, to borrow a phrase from the lesbian mother and poet Adrienne Rich, "outlaws from the institution of motherhood." In her landmark book *Of Woman Born* (1976), Rich distinguished between "two meanings of motherhood, one superimposed on the other: the *potential relationship* of any woman to her powers of reproduction and to children; and the *institution*," reflected in social processes such as devaluing the everyday tasks of mothering, the isolation from which most women mother, and the prevalence of theories attributing psychological and social problems to various kinds of bad mothering. Rich saw the institution of motherhood as inextricably bound to the institution of heterosexuality and the oppression of women. She pointedly questioned the nature of motherhood in our society. What ideas about mothering do women bring to the experience of raising children? How do these ideas affect family relationships? Where do these ideas come from? And most important of all, What other possible ways of constructing motherhood are available? Describing time spent alone with her three young sons, she wrote:

> . . . we fell into what I felt to be a delicious and sinful rhythm. It was a spell of unusually hot, clear weather, and we ate nearly all our meals outdoors, hand to mouth; we lived half naked, stayed up to watch bats and stars and fireflies, read and told stories, slept late. I watched their slender, little-boys' bodies grow brown, we washed in water warm from the garden hose lying in the sun, we lived like castaways on some island of mothers and children. At night they fell asleep without murmur and I stayed up reading and

writing as I had when a student, till the early morning hours. I remember thinking: This is what living with children could be—without school hours, fixed routines, naps, the conflict of being both mother and wife with no room for being simply myself. . . . We were conspirators, outlaws from the institution of motherhood; I felt enormously in charge of my life. Of course, the institution closed down on us again, and my own mistrust of myself as a "good mother" returned, along with my resentment of the archetype. But I knew even then that I did not want my sons to act for me in the world, any more than I wished for them to kill or die for their country. I wanted to act, to live, in myself and to love them for their separate selves.

As an "outlaw from the institution of motherhood," Rich discovered the pleasure of being in charge of her own life and the joy of being able to be herself along with her children, who also were able to be themselves. Noting these feelings as extraordinary, she thought about how her usual experience of mothering made her feel less in control of her life. She recognized that this loss of control was not a necessary corollary of motherhood, but rather a direct consequence of particular societal expectations of mothers— expectations quintessentially linked to women's oppression.

Feminists like Rich were among the first to challenge the pervasive notion that a "good" mother is, by definition, self-sacrificing. Central to that notion is an image of the mother's and children's needs in opposition to one another. In describing her brief respite from the institution of motherhood, Rich turned that idea on its head, suggesting instead that when a mother extricates herself from the experience of oppression and begins to value her capacity to act from a strong sense of herself, both she and her children can thrive. Frequently what society declares to be in the interests of children might better be understood as the interests of the larger culture projected on to children. In those instances, teasing apart the child's needs from society's demands can put mothers and children on the same, rather than opposite, sides of the fence.

The vision of authenticity that drives anyone's coming-out process takes on particular significance when the person coming out is a mother. As long as motherhood is characterized by selflessness, to speak and act authentically—that is, from a strong sense of one's self—is to fly in the face of the "good mother" archetype. Can a woman who speaks in her own voice and acts on her own behalf be a good mother? A resounding "No!" reveals itself in the form of guilt that a mother struggling to come out might feel or rage that others may direct at her. As society enforces the split between lesbian and mother, many face an impossible choice.

Minnie Bruce sat in the dimly lit stairwell trying to figure out her next move. The problem was, she couldn't predict the future. In that moment so fraught with uncertainty and grave consequence, all she could do was assess the risks and look deeply into her soul. Truths about lesbian mothers were rarely told, and even less often heard; instead, a cloud of silence and myth enveloped the nation. As she sat in the stairwell contemplating her family's future, Minnie Bruce knew that this cloud would exert a destructive force wherever it appeared, whether in her own imagination or that of her husband, children, neighbors, and the North Carolina courts. But she also knew that there was no turning back and, underneath her fear, she had faith. In the end, it seemed there was no choice really; as a human being and as a mother, only a life of integrity made sense. So she rose from the stairwell and turned toward the unknown.

Days later Minnie Bruce would sit in this same place and watch as her older son screamed "No! No! No!", running in circles around the room like a trapped bird bouncing from wall to wall in search of a way out. The younger boy sat so calmly that she wondered if he had taken in the news. Minnie Bruce and her husband had already had their words—the accusations, the smashed chairs. When it was all over, they'd decided she would move out. They'd continue to share child care, and they would tell the boys together. So here they were. She'd thought so deeply about how to help them through it, how to let them know they'd both be there loving them no matter what. But now one boy sat in Sphinxlike silence while the room swelled with his brother's panicked cries.

In the new house, life was pared down to essentials—a stove, a bed, books, her journals. At first she cared for the boys as they had arranged, but soon it became clear that this was not to be. Her husband said she was a bad mother. He didn't want them to visit when her lover was there. He never said the word *lesbian*, but it hovered over all of them in the deafening way that unspoken words do. Once, early on, her older son asked her if she were in love with Star. "Yes," she answered. "Oh," he said. It seemed so simple. But when the arrangements became strained, she dared not speak of it. She was up against the wall; everywhere she looked, loss loomed large.

"He has a good case against you," the Raleigh lawyer said as she opened the book of statutes. "You shouldn't have moved out. You should have made him move out, or you should have taken the children with you. He can get you for desertion, for abandonment." Then she read the state's sodomy statute out loud: "If any person shall commit the crime against nature, with mankind or beast, (s)he shall be guilty of a felony, and shall be fined or imprisoned in the discretion of the court." Another lawyer said simply this: "The world is not ready for someone like you."

Indeed, the world was not ready. Embedded in every social institution, homophobia is often indicated only by silence—that is, until the silence is broken by lesbians and gay men themselves. When lesbian and gay parents first began to declare themselves, they moved from a position of invisibility to one of castigation as previously covert homophobia burst violently on to the scene. A societal struggle was under way, which would yield many casualties along with transformation. Minnie Bruce and her family were among thousands on the front lines of that struggle.

Of all the institutions where fear and hatred of homosexuals flourish, the legal system has perhaps the greatest impact. While the church or media may comment harshly, the courts actually shape and determine the fates of families. Divorce is one occasion when the state's powerful role in family life is explicit: relationships that may have seemed a matter of private consensus become clearly subject to state law. In that moment it is obvious that families are not naturally occurring, isolated and autonomous units. They are socially constructed arrangements embedded in and formed by the power relations of the surrounding culture.

Thus the warning that the world was not ready for someone like Minnie Bruce. She was trying to find a way to maintain her relationship with her children in a time when lesbian mothers were anathema. In the eyes of the state, by definition, *lesbian* and *mother* canceled each other out. Feminists were not the only ones to recognize the threat lesbian mothers posed to the status quo; judges also saw all too clearly the potential for lesbian mothers to redefine the family.

It is not surprising that some judges' most castigating views of lesbian mothers decried their "selfishness." From this perspective, lesbianism is an affront because it reveals the mother as a person who declares her own sexual identity and so pursues fulfillment of her own needs and desires—the implication being that she does so in opposition to the needs of her child. This "selfishness" is seen as incompatible with the "selflessness" of proper motherhood. As one judge commented about an openly lesbian mother, "While mother's homosexuality may be beyond her control, submitting to it and living with a person of the same sex in a sexual relationship is not. Just as an alcoholic overcomes the habit and becomes a non-drinker, so this mother should attempt to dissolve her alternative lifestyle of homosexual living." He went on to juxtapose the image of the selfish lesbian with the virtuousness of the selfless mother: "Such is not too great a sacrifice to expect of a parent in order to gain or retain custody of his or her child. This Court can take judicial notice of the fact that throughout the ages, dedicated, loving parents have countless times made much greater sacrifices for their children."

Another judge expressed a similar sentiment as he found a lesbian mother unfit: "I don't say that a mother cannot be fit to rear her children even if she is a lesbian, but I wonder if she is fit when she boldly and brazenly sets up in the home where the children are to be reared the lesbian practices which have been current there, clearly to the detriment of the children." In this particular case, there was no evidence of neglect and the judge didn't explain the allegation. Apparently, the mother's "brazen lesbian practices" were themselves "detrimental."

In 1975, in Fayetteville, North Carolina—a conservative town that was home to the 82nd Airborne Division and to country clubs that were closed to blacks and Jews, a town where news of women being beaten or murdered by their husbands was not uncommon— Minnie Bruce, a lesbian and active feminist, faced a decision about whether to enter the local courts and fight for custody of her children.

Her vulnerability within the local community and larger legal structure seeped into all aspects of the negotiations between Minnie Bruce and her husband. Initially he asked her to sign a document saying she had no rights and that he would decide when she could see the children—period. Either she would agree to that, his lawyer said, or not see her children at all.

She refused to sign. They went through another round of negotiation, this one yielding a settlement that said she couldn't have the children in her home if she were living with anyone else, and couldn't take them out of state except in the company of her mother or one of her aunts. She was allowed to see her sons weekly, and for two weeks in the summer and some alternating holidays. The restrictions in this pact were far more limiting than typical visitation agreements, which usually allow unrestricted access to children if the custodial parent is given notice, and do not stipulate living arrangements or travel plans.

"The lawyer said he just didn't think that we could go to court," Minnie Bruce recounted. "He said I would lose them completely because people weren't ready for someone like me. He said maybe some time down the road people will be able to accept this, but they weren't ready then. Everything around me seemed to indicate that that was true. I felt intensely isolated. I knew no other lesbian mothers. My lover said that if we ended up in court, she didn't want to testify because she didn't want to be open about being gay. My husband said he was going to call my mother to testify on his side and I think she probably would have—to this day she is sickened by the thought of my lesbianism. At the time I wasn't out to my mother because I was afraid. By the time I was in the middle of the divorce negotiations I wasn't telling anyone. I wasn't talking to the children or my mother about it because I was afraid that they could all be called into court and then the words out of my own mouth—the fact that I'd said I was having a relationship with a woman—would be used against me. There was no sense that there were other legal strategies to take or somebody to go to bat for me."

Minnie Bruce accepted the settlement. It seemed to be the best she could get. Soon after, their father took the children to Kentucky. Thus began the years of absence, their separate lives bridged only by sixteen-hour car rides, long-distance phone calls, letters sealed with tears. This is what they remember of that time: the absences, the bridges.

Often those in the vanguard of a critical social shift experience themselves not as an integral part of history, but rather as isolated, outside the realm of human community. Though there were thousands of women throughout the country similarly struggling, Minnie Bruce like most of them, felt completely alone. In proclaiming her true self, she crossed a line to become a seeming contradiction in terms: a lesbian mother.

The experiences of parents who, like Minnie Bruce, came out during the early 1970s were largely shaped by the fact that they were moving in a cultural vacuum—there was no precedent, no dialogue. But as more and more parents came out, the cultural landscape was irrevocably transformed. These women made society take its first steps toward recognizing that *lesbian* and *mother* are not mutually exclusive terms. Now that the world could see there was such a thing as lesbian and gay parents, would they be allowed to exist? Could you come out and remain a parent?

Over the years that followed her sons grew up in the shadow of their mother's absence and Minnie Bruce struggled to make sense of her life shorn of children. All the while, throughout the nation a battle was brewing. Although the struggle would yield change too late to help Minnie Bruce and her children directly, they were an integral part of the spirit of change. The silence had been broken and the challenge was made.

It is almost twenty years since Minnie Bruce came out and lost her children. Stories like hers mark the beginning of a struggle that continues today. Though people in the 1990s are more able to live as openly lesbian or gay parents, many still suffer losses such as Minnie Bruce's or try to avoid them by staying in the closet. The fact that there are any openly lesbian or gay parents is a direct result of the courage of people like Minnie Bruce, who took the first steps. We should not be surprised that their stories are often tales of loss. Like all struggles to overcome oppression, the story of lesbian and gay parents begins with courage in the face of great danger.

Breaking the Silence

A recent rash of murders in the Boston area prompted the local media to focus on battered women. Among the many horrifying aspects of such domestic violence that these murders brought to light was the fact that leaving an abusive situation can pose as much danger as staying. Many of the women murdered each year are killed just after they take steps to free themselves. The failure of our communities to protect women at this stage is literally deadly, since frequently it is the moment after a woman leaves her abuser that he is most likely to kill her.

Other women, in the face of such grim stories, must nonetheless continue to find the courage to leave and the protection to help them survive the move. If they don't leave, they remain not only in constant danger but also sentenced indefinitely to a living death—to the spiritual erosion that comes of constant degradation and threats.

The violent dramas enacted in so many American homes parallel those that occur on a larger societal level. Intimidation whittles away the human spirit and fear keeps people locked in degrading circumstances. Resistance requires tremendous courage because it is inevitably met with violent backlash. The maintenance of all relations of domination and oppression stems largely from one awful fact: the threshold to freedom is the most heavily guarded and perilous place to stand.

When people first move from tacit acceptance of domination toward active resistance, they often face increased terrorization. In fact, frequently their only hope lies in their willingness to confront the backlash head-on. History is rife, not with stories of smooth and effortless blossoming of freedom, but with bloody battles marked by tragic losses that only sometimes lead to self-determination. For instance, the civil rights movement in this country, like so many struggles throughout the world, was shaped by people who were willing to take great risks in the effort to extricate themselves and others from the bonds of oppression.

All liberation struggles are endangered by the pull toward fearful retreat, but the battle for lesbian and gay rights has been plagued by a particularly insidious form: the closet. In a world of threats, closets seem to be the only sanctuary. Alas, their apparent safety is a deceit, for closets are the place where all is lost.

When people begin to identify lesbian or gay desires in themselves, they confront their very existence. Do they live honestly in relation to their desires, or do they turn away from that part of themselves, suppressing their homosexuality? The process of coming out is a move toward authenticity—not only a profound personal experience but also a societal one. As lesbians and gay men speak the truth, society is also pushed toward authenticity, replacing public myths of both homosexual and heterosexual existence with acknowledgment of more nuanced, complex—and heretofore hidden—realities.

A popular fantasy in lesbian and gay circles invites us to imagine what would happen if even just for one day all homosexuals woke up with purple skin. No doubt many assumptions would be shaken,

as the ranks of supposed heterosexuals were revealed to be pep-
pered with queers. This fantasy is about freedom from constant
tension and fear. It is compelling in direct proportion to its distance
from reality.

Homophobia works not just to keep lesbians and gay men silent
and underground but also to prescribe heterosexuality itself. Many
people who might otherwise be inclined toward same-sex relationships will never sense that possibility in themselves given a homophobic climate. In this way, homophobia curtails the very
existence of lesbians and gay men. Then there are those who,
aware of their homosexual desires, don't dare act on their feelings,
or if they do, do so in secret. In these instances, it is not the
existence but rather the visibility of homosexuality that is in question. As long as homosexuality is bound by a continuum ranging
from nonexistence to invisibility, oppression is easily maintained.
Some go through life cut off from their most essential selves, while
others live in constant fear of discovery. To fight the homophobic
threat, lesbians and gay men must recognize the truth about themselves and be willing to speak about it. Only when they move
beyond invisibility to public existence can lesbians and gay men
challenge the status quo.

The range of lesbian and gay oppression is matched by a parallel
range of manifestations of homophobia. At their most extreme,
homophobes decry the very existence of lesbians and gay men.
The more subtle homophobes attack speech rather than existence.
Many claim not to have anything against lesbians and gay men, and
even to believe they should be able to live in peace, "if only they
wouldn't flaunt their sexuality, throwing it in everyone's face."
Much current debate revolves not around the issue of existence but
around the issue of speech. Witness how quickly the question of
whether lesbians and gay men should be allowed to serve in the
military became instead a question of whether to establish a policy
of absolute silence about their presence.

Of course, questions of existence and speech are not so far apart
as some may imagine. If it really were okay to be lesbian or gay, it

would be okay to talk about it. It is speech that most profoundly threatens the status quo.

All lesbian and gay struggles can become bogged down by fearful retreat to the closet or, conversely, pushed forward by the willingness to venture out, but both the difficulties of emerging and the profound impact of public declaration are especially clear in the case of lesbian and gay parents.

The struggle of lesbian and gay parents must be seen both as part of the larger struggle of lesbians and gay men and on its own terms. Although the parents who came out in the early 1970s were embedded in the gay rights and feminist movements, their experiences were also unique. They were not simply men and women coming out; they were *parents* coming out. As such, they faced two of the most powerful facets of homophobia: abhorrence of any association between homosexuals and children; and the belief that lesbians and gay men exist in opposition to family life. Often their lives seemed anomolous. These men and women fit into neither the world of lesbians and gay men, which appeared to exclude children, nor the world of parents, which apparently excluded homosexuals.

The split between homosexuality and children is self-perpetuating, despite its lack of connection to reality. Long before there was public awareness of homosexual parents, there were parents who were lesbian or gay. Many lived as heterosexuals because other options were unimaginable. Wanting children, others chose to get married because it seemed the only way to become a parent. Still others realized their sexual orientation later in life, after having had children in heterosexual unions.

With the dynamics of the closet entrenched in lesbian and gay experience, it took little overt expression for homophobia to exert control. At first, with almost no legal precedents one way or the other, simply the knowledge that a negative response was lurking in the wings, kept many homosexual parents confined to the closet. The situation might have remained static indefinitely. But during the early 1970s, despite tremendous isolation and vulnerability, record numbers of parents like Minnie Bruce came out.

When Minnie Bruce left the bottom of the stairwell, she began to inch her way out of the closet. She knew that she wanted to be with a woman. At that point, she could have turned away from that knowledge and remained, for all intents and purposes, a heterosexual mother. Or she could have chosen a double existence—wife and mother by day, lesbian by night. If she had made either of those decisions, and if no one else revealed her secret, she wouldn't have challenged the status quo. But Minnie Bruce made a different decision, acknowledging to herself and to others that she—a mother—was also a lesbian.

As Minnie Bruce and others moved from silence to speech, a most interesting dynamic emerged: as parents came out, so too did homophobia. While we readily recognize the closets of homosexuals, we are much less often aware of the closeted nature of homophobia. However, in the case of lesbian and gay parents, this dimension is hard to miss. No one explicitly said that lesbians and gay men couldn't be parents until parents began to come out publicly and their cases entered the courts. Only at that point did increasingly violent homophobic sentiments emerge. In fact, before 1974 there were virtually no documented custody hearings involving lesbian and gay parents. As increasing numbers of openly lesbian or gay parents entered the courtrooms, previously intangible homophobic and heterosexist views became quite clearly articulated. It was this articulation itself that provided the basis for challenge. It is much easier to fight an enemy one can clearly see, than to struggle against an ominous but hidden threat.

The 1970s were a critical juncture for lesbian and gay parents. It was the moment they moved beyond the continuum of nonexistence and invisibility to the point of public emergence. Speaking out brought Minnie Bruce and others like her to the threshold of freedom—that most perilous place. Not surprisingly, once there, many lost their children. The move into the public arena was met with a powerful backlash. As lesbian and gay parents emerged from the closet, so too did attempts to push them back in and even to disallow the coexistence of parenthood and homosexuality altogether.

It was a vulnerable time for the struggle since the heightened threat provided strong impetus for parents to return to the closet. If one thought of the first openly gay parents who entered the courts as canaries in the coal mine it would make little sense to go in after them. Indeed for many that was exactly the case. Negative custody decisions had ramifications well beyond the people they directly involved. As long as the outcomes were mostly custody losses and severe visitation restrictions, a psychological terrorism flourished. Even today, in the face of such threats, many don't come out or dare leave their marriages. Others remain closeted through custody battles and thereafter live in fear of being discovered. And others, like Minnie Bruce, who don't dare enter a courtroom, accept unsatisfactory out-of-court settlements. Not surprisingly, one researcher found that lesbian mothers who maintain custody of their children are less likely than their heterosexual counterparts to pursue child support, for fear of rocking the boat.

A little terrorism goes a long way. With such powerful threats and so many possible points of retreat, the advancement toward fair treatment of lesbian and gay parents has been erratic. And yet people persevere. By the mid-1970s, the gay rights and feminist movements were well established. Though many parents were frightened, others stood their ground and even pushed forward.

Coming out was just a first step—one that, in fact, made parents extremely vulnerable in legal settings. Just as a woman venturing out of an abusive relationship is far more likely to survive if she finds support, openly lesbian and gay parents entering the courts needed much more than a willingness to do battle. Without a well-developed strategy to counter homophobic processes, these parents would not fare well. Spurred on by visions of more truthful and fulfilling lives, lesbian and gay parents had finally stepped out of their closets. Thus they began the long journey toward an unknown place.

In the Halls of Justice?

Lesbian and Gay Parents Enter the Courts

*That life is complicated is a fact of great analytic impor-
tance. Law too often seeks to avoid this truth by making up
its own breed of narrower, simpler, but hypnotically powerful rhetorical truths. Acknowledging, challenging, playing
with these as rhetorical gestures is, it seems to me, necessary
for any conception of justice. . . . One of the most important
results of reconceptualizing from "objective truth" to rhetorical event will be a more nuanced sense of legal and social
responsibility. This will be so because much of what is spoken
in so-called objective, unmediated voices is in fact mired in
hidden subjectivities and unexamined claims that make
property of others beyond the self, all the while denying such
connections.*

Patricia Williams
The Alchemy of Race and Rights

When lesbian and gay parents started coming out, they leapt out of
the frying pan and into the fire. Before 1974 there were virtually no
lesbian or gay custody cases in the courts, but within just a few
years lesbian mothers were losing custody in near-epidemic proportions. As negative custody rulings proliferated, it became obvious that there was a critical gap: parents were coming out but they
had no power to do so safely. By the late 1970s, there was dire need
for some organized legal response. But where was that response to
come from?

At the time, organizations promoting gay civil rights—such as the
National Gay Rights Advocates and the Lambda Legal Defense
and Education Fund—were largely male dominated. In keeping

with broader social patterns, they didn't put much emphasis on children or family concerns, though Lambda did handle some parenting cases. In many ways, gay male circles, as much as straight society, maintained the split between homosexuality and children.

The gender patterns in custody disputes were quite pronounced when lesbian and gay parents first entered the courtroom. Lesbians were frequently in custody battles while gay men more often were embroiled in visitation struggles. Though the legal issues overlapped, as women, lesbians were more often at the center of the initial questions about the homosexual parent's relationship to his or her children. Because gender so powerfully shaped the experiences of lesbian and gay parents it is not surprising that lesbian feminists rather than male-dominated gay rights groups were first to recognize that family issues are crucial to lesbian and gay civil rights.

In 1977, appreciating the need for an organized legal strategy to stem the tide of lost custody suits, Donna Hitchens founded the Lesbian Rights Project, the first organization in the country to focus on lesbian and gay parenting. But it would be almost a decade before such family concerns would become central to the gay rights movement. Not until the mid-1980s did lesbian and gay advocates begin working together on the issue. But then things moved quickly. In 1986, Paula Ettlebrick, an attorney profoundly influenced by the work of the Lesbian Rights Project, joined the staff of the Lambda Legal Defense and Education Fund. Ettlebrick developed a strong emphasis on family issues, and in 1989 established the Family Rights Project as part of Lambda. Meanwhile, the Lesbian Rights Project had grown so much that, though initially a subdivision of the Equal Rights Advocates, a feminist organization, by 1989 it became independent and was renamed the National Center for Lesbian Rights.

In contrast to the growing consciousness about lesbian and gay family issues evident in the 1980s, during the 1970s only a few advocates were beginning to address the plight of lesbian and gay parents. Operating in an atmosphere of silence and ignorance, these pioneers had their work cut out for them.

Like lesbian and gay parents themselves, lawyers working on their behalf were breaking silence. They were trying to clear a space in the legal arena for the hitherto absent voices of lesbian and gay parents. As they did this, they also broke silence at another level: they unearthed the discourse of homophobia in the courts, revealing the prejudices that had so powerfully shaped negative outcomes, and continue to do so today. These attorneys helped move those prejudices out of the realm of certainty into the realm of dialogue.

At about the same time as the Lesbian Rights Project was founded, legal scholars began to investigate lesbian and gay custody proceedings. These advocates knew that they would have to understand both the process and the content of negative custody outcomes before they could successfully fight such rulings.

Their task certainly was not easy. Even the most basic level of information gathering was hampered by the silence that homophobia perpetuates. For example, judges often make homophobic decisions without clearly articulating their prejudices. They also frequently order proceedings to be closed, reasoning that the issues are so sensitive that public disclosure would be harmful to the children involved. These practices make it difficult to identify the exact influences on custody outcomes.

The structure of family law itself further complicates the task of amassing data. Only decisions made at the appellate level set precedents and are formally gathered or documented, but there are very few appellate-level custody rulings. Unless circumstances change significantly following a trial-court decision, the ruling is difficult to overturn on appeal. Appellate-level judges reason that the trial-court judges had full access to the relevant facts, and therefore defer to their opinions. And because appeals are so seldom worth pursuing, there are few precedents and few documented lesbian and gay custody cases. Legal advocates for lesbian and gay parents in the 1970s often had to start from scratch for each case.

The first legal scholars to examine lesbian and gay custody battles filled in the gaps. Their work was crucial well beyond its immediate aim of helping parents maintain their relationships with their children. As lawyers began to analyze the mechanisms and content of lesbian and gay custody proceedings, they revealed the ways that prejudice shapes our lives. Like taking apart a watch and demonstrating how the gears function, they showed how the legal system works to curtail certain lives while allowing others to flourish.

The law is filled with contradictions, and much of the effort to change how lesbian and gay parents are treated in the courts involves mobilizing those contradictions within the legal system itself—stirring them up and rearranging their relations to each other. For instance, sodomy statutes exemplify the discrimination built into the law; but at the same time, discrimination, if recognized as such, violates our most basic concept of justice. Lesbian and gay parents fighting for custody expose these kinds of contradictions. Their advocates must make judges recognize homophobic prejudice for what it is and bring to bear basic values of fairness and justice.

Lesbian and gay parents, struggling to transform their lives run into a formidable obstacle: the very different paces at which law and society incorporate change. As our culture develops, the past and present collide in the courtroom. The law is a peculiar amalgam of history. On the one hand it is a crystallization of the past; on the other hand it is shaped by current social mores through new legislation and new interpretation of existing laws. However, society changes much more rapidly than the law, yielding an ever-widening gap between how we actually live and the legal guidelines we turn to in times of conflict. Existing law often fails to encompass the complex issues that our changing social arrangements raise.

Fighting in an arcane and resistant legal context, lesbian and gay parents must grapple with both institutional and individual levels of discrimination. People, not just laws, make the legal system function. Legal discourse is not simply a matter of what is written; it is also how that writing is interpreted in any given instance. While some aspects of homophobia are embedded in legal procedures and in the language of the law itself, others are enacted by individuals endowed with great legal power, who go beyond procedural limits and act against the spirit of the law.

As they develop new forms of the family, lesbian and gay parents run up against both individual and institutional notions of how men and women should behave and what relationships are socially acceptable. Their fate hinges on this key question: will the state acknowledge and honor diverse forms of intimacy?

Homosexual Relationships versus Homosexual Identity

When legal advocates began to examine what was happening to lesbian and gay parents, they discovered what continues to be true: losing custody outright is not the only danger. Judges frequently award custody or visitation rights on a contingency basis, with homosexual parents essentially having to stay closeted in order to maintain contact with their children. In deciding such cases, judges view homosexuality as both an identity and a behavior. They may recognize that they can't disallow the identity, so they focus instead on disparaging and curtailing the behavior. In a 1973 California case, a lesbian mother's parental rights were terminated by the state on the grounds of her lesbianism. The judge said that this move was necessary in order to "assure [the children's] adjustment to a 'dominantly heterosexual society.' " He went on to declare that the "continuous existence of a homosexual relationship in the home where the minor is exposed to it involves the necessary likelihood of serious adjustment problems."

The idea that children should not be exposed to lesbian or gay relationships may, as in this California case, cause a parent to lose custody outright; but it also commonly leads to granting custody contingent on the parent's abstaining from relationships or from sharing a household with his or her partner. Similarly, judges often impose visitation restrictions on noncustodial parents, including no overnight visits, supervised visits only, or no visits in the presence of same-sex partners. In these ways judges shape families, legitimizing some while virtually forbidding others even to exist.

Judges may restrict not only relationships but also other aspects of behavior, such as political activity or being forthrightly homosexual. In a 1974 case in which two women had made a film about their family, the judge warned: "I would caution Miss Schuster and Miss Isaacson that if in the future they put the children on exhibition for the cause of homosexuality or if they spend too much time on that cause to the neglect of the children, these circumstances could jeopardize future custody."

In many instances, simply the parent's openness comes under fire, as this judge's comments illustrate: "the mother has . . . behaved affectionately toward . . . women in front of the children, although she insists such activity is merely friendly, not passionate or sexual . . . [during visits she may] not have with her, in her home, or around the children, any lesbians."

Judges also often bar parents from participating in community activities or from having their children with them at such events. As one judge opined, the "mother's lover has chosen not to make her sexual preference private but invites acknowledgment and imposes her preference upon her children and her community. We are not forbidding Wife from being a homosexual, from having a lesbian relationship, or from attending gay activist or overt homosexual outings. We are restricting her from exposing those elements of her 'alternative lifestyle' to her minor children."

As judges articulate their reasons for custody denials or restrictions, they reveal the link between controlling speech and curtailing homosexual existence. In these cases, judges hold lesbian and gay parents to a standard of silence, decreeing that if they want to remain active parents, they must stay in the closet.

Rulings like these hurt, rather than help, the very children they are supposed to protect. They either pull parents and children apart or they greatly impair the quality of family life. Parents forced to stay closeted have more difficulty maintaining a sense of pride and helping their children do the same; the relationships between children and their parents' same-sex partners are abridged. Thus, homophobic decisions burden children with loss and increased family stress.

These rulings blatantly damage the families they are directed at, but their destruction extends far beyond those particular families.

The decisions undermine essential American values. By impinging on people's personal choices and intimate ties—in violation of basic constitutional rights—they eat away at the potential for a just society, thus indirectly diminishing all of our lives.

Faced with a range of antihomosexual sentiment, advocates who initiated the battle against homophobic custody rulings had to begin by exploring two crucial issues. First, they needed to examine the processes through which prejudice comes to hold sway. What mechanisms allow homophobic views to determine custody outcomes? Are these ways of proceeding fair and just? Are there any legal principles that can be brought into play to disallow prejudicial judgments? Second, advocates had to look closely at the content of homophobia itself. What particular beliefs, myths, and fears dominate? Can they be dispelled through dialogue and education? Throughout the 1970s and 1980s exploration of these two issues established the basis for a powerful challenge to homophobia in the legal arena.

The Mechanisms of Lesbian and Gay Custody Determinations—From *Per Se* to Nexus Standards

In one of the earliest documented lesbian mother custody cases, Doris Nadler lost custody of her four-year-old daughter when she and her husband divorced in 1967. The court ruled that "as a matter of law," her homosexuality rendered her "unfit." In reaching this conclusion, the judge saw no reason to explain how Doris Nadler's lesbianism rendered her unfit, and no reason to question the relevance of a mother's lesbianism to the well-being of her child. In legal terms, the ruling constituted a *per se* finding of unfitness—that is to say, it established that lesbianism in and of itself was sufficient reason to deny custody. However, on appeal a higher court reversed the ruling, holding instead that the trial-court judge should have considered all the evidence and in ruling "as a matter of law," had failed to exercise judicial discretion. This appellate-level decision essentially established that a *per se* finding of unfitness is not acceptable. That was a start; homophobes would at least have to try to prove their case.

But having given lip service to the idea that all evidence must be considered, and that homosexuality should be considered only insofar as it is truly relevant to the best interests of the child, the higher court went on to deny Doris Nadler custody and to grant her quite restricted visitation consisting of once-weekly visits to occur only in the presence of another adult. The court did not document any evidence to support the notion that Doris Nadler's lesbianism was harmful to her child. Having established the need for evidence to be presented, the higher court made its decision without that evidence. Homophobia influenced not only the outcome but also the process of the hearing.

The entire trial was rife not only with gross ignorance but also with hostile voyeurism. According to one account:

> At her second trial, the mother was required to give the names and addresses of anyone with whom she had sexual activity during the previous two years, state how often she had sexual relations, and answer unfounded questions about whether she had ever been a prostitute. At one point during the examination of the mother, the judge asked her, "Ma'am, will you explain to the Court exactly what occurs—we talk here of a homosexual act. Just what does this entail? What do you do?" The mother responded: "I refuse to answer on the grounds that it may incriminate me". . . . In response to objections about his line of questioning the judge declared: "But my point is as a trier of fact here, that in a contested custody matter in which this issue of homosexuality is a main thread, the Court has to have some detailed knowledge of what these activities are in aiding it in many things. . . . Now depending on what type of background and experience you have—to some people holding hands is a homosexual act. I don't know. . . . Everybody bandies this word

about, and yet we don't have a definition. Now I
would like to know what she does with other women
that constitutes the act. Maybe she just shakes hands
with them. I don't know."

The judge was eventually persuaded not to pursue this line of
questioning. His prejudice, however, was also obvious in his decision. His closing comments were: "Frankly ma'am you should take
therapy, as the doctor suggested, if you are going to overcome your
. . . beat your psychological problem. And the Court—we are dealing with a four-year-old child on the threshold of its development—
just cannot take the chance that something untoward should
happen to it. . . . I'm sincere in saying that I want this child protected, and if the lady takes therapeutics, and the psychiatrist can
assure me, then I will look for unrestrained visitation. It would
depend on the factors. Right now I just can't take the chance."

Court records all across America are filled with decisions that,
like the Nadler appeal, claim to be considering the evidence, but
nevertheless after failing to establish a clear connection between a
parent's homosexuality and detriment to the child, go on to assert
vague assumptions of unfitness or harm. These are not technically
per se decisions, but in practical terms they function the same way.

Clearly, in both the Nadler trial-court and appellate-level cases,
the judges' homophobia held sway. What enabled this to happen?
Is custody supposed to be determined simply by an individual
judge's personal opinion? Are there any legal mechanisms that prevent such impositions of prejudice? Ironically, contradictory answers to these questions emanate from the same place: the best-
interests-of-the-child standard that guides custody rulings.

For any parent, gay or straight, the basic mechanisms for determining custody and visitation arrangements are at least superficially
the same. Family law rulings are governed by statutes that vary from
state to state. However, all state statutes have some critical elements
in common. The legal standard for deciding custody disputes between two parents is to rule in "the best interests of the child"—a
term defined by state statutes whose vague language tends to offer

few firm legal guidelines. Generally, judges consider factors such as the parents' financial status; the environment of home and neighborhood; what the children prefer; the quality of emotional bonds among parents and children; and the age, sex, and health of parents in relation to the age, sex, and health of children. When a parent is lesbian or gay, homophobic courts may focus on whether opposite-sex role models are available, the extent of a parent's openness about sexual orientation, his or her degree of political activity, and whether a same-sex lover lives in the household.

Sometimes custody disputes don't involve two parents, but instead arise between a parent and the state or between a parent and a relative such as a grandparent. In order for the state to terminate a parent's rights, it must prove that parent unfit. Here, the state must not only meet the best-interests-of-the-child standard, but must also show that the child is not cared for properly or that the parent is depraved. Though one might expect that this more stringent standard is clearly defined, in fact it is also guided by vaguely written statutes that vary state to state. Disputes between parents and relatives constitute an unsettled arena in which the choice between best interests and unfitness standards has not been clearly and uniformly established.

Since the statutes are so vague, decisions do end up hinging largely on the individual judge's personal interpretation of the best-interests and unfitness standards. This, of course, leaves a great deal of room for prejudice to flourish. In 1976, Nan Hunter and Nancy Polikoff wrote a landmark law-review article about the mechanisms through which lesbian-mother custody cases are decided. They zeroed in on the fact that the vague language of the best-interests standard poses great danger to lesbian and gay parents in a homophobic society. "From this maze of factual information, a court must focus on what it considers to be the most essential and . . . then place the child accordingly. While this latitude protects parents and children from inflexible rules which might preclude the essential human aspects of a custody dispute, it also permits—perhaps even encourages—the biases of a judge to be given free rein. When the issue in question is lesbianism, in a society in which homosexuality is often viewed as immoral or unhealthy, the possibilities for abuse are clear." Though Hunter and Polikoff recognized that the vague wording of the best-interests statutes gives judges the latitude through which to inject prejudice, they simultaneously saw that the key to prohibiting such discrimination also lies in the best-interests standard—in the spirit of the law itself: "To deprive a parent of custody because of what one judge may consider misconduct offends the belief that cases should be decided on rational and predictable rather than arbitrary grounds."

Lesbian and gay custody outcomes hinge on the question of what constitutes the best interests of the child. Are judges free simply to impose their personal prejudices, or are they obligated to assess the question independently of such prejudices? When Hunter and Polikoff examined how judges arrive at gay and lesbian custody decisions, they saw that a continuum of interpretations of the best-interests standard results in three basic ways that courts determine lesbian and gay custody outcomes.

The first, exemplified by Doris Nadler's original trial-court case, yields decisions that are made as a matter of law—where homosexuality *per se* justifies custody loss. This kind of ruling establishes an irrebutable presumption that homosexuality in and of itself constitutes "unfitness." *Per se* rulings essentially codify homophobic prejudice into the law itself. Is this approach legally sound? Many who think not nonetheless proceed in a way that is closely aligned with the *per se* standard. Such was the case in the 1967 Nadler appeal. There the judge found that declaring a lesbian mother unfit "as a matter of law" was not acceptable and that instead evidence must be considered. However, the judge went on to rule against the lesbian parent without documenting a connection between her lesbianism and presumed harm to the child. This typifies a second, and more common, approach to lesbian and gay custody cases—one characterized not by a *per se* perspective but rather by a presumption of harm.

Both the *per se* and the presumption-of-harm standards fly in the face of the spirit of the law. They preempt serious and accurate appraisal of the best interests of the child by forgoing a thorough evaluation of the specific family in favor of prejudicial presumptions. Furthermore, they violate a parent's constitutional rights, most obviously the right to due process (since the irrebutable presumption replaces a fair hearing), but also the rights to freedom of association, privacy, and equal protection.

The third standard contrasts sharply with the *per se* and presumption-of-harm standards. It holds that a parent's sexual orientation can be considered relevant only if there is a clear connection—or nexus—demonstrated between the parent's homosexuality and harm to the child. Though homophobia is always a force to contend with, only the nexus standard requires that homophobic assumptions be examined and allows a parent the chance to rebut them. With nexus, it is not sufficient to base a decision on a presumption of harm to the child; instead, the court must clearly document evidence of such harm. Furthermore, in accordance with the custody statutes, the harm factor is to be considered only as one of many on which a decision hinges.

Hunter and Polikoff argued strongly that only the nexus standard is legally sound because only nexus replaces prejudice with a true appraisal of the best interests of the child and doesn't infringe on a parent's basic constitutional rights. Generally, lesbian and gay parents lose custody when the courts fail to employ a true nexus standard. Therefore, the critical element in such custody cases is the push for this nexus or, as others call it, detriment standard. Taken to its logical conclusion, the nexus standard ultimately means that the sexual orientation of a parent is irrelevant to a custody proceeding, once there is an understanding that its assumed relevance stems from prejudice rather than demonstrable harm to the child.

In 1976, a time when most lesbian and gay parents lost custody, Nan Hunter and Nancy Polikoff posed a profound challenge. They demonstrated the legal and ethical necessity for courts to question rather than rely on homophobic assumptions. The shift they pushed for in the legal arena is also crucial to the more general effort to purge society of prejudice. *Prejudice* means both "a judgment or opinion formed before the facts are known" and "hatred or dislike for a particular group, race, religion, etc." Of course, these two meanings are closely related. Marginalized groups suffer precisely from being unseen because derogatory myths obscure the realities of their lives. This dehumanizing process of distorted perception is often both the basis and justification for maltreatment. Hunter and Polikoff showed how families are torn apart when the state does this to lesbian and gay parents and how such practices violate our most basic sense of justice.

While establishing the logic of a nexus or detriment standard was a critical first step, it still left the matter of content to be dealt with. Having identified which ways of proceeding allow prejudice to enter the decision-making process and which ways don't, legal advocates still needed to examine and address the specific homophobic beliefs and fears that often hold sway in court.

A Question of Morals—Homosexuality as Sin

Understanding prejudice of any kind is not so much a matter of grasping its logic as it is of recognizing how particular social forces generate and perpetuate senseless hatred. Like other forms of bigotry, the core of homophobia is a tautological belief that is, in many ways, immune to rational questioning because it confirms itself: homosexuality is wrong because it is wrong. In our culture biblical references are often the sole justification for antihomosexual sentiments: "If a man also lie with mankind as he lieth with a woman, both of them have committed an abomination: they shall be put to death." During the Middle Ages, Thomas Aquinas further consolidated the foundation of Western Christianity's condemnation of homosexuality, declaring that since it involves nonprocreative, pleasure-seeking sexual behavior, homosexuality is a "sin against nature." In our current society, the religious right's relentless antihomosexual campaigns carry on the centuries-old tradition of religious condemnation.

Perhaps more subtly but no less significantly, homosexuality is seen as an abomination not just in theological circles but in secular life as well. Employing their own form of moral righteousness, many who are not at all religious believe, again in tautological fashion, that homosexuality is simply immoral. The theological basis of homophobia thus influences society in two key ways: both through organized religion's antihomosexual crusades and through secular language that casts homosexuality as immoral.

There is no doubt that the religious right has built a powerful political and economic base rooted in antihomosexuality. The religious right emerged in full force around the same time as lesbian and gay parents became more visible; not surprisingly it targeted those parents. In the religious right's propaganda, homosexual parents, having transgressed the sanctity of the nuclear family, threaten the very foundation of civilization and must be kept from destroying their own children.

As soon as lesbian and gay parents emerged on the scene, their private struggles often became public vehicles through which the religious right could bring its message to the world. Such was the fate of Brian Todd Batey, whose parents divorced when he was three years old, at which time Brian's father began to come out and Brian's mother became increasingly involved in the Pentecostal church. Though Brian was very attached to his father, Frank, his mother forbid visitation and, using the worst stereotypes of gay men, supported her refusal by falsely accusing Frank of being a child molester. After a lengthy trial a judge found no reason to restrict Frank's visitation, but Brian's mother continued to keep father and son apart. In response, the court eventually awarded Frank custody. Six-year-old Brian lived with his father for only a week before his mother kidnapped him and left the state. At that point the religious right seized upon Brian as the perfect symbol through which to advance its cause. A private family struggle thus became a public debacle as the religious right took up the crusade to keep Frank and Brian apart, providing massive funding and media coverage for what would become a highly publicized seven-year custody battle. During most of that time, after Brian's mother revealed his whereabouts, Brian bounced from foster home to foster home, unable to thrive in any. Since the court succumbed to the religious right's insistence that he be placed only in religious homes and schools, Brian was constantly subjected to virulent antihomosexual campaigning. Ultimately, unable to find any reason to do otherwise, the court awarded Frank custody of Brian. By the time he arrived at his father's house, at age thirteen, Brian was a deeply troubled boy, but eventually he settled comfortably into his new life. In a sad twist of fate, Brian lived with his father only two years before Frank developed AIDS. Within days of Frank's death, Brian's mother once again kidnapped Brian, but this time, sixteen-year-old Brian took matters into his own hands. He asked the court to make Craig his legal guardian, and the court, recognizing the fact that Craig was indeed Brian's "psychological parent," granted the request.

The religious right's zealous interference with Frank and Brian's relationship was a foreshadowing of things to come. Like others encroached upon by the self-appointed moral guardians of our time, Brian's childhood was effectively destroyed in a dramatic public process. Meanwhile, many other childhoods are more quietly obliterated—if not in the name of God, then in the name of morality.

Sodomy Statutes—Homosexuality as Crime

Judges often bring moral condemnation to bear in lesbian and gay custody cases. One judge denied a lesbian mother custody and granted her only restricted visitation, justifying his decision by saying: "Homosexuality has been considered contrary to the morality of man for well over two thousand years. It has been and is considered to be an unnatural, immoral act."

Sometimes judges explicitly use religious language to support their moral condemnation, as one North Carolina judge did in dissenting from a majority decision to award a lesbian mother custody of her children. This judge, like many, linked antihomosexual sentiments to his more general disgust about the changing roles of men and women brought on by feminism.

> It is not a light thing to take children from the custody of a mother—or a father. . . . It has been customary,

when children are small, to regard the mother as the more natural custodian when divorce disrupts the home. In part this is tradition, stemming from the fact that the father is normally the provider of support and so is unable to spend as much time at home, and from the unusually greater tenderness of a woman's nature. It is due in part to the ingrained habits of chivalry and to the resulting sheltered protection of women from contact with degrading influences. Now however, a permissive society has "liberated" women, if so inclined, to inquire into, discuss, experiment with, condone and practice all the vices which the most depraved of men have practiced since the days of Abraham. Consequently, courts of the present day must put into practice in custody cases the realism on which current society prides itself. In awarding custody of children we must remember that the process of giving birth does not automatically transform a woman into an exemplification of the 31st Chapter of Proverbs.

Whether explicitly religious language is used or not, all custody decisions that hinge on a moral stance against homosexuality seriously transgress a value that is fundamental to our country's very existence—namely, the separation between church and state. Though judges often deny custody based on their personal moral condemnation of homosexuality, this kind of reasoning is difficult to justify legally since it defies the spirit of the best-interests standard by precluding an impartial assessment of the child's well-being. However, the argument that judges are obligated to leave their antihomosexual opinions out of the decision-making process is considerably weakened by the fact that a religious moralistic perspective is incorporated into the law itself in the form of sodomy statutes.

In 1553 the ecclesiastical framing of nonprocreative, nongenital sex as an "abominable crime against nature" became codified in

British secular law, which later carried over to American law. Though the laws were not originally intended so narrowly, they have more recently been interpreted as referring essentially to homosexuality, making it not only a sin but also a crime. Of course these laws, originating in religious doctrine, themselves violate the American separation between church and state.

Generally, sodomy statutes aren't enforced, but their continued existence has great symbolic and practical significance that is amply evident in lesbian and gay custody battles. While casting homosexuality as "immoral" is technically not a sound basis for denying a parent custody, such thinking seeps into the decision-making process anyway, frequently bolstered by sodomy statutes that many judges cite as evidence of lesbian and gay parents' criminality. As the lawyer that Minnie Bruce Pratt contacted in Raleigh pointed out, in the states where sodomy statutes exist they are often used against lesbian and gay parents in custody battles. One judge denying a lesbian mother custody in 1975 noted:

> The commission of certain homosexual acts is a criminal offense in California (Penal Code 286, 288a) albeit an offense not readily susceptible to criminal prosecution. The fact that in certain respects enforcement of the criminal law against the private commission of homosexual acts may be inappropriate and may be approaching desuetude, if such is the case, does not argue that society accepts homosexuality as a pattern to which children should be exposed . . . or as an example that should be put before them for emulation. In exercising a choice between homosexual and heterosexual households for purposes of child custody, a trial court could conclude that permanent residence in a homosexual household would be detrimental to the children and contrary to their best interests.

While this judge incorporates the sodomy statute into an overall perspective that homosexuality is immoral, some courts hold that simply the fact of the statutes, and by implication lesbian or gay parents' "criminality," is sufficient reason to deny custody. However, this point is hotly debated. Though some argue that in legal terms "criminality" is in and of itself against the best interests of the child, others point out that such a position has not been held with respect to other criminal offenses and that, even where sodomy statutes exist on the books, the explicit relevance to the child must be established before custody is denied.

There is no doubt that the existence of sodomy statutes is quite detrimental to lesbian and gay parents. It is generally more difficult to argue in legal terms with the criminality position than with the more vaguely defined concept of immorality. In fact, the law is clear that judges are not supposed to make custody decisions based on their own moral views. Many acknowledge this more readily when their moral judgments are not bolstered by the legal sanction of the sodomy statutes.

Sodomy statutes are widely used in blatantly discriminatory ways, a fact which is especially apparent as the statutes crop up in lesbian and gay custody cases. In general the statutes don't name homosexuality itself as illegal, but rather delineate certain sexual acts, whether performed by heterosexual or homosexual couples. Furthermore, a significant percentage of homosexuals (particularly lesbians) don't engage in these practices. Nonetheless, sodomy statutes are often brought to bear on lesbians and gay men, but not on heterosexuals. For example, in custody cases it is common to see sodomy statutes cited with respect to the lesbian or gay parent, while the statutes are virtually unheard of with respect to a sexually active heterosexual parent. In fact, in many cases where custody denials are attributed to sodomy statutes there is neither evidence that the lesbian or gay parent committed sodomy nor that the heterosexual parent did not.

Homophobia and the state's undue interference with personal choices about intimacy converge in the sodomy statutes. In addition to specifically damaging lesbians and gay men, these laws raise the specter for all citizens of an Orwellian nightmare, in which the state's presence invades our hearts and homes. Not surprisingly there has been a strong push during the past three decades to eliminate the sodomy statutes. At the beginning of the 1960s all states had some form of sodomy statutes, but then a trend toward repeal took hold. By 1980 only half the states in the country still had sodomy statutes on the books, and at the time of this writing, the statutes exist in only twenty-two states. Despite the steadily diminishing number of states with sodomy statutes on the books, the 1986 Supreme Court *Bowers* v. *Hardwick* decision dealt a serious blow to those fighting the statutes. That decision, which upheld the constitutionality of the Georgia sodomy statute, was particularly damaging to lesbians and gay men. It essentially sanctioned the continuing use of sodomy laws to further homophobic discrimination. The right to privacy for lesbian and gay people with respect to these issues was thereby emphatically eliminated at the federal level.

The Psychiatric Perspective— Homosexuality as Sickness

The view that homosexuality is a sin formed the basis for the construction of homosexuality as crime. Both perspectives contribute to lesbian and gay custody loss through judges' personal opinions and through the codification of homophobia in law itself. However, the influence of Western Christianity does not end there. Just as religious condemnation of homosexuality seeped into secular morality and legal parameters, so too it spread to another powerful cultural influence: the modern-day religion of psychiatry.

In the nineteenth century the medical community turned its attention to homosexuality, recasting the language of sin as the language of sickness. Psychiatric perspectives distinguished themselves from the religious view by framing homosexuality as the end result of pathological influences on the individual, rather than as willful transgression. However, they did not depart from the fundamental, tautological view of homosexuality as wrong. Taking for granted the belief that homosexuality is if not an abomination then a perversion, those looking at it from a so-called scientific perspective sought to explain its origins and search for a cure. Some schools of thought declared a propensity toward homosexuality as primarily biological in origin, while others maintained that environmental factors were more salient. Likewise, some conceptualized homosexuality as an intractable disease, while others saw it as treatable.

Though many schools of psychology cast homosexuality as a form of deviance, the psychoanalytic perspective has been most influential in this regard. Freud saw all human beings as starting out with bisexual tendencies that, in normal development, become channeled in a heterosexual direction. In his model, homosexuality is a form of arrested development, and is, in that sense, pathological. However, unlike many of his followers, Freud didn't think of homosexuality as incompatible with an otherwise normal and productive life. In a now-famous letter written to the mother of a gay man, he said "Homosexuality is assuredly no advantage, but it is nothing to be ashamed of, no vice, no degradation, it cannot be classified as an illness; we consider it to be a variation of the sexual function produced by a certain arrest of sexual development. Many highly respected individuals of ancient and modern times have been homosexuals, several of the greatest men among them (Plato, Michelangelo, Leonardo da Vinci, etc.). It is a great injustice to persecute homosexuality as a crime, and cruelty too."

As Freud walked the delicate line between viewing homosexuality as a normal aspect of human sexuality and seeing it as outright pathology, he often contradicted himself. Building on the part of Freud's theory that cast homosexuality as deviance, many of his followers developed far more vehemently homophobic ideas. In the 1940s Sandor Rado, and in the 1950s and 1960s Irving Bieber, rejected Freud's notion of constitutional bisexuality, and asserted instead that heterosexuality was the "biologic norm." Following this line of thought, Bieber declared that "all psychoanalytic theories assume that homosexuality is psychopathologic." Basing his ideas on this assumption Bieber conducted a study in which psychiatrists provided data about their homosexual and heterosexual patients. From this work, Bieber developed a portrait of homosexuality as deep psychological disturbance resulting from "highly pathologic parent-child relationships," most often including over-bearing, "desmasculinizing" mothers and detached or hostile fathers. Bieber saw no need to question the premise that homosexuality is a disease; and likewise, he saw no problem with basing his conclusions about the general population on a study of psychiatric patients.

During the 1960s and 1970s Charles Socarides took the pathologizing of homosexuality one step further. He saw homosexuality as resulting from even earlier and therefore more pervasive disturbance than his predecessors had suggested. He declared that "Homosexuality is based on the fear of the mother, the aggressive attack against the father, and is filled with aggression, destruction and self-deceit."

Though the dominant psychiatric perspectives on homosexuality characterized it as pathological, there were always dissenting views both from other social scientists and from within the mental health profession. Alfred Kinsey's 1948 study of American sexuality revealed homosexual behavior to be far more prevalent than was previously imagined. Kinsey argued that his data provided no evidence of a link between homosexuality and psychopathology. Furthermore, he suggested that heterosexuality was no more natural than any other form of sexual expression. Instead he believed that the "capacity of an individual to respond erotically to any sort of stimulus . . . is basic to the species." This perspective was supported by other sociological and anthropological studies that found evidence of socially accepted homosexual behavior among a variety of human cultures as well as animal populations.

In 1954, from within the psychiatric profession itself, Evelyn Hooker profoundly challenged the idea that homosexuality is a disease. Unlike previous theoreticians, Hooker based her work on the general population rather than on psychiatric patients. She administered a battery of psychological tests to both homosexual and heterosexual men and then had other clinicians determine whether any sort of pathology was evident. The judges, who didn't know which test data belonged to which individuals, ended up classifying two-thirds of both the heterosexual and homosexual subjects as psychologically well adjusted. Furthermore, they were unable to guess from the test material which were gay and which were straight. Hooker's work strongly undercut previous psychological theorizing about homosexuality that had been based on the assumption of pathology.

Around the same time as Hooker's work was published Thomas Szaz began to develop a powerful critique of psychiatry in general, which would later become the basis of his more specific critique of psychiatric views on homosexuality. For Szaz, psychiatrists mistakenly applied a medical model to the realm of human behavior, thus disguising their value-laden theories in the supposedly neutral language of science. From this perspective psychiatric labeling was best understood as a form of social control. In Szaz's view, psychiatry had taken over the repressive function of the church. "The psychiatric perspective on homosexuality is but a thinly disguised replica of the religious perspective which it displaced," he contended. In a scathing critique of the profession's attitude toward homosexuality, Szaz said:

> Psychiatric preoccupation with the disease concept of homosexuality—as with the disease concept of all so-called mental illnesses . . . conceals the fact that homosexuals are a group of medically stigmatized and socially persecuted individuals. The noise generated by their persecution and their anguished cries of protest are drowned out by the rhetoric of therapy—just as the rhetoric of salvation drowned out the noise generated by the persecution of witches and their anguished cries of protest. It is a heartless hypocrisy to pretend that physicians, psychiatrists, or normal laymen for that matter really care about the welfare of the mentally ill in general, or the homosexual in particular. If they did, they would stop torturing him while claiming to help him.

Though the disease model of homosexuality was debated among social scientists, it remained unquestionably the dominant view until the early 1970s. This was reflected in the *Diagnostic and Statistical Manual of Mental Disorders*, the bible of modern psychiatry. In the first edition, the *DSM I* published in 1952, homosexuality was listed under the category of sociopathic personality disturbances. This category explicitly referred to illnesses that included a problem with "conformity with the prevailing cultural milieu." In 1968, the revised *DSM II* listed homosexuality not as a sociopathic personality disturbance, but rather as a sexual deviation, along with pedophilia, voyeurism, and other "non-psychotic mental disorders."

During the late 1960s the gay rights movement began to actively challenge the psychiatric position, and professionals increasingly recognized that there was no sound basis for conceptualizing homosexuality as an illness. Finally, in 1973 the American Psychiatric Association (APA) voted to remove homosexuality from the *DSM III*. However, heated debate and ultimate ambivalence about the decision resulted in the invention of a new diagnosis at that time— "ego dystonic homosexuality," a label for people who were unhappy about their sexual orientation. By maintaining the possibility of considering those who are unhappy about their homosexuality to be psychiatrically ill, professionals who created this diagnosis missed a crucial point about the place of homosexuals in society: thanks to the weight of homophobia in our culture, many lesbians and gay men are unhappy at some stage of their coming-out process. Categorizing the social problem as individual pathology, particularly with the implicit idea that cure means becoming heterosexual, supports society's homophobia. Eventually, psychiatric discourse evolved to recognizing this point, and the updated manual, the 1987 *DSM III-R*, does not include the diagnostic category of ego dystonic homosexuality.

Psychiatry is not monolithic, and many continue to pathologize homosexuality despite the shift in the American Psychiatric Association's official position. Furthermore, the view that homosexuality is a disease is quite entrenched in our society, having seeped just as deeply into public consciousness as the idea that homosexuality is a sin. Since courts are part and parcel of society, the casting of homosexuality as sickness has profoundly influenced lesbian and gay custody outcomes. For instance, in the Nadler appeal the judge drew on a pathologizing perspective when he commented that Doris Nadler should "seek therapeutics" and that until she was cured he would not consider granting unsupervised visitation with her daughter. The following characterization, expressed in a divorce proceeding, typifies a judicial stance on homosexuality that draws on both the sin and sickness perspectives:

> Added to the insult of sexual disloyalty *per se* (which is present in ordinary adultery) is the natural revulsion arising from knowledge of the fact that the spouse's betrayal takes the form of a perversion. . . . Few behavioral deviations are more offensive to American mores than is homosexuality. Common sense and modern psychiatric knowledge concur as to the incompatibility and the subsistence of marriage between one so afflicted and a normal person.

Despite ongoing differences of opinion, the APA's official shift away from a pathology model has had great impact on lesbian and gay custody cases. Though some "experts" may testify about homosexuality as a disease, in fact most mainstream organizations and current psychiatric knowledge do not support that stance. From the time lesbian and gay custody cases first began to appear in the courts judges have turned to mental-health professionals for guidance. Since the idea that homosexuality is a disease was strongly refuted, many mental-health professionals have been able to play a positive role in the lives of lesbian and gay parents and their children.

Children Raised by Lesbians or Gay Men

To frame homosexuality as "immoral," "criminal," and "abnormal" is essentially to focus on lesbians and gay men themselves. But in custody battles another question is key: What are the experiences of children raised by homosexual parents? Since homophobia is so pervasive in our culture, advocates must be able to respond to beliefs that lesbian and gay parents, simply by virtue of their homosexuality, harm their kids. They have their work cut out for them, even when courts are ready to deploy a nexus or detriment standard. In 1978 Donna Hitchens and Barbara Price analyzed the content of judges' justifications for denying custody and restricting visitation. Hitchens and Price identified and refuted three myths and fears that contribute to negative custody outcomes: (1) children will themselves become gay, (2) children will suffer psychological damage as a result of stigmatization, and (3) lesbian and gay parents are likely to sexually molest their children.

Will the Kids Be Gay?

As people first began to consider the phenomenon of children being raised by homosexual parents, the main question on everyone's minds was: Will the kids grow up to be gay? Another set of questions was closely tied to this one: Would boys be less masculine? Would girls be less feminine? In short, would the children of lesbian and gay parents be confused about their gender identities and unable to take on their proper social roles?

One psychologist testifying in a 1978 lesbian-mother custody dispute certainly believed this was the case. He said that if the children were to live with their mother and her lover, they might "pick up mannerisms, the behavior, and the way of speaking and talking, and gait, and other things that are likely to be decisive in which way these girls will go with their sexual identification at this particular time and over the next few years."

A cross-examination of a psychiatrist testifying in another lesbian-mother custody trial illustrates how forcefully the culture and the law may be determined to categorize people as masculine or feminine and to keep them in traditional sex roles.

ATTORNEY: Doctor, you made allusion to the fact that Richard Risher came to your office wearing a YWCA T-shirt, did you not? And from that incident you drew the conclusion that that was poor judgment on the part of Mary Jo Risher?

PSYCHIATRIST: I certainly did. I thought it was ridiculous.

ATTORNEY: Would it surprise you to know that Richard Risher goes to the YWCA to take gymnastics lessons?

PSYCHIATRIST: No it would not.

ATTORNEY: Would it surprise you to know that he wears a YWCA T-shirt to go there?

PSYCHIATRIST: I have observed him wearing it. But I must say that when you're dealing with this particular issue—and I'm not criticizing sexual preference, but the manner in which the parent is dealing with it—I think that is most ill advised.

ATTORNEY: So it would be better advised if he was told not to wear his YWCA shirt to the YWCA where he is to wear it.

PSYCHIATRIST: No, it would be better for him to have matriculated into a YMCA program. And it would be much better for a mother to encourage those kinds of masculine identifications.

ATTORNEY: Doctor, are you aware or do you know that there are programs offered at the YWCA centers for boys?

PSYCHIATRIST: I was not aware of that, but it doesn't change my view of things one whit, if you're dealing with a child with problems. Now I don't see anything wrong in the ordinary sense with a boy attending programs at the YWCA or a girl attending programs at the YMCA; that's perfectly fine as far as I'm concerned. But when you have a particularly sensitive issue here that Mary Jo Risher is cognizant of—she is an intelligent, sensitive, bright lady—she owes the responsibility in my judgment to try to meet this special need, and not advance, in my view, the YWCA experience.

Here, the psychiatrist views any digression from purely masculine affiliations as a major threat to the boy's well-being, particularly because his mother is a lesbian. What exactly is he saying? If we don't make sure that boys and girls act in stereotypical masculine and feminine ways, if we let gender categories break down, there will be terrible consequences. Yet, what are those consequences? They remain unnamed. Diverging from rigidly constructed gender roles is seen as terrible in and of itself. Thinking along these lines, people often presume that heterosexual "role models" are vital to children's well-being, without looking particularly carefully at whether this is so.

In one case a lesbian mother lost custody of her children specifically because, in the household she shared with her lover, she would not be providing a heterosexual role model. The judge reasoned:

> The Court observes that the situation in the home occupied by petitioner and [her partner] is now the optimum which the petitioner can hope to offer. This is not true in the case of the respondent. He may remarry and establish a home where the children would have the attention of both a father and a step-mother. The Court realizes that this might turn out to be a situation worse for the children than is presently offered them. It also might be substantially better. In the home of the respondent any changes may create either a better or a worse environment for the children. Any changes in the home of the petitioner and [her partner] can only be in the direction of a deterioration of the present situation. Both would of necessity involve the employment of baby-sitters. At the home of the petitioner the children would be in an all-female environment. At the home of the respondent they will be in a male environment, but on occasions when with the baby-sitter they will be in a female environment in a heterosexual home.

This judge considers "a heterosexual home" to be, by definition, better than a lesbian one. Having implied that children need role models of both genders, the judge doesn't suggest that the mother could provide male role models through hiring a baby-sitter—but he says exactly that about the father. His suggestion that the potential change in the father's environment makes that a more optimal rather than less optimal situation when compared to the mother's established household is homophobia, pure and simple. Issues such as the quality of parents' relationships to their children take second place to the idea that parents' gender matters most. Furthermore, in discussing gender, the judge simplistically assumes that what children need in terms of parents is one of each flavor. This is set forth as so self-evident that no reasons need be provided.

Judges sometimes combine their fetishism of traditional gender roles with misconceptions about the relationship between sexual orientation and gender identity. For example, many incorrectly assume that lesbian and gay relationships mimic stereotypical heterosexual husband-wife role delineations, or that lesbians and gay men take on gender roles that are the opposite of their biological sex. Given the tremendous value many place on upholding traditional gender roles, both these possibilities are of course seen as dangerous and warped. In one case a judge "maintained that there was a husband and wife relationship between the mother and her partner since the partner took the son to Cub Scout meetings like a father would. The witness responded that the woman took the child to Cub Scouts the way an aunt or grandmother would. The judge responded to the witness by saying 'Oh come on now, you and I both know what's going on.' "

When lesbian and gay custody cases first began to appear in the courts, myths and fears were rampant. As judges turned to mental-health professionals to find out about the impact of parents' homosexuality on children, they found a dearth of information. Just as families headed by lesbians and gay men had been previously invisible in the courts, so too were they absent from the psychological literature. Judging from a careful reading of professional journals published prior to the late 1970s, there seemed simply to be no such thing as lesbian or gay parents. The first psychological studies stemmed directly from questions initially raised in courtrooms. The sudden emergence of lesbian and gay parents in psychological literature underscores the extent to which psychology is linked to its social context. Beginning in the late 1970s, lesbian and gay parents moved from complete absence in the psychological literature to a presence that was peculiarly close to that absence: research was fundamentally shaped by the very same homophobic and heterosexist assumptions it was designed to refute. Instead of describing the children of lesbian and gay parents as they were, the studies depicted what they were not.

Not surprisingly, the researchers who first looked at families headed by lesbians and gay men focused most on the question of whether children raised by homosexual parents would themselves grow up to be lesbian or gay. Across the board they found that this was not the case. Furthermore, they saw that kids raised in such households were no more prone to confusion about their gender identities or to emotional disturbance of any kind. Study after study revealed that there were essentially no differences between children reared by heterosexuals and those raised by lesbian or gay parents. Besides these studies, common sense argued that the development of sexual orientation is not purely a matter of imitation of one's parents: the vast majority of lesbians and gay men have been raised by heterosexual parents.

Refuting the worry that children raised by homosexuals will themselves grow up to be gay was a pivotal step in the legal advocacy for homosexual parents. These studies relieved many who had worried about how lesbian and gay parents might influence their children and thwart their development. While the reassurances have been crucial to positive lesbian and gay custody outcomes, it is disturbing to recognize how deeply homophobia informs both legal and psychological discussion of these questions. Clearly, the fear that children raised by homosexuals will grow up to be lesbian or gay suggests that it would be awful if that were the case. In other words, in order to prove that they are worthy parents, lesbians and gay men have had to prove that they are not likely to raise children who will grow up to be like them. The idea that lesbian and gay parents are by definition poor role models is implicit in the discussion. Those advocating for lesbian and gay parents have not challenged this aspect of homophobia in legal or psychological arenas. In this area, people wanting to help lesbian and gay parents took up homophobic questions on homophobic terms. It seems society is not yet ready for a more deeply challenging response to the question of whether the kids of homosexuals will grow up to be gay— namely, so what if they do?

Will the Kids Be Stigmatized?

In the same case in which a lesbian mother was denied custody because she couldn't provide a heterosexual role model, the judge also stated: "the petitioner and her partner live very much to themselves as far as the neighborhood is concerned, this being a normal result of what would be considered by many their abnormal relationship. The court feels that with the respondent, the children would have more numerous and more satisfying contacts with their peers and the neighborhood adults than would be true in the neighborhood to which the petitioner would take them." Here, the lesbian parents were caught in a classic *Catch-22*. In the eyes of the court, their social reticence was a "normal" result of their "abnormal" relationship. Presumably, if they were more open and socially visible, they would have been criticized for flaunting their homosexuality, as many are. However, in this instance the judge seized upon their tendency to "keep to themselves" as evidence that their household wasn't suitable for children.

Other judges have similarly seen societal prejudice as inevitable and beyond criticism or challenge. Assuming that children will be stigmatized, they go on to deny custody in terms that claim to be protective of those children. In 1985, for example, one judge declared "the conditions under which this child must live daily . . . impose an intolerable burden upon her by reason of the social condemnation attached to them, which will inevitably afflict her relationships with her peers and with the community at large." In another case, the judge said "living in the same house with their mother and her lover may well cause the children to 'suffer the slings and arrows of a disapproving society' to a much greater extent [than would the father's custody]."

Though advocates for lesbian and gay parents handled the question of children's sexual orientation without seriously challenging its underlying values, they approached the question of whether children would be damaged by stigma in a much more complex way, challenging it on both empirical and philosophical grounds.

As with the question of sexual orientation, studies have demonstrated that children of lesbians and gay men don't necessarily experience as much stigmatization as judges may imagine. These studies suggest that the presence of stigma must be evaluated on a case-by-case basis rather than assumed across the board. But beyond this question lie two critical issues that cut to the very core of how stigmatization is viewed.

First, is it always by definition damaging for a child to be stigmatized? An alternative view suggests that what really matters is the kind of support children get, particularly from their families, in dealing with whatever prejudices they are subjected to in the world. Children who are helped to deal constructively with discrimination are likely to develop significant strengths; they can think independently and stand up for what they believe. Furthermore, as some courts have recognized, children with lesbian or gay parents will not be spared the ravages of homophobia simply by being removed from the custody of those parents; the issue will be part of children's lives no matter whom they live with. This too supports the idea that rather than attempt to completely shield children from prejudice, responsible adults should make efforts to help them deal with it.

Second, who bears responsibility for the destructiveness of society's bigotry? Those who argue that children should be protected from stigmatization by being separated from their lesbian or gay parents essentially shift the burden of responsibility from society onto parents—onto the victims rather than the perpetrators of bigotry. This is a key issue in the legal arena, where some courts have recognized that to deny custody on the basis of stigmatization is tantamount to supporting prejudice.

In fact, a 1984 U.S. Supreme Court decision established that basing custody decisions on fear of social prejudice is unconstitutional. In *Palmore* v. *Sidoti*, a Florida court denied custody to a white mother because she married a black man. The judge asserted that if custody were retained, the child would suffer discrimination. The judge stated:

> The father's evident resentment of the mother's choice of a black partner is not sufficient to wrest custody from the mother. It is of some significance, however, that the mother did see fit to bring a man into her home and carry on a sexual relationship with him without being married to him. Such action tended to place gratification of her own desires ahead of her concern for the child's future and welfare. This Court feels that despite the strides that have been made in bettering relations between the races in this country, it is inevitable that Melanie will, if allowed to remain in her present situation and attains school age and thus more vulnerable to peer pressures, suffer from social stigmatization that is sure to come.

The U.S. Supreme Court, in a unanimous decision, disagreed with the trial court's reasoning and found it to be in violation of the Constitution:

> It would ignore reality to suggest that racial and ethnic prejudices do not exist or that all manifestations of those prejudices have been eliminated. There is a risk that a child living with a step-parent of a different race may be subject to a variety of pressures and stresses not present if the child were living with a parent of the same racial or ethnic origin.
>
> The question, however, is whether the reality of private biases and the possible injury they might inflict are permissible considerations for removal of an infant child from the custody of its natural mother. We have little difficulty in concluding that they are not. The

Constitution cannot control such prejudices but neither can it tolerate them. Private biases may be outside the reach of the law, but the law cannot, directly or indirectly, give them effect.

Judges now often acknowledge the relevance of *Palmore* v. *Sidoti* to lesbian and gay custody proceedings. That precedent prohibits courts from denying custody because a child might be stigmatized. As one Alaska court put it, "It is impermissible to rely on any real or imagined social stigma attaching to [the] Mother's status as a lesbian [applying *Palmore*]."

Some judges have quite sensitively appreciated the complexity of stigma as an issue in children's lives. In upholding a lesbian mother's custody rights, a judge eloquently framed the issues in a 1979 decision:

> Within the context of a loving and supportive relationship, there is no reason to think the girls will be unable to manage whatever anxieties may flow from the community's disapproval of their mother. . . .

> If defendant retains custody, it may be that because the community is intolerant of her differences, these girls may sometimes have to bear themselves with greater than ordinary fortitude. But this does not necessarily portend that their moral welfare or safety will be jeopardized. It is just as reasonable to expect that they will emerge better equipped to search out their own standards of right and wrong, better able to perceive that the majority is not always correct in its moral judgments, and better able to understand the importance of conforming their beliefs to the requirements of reason and tested knowledge, not the constraints of currently popular sentiment or prejudice.

> Taking the children from defendant can be done only at the cost of sacrificing those very qualities that they will find most sustaining in meeting the challenges

inevitably ahead. Instead of forbearance and feelings of protectiveness, it will foster in them a sense of shame for their mother. Instead of courage and the precept that people of integrity do not shrink from bigots, it counsels the easy option of shirking difficult problems and following the course of expedience. Lastly, it diminishes their regard for the rule of human behavior, everywhere accepted, that we do not forsake those to whom we are indebted for love and nurture merely because they are held in low esteem by others.

We conclude that the children's best interest will be disserved by undermining in this way their growth as mature and principled adults. Extensive evidence in the record upon which we have commented amply confirms the trial judge's finding that defendant is a worthy mother. Nothing suggests that her homosexual preference in itself presents any threat of harm to her daughters or that in the ordinary course of their development they will be unable to deal with whatever vexation may be caused to their spirits by the community.

This opinion contains a view of family that is strikingly different from many quoted earlier. Here, personal values such as integrity, love, and courage are linked in a primary way to ideal family life, while questions of gender and sexual categorization are absent. Furthermore, the judge clearly started from the premises that prejudice is a societal problem, and the consequences of it for any given individual are something to be dealt with rather than avoided. In framing a decision around these understandings, this judge upheld profound and essentially human values.

Will the Kids Be Molested?

To understand the multitude of false allegations the issue of lesbian and gay parents inspires in our culture, we must recognize that homophobia is a complex weave of anxious preoccupations with sexual categories and tendencies to project malice and violence onto marginalized groups. These features of homophobia are magnified tenfold when relationships between lesbians or gay men and children are under consideration, because conservative forces tend to project their own moral righteousness onto children. So-called pro-family rhetoric declaring exactly what children need is often a thinly masked diatribe against anyone who challenges the primacy of traditional heterosexual arrangements.

One of the clearest examples of this thinking is the persistent myth that homosexuals are likely to molest children. This myth is deeply entrenched in our society, seemingly impervious to the vast evidence that it is heterosexual men who are most likely to be pedophiles. Gay men tend to be tarred most by the specter of pedophilia, but lesbians are burdened by it as well. In the Nadler appeal, the judge asked the testifying psychiatrist point-blank: "Could she harm her own child, the daughter, by this activity? Is there any potential that she might use the child in this activity?"

Without a doubt, sexual abuse of children is a horrendous and frighteningly common phenomenon in our society, and concern for a child's safety should be paramount. However, the automatic reflex to bring this issue up in the context of a lesbian or gay custody proceeding, and to raise it much less often with respect to heterosexual parents, is extremely misguided. Study after study has shown that the vast majority of perpetrators are heterosexual men. Society's conflation of pedophilia with homosexuality burdens lesbians and gay men in their parental and professional relationships to children. The myth obscures both the humanity of homosexuals and the darker side of heterosexuality.

HIV and AIDS in Custody Proceedings

Throughout the 1970s and early 1980s the primary issues that lesbian and gay parents in custody battles had to contend with centered on the meanings society ascribed to homosexuality in and of itself. However, by the mid 1980s, with the advent of AIDS, a whole other dimension of homophobia emerged. Hysteria and ignorance about the disease combined with already prevalent antihomosexual sentiments to unleash a new and extraordinarily virulent form of homophobic hostility. During the past decade issues of AIDS and HIV status have increasingly appeared in divorce and custody disputes. Legal experts suggest that we will be seeing more and more of this in the years to come.

AIDS and HIV status may become custody issues in two ways. When a parent's HIV status is unknown, there is sometimes a question about whether courts can mandate testing. Often this is part of a gay-baiting mentality. It is not a logical requirement, since HIV status in and of itself does not have an impact on parenting abilities. Furthermore, the test is of limited value, with a negative result having to be continually reaffirmed through repeated testing, if there is any question of ongoing risk of exposure. In a 1986 Chicago case a judge mandated testing of a gay father prior to granting visitation rights, but the decision was appealed. In this case, the attempt to require testing was clearly part of a larger homophobic attack on the father. The mother's attorney stated that regardless of how the AIDS question was resolved, the father would be challenged on other aspects of his lifestyle. Mandatory testing in these kinds of cases has generally so far not been upheld. More commonly, decisions employ reasoning, as that of a 1988 New York court that denied the maternal grandparents' request for mandatory testing of a father. The decision was based on recognition that HIV infection was relevant to the proceeding only insofar as it affected the child.

The other way AIDS or HIV status may become an issue in a custody case is when a parent is known to be HIV positive or to have AIDS and someone sees this as a reason to disrupt the parent-child relationship. That's the situation Elliot found himself in when, after years of a joint-custody arrangement, he became ill and was suddenly threatened with the loss of his son.

Elliot had always been aware that he was attracted to men. Confused about the meaning of this and encouraged by others to pursue heterosexuality, he married at age twenty-two. He and his wife, Karen, had a son, Mark. During the early years of his marriage, Elliot became increasingly aware that his being attracted to men was an essential part of his identity; there was no doubt in his mind that he was gay. When Mark was three years old, Elliot came out and separated from Karen amicably, with the two agreeing on joint custody of Mark. Not long after the divorce Elliot met Larry, who became his life partner and another parent to Mark. For six years they lived a rather ordinary family existence. The shared-custody arrangement went smoothly, and Mark thrived.

Then in 1986 Elliot began to notice physical problems—he was forgetful and experienced strange sensations in his arms and legs. A visit to his doctor confirmed his fears: he was HIV positive and suffering from neurological symptoms. At first Elliot was able to carry on with his work and parenting responsibilities, but after a while he was too exhausted to function at full tilt in both arenas. Elliot talked with his wife about his condition, and they made a temporary, informal agreement that Mark would stay with Karen more during the summer. Soon after that Elliot was diagnosed with AIDS dementia and began AZT treatment, which considerably diminished his symptoms, eliminating altogether the neurological problems he'd had. Around the same time, he made a decision to stop work temporarily in order to be able to focus his energies on his relationship with Mark. Elliot also sought counseling about how to help Mark deal with his father's AIDS diagnosis.

With the situation more under control, Elliot let Karen know that he expected to resume the joint-custody arrangement in the fall. But Karen and her new husband, Michael, had other ideas. She told Elliot she would not return to the arrangement and she told Mark's school not to allow Elliot to pick him up. Karen had no legal right to assert this position since Elliot still had joint legal and physical custody. Elliot picked Mark up from school at the beginning of the week that was officially their time together, bringing with him the documentation of his legal custody arrangement. At that point, Karen went to court to get an *ex parte* injunction giving her sole custody of Mark. Elliot had no legal representation, and ignorance about AIDS dominated the proceeding. A psychiatric social worker who had never met Elliot and who had no experience with AIDS nonetheless testified that, since according to his own report Elliot had suffered from AIDS dementia, he was undoubtedly unfit to parent Mark. The social worker relied on a description of senility in defining Elliot's condition, when in fact his neurological symptoms had nothing in common with that condition and furthermore had responded favorably to the AZT treatment. Meanwhile, nine-year-old Mark vociferously expressed his wish to return to the old custody arrangement. Nonetheless, the judge, assuming Mark was jeopardized by remaining in Elliot's custody though having no actual evidence to this effect, granted the injunction. Elliot's custody was revoked and he was allowed to visit Mark only in Karen's presence.

Eventually Elliot was able to find funding and a lawyer to handle his appeal. It was in this appellate court that the arguments vital to parents with AIDS in custody struggles were set forth.

Essentially, as with other lesbian and gay custody issues, a nexus standard is the only one that allows for a reasonable appraisal of custody involving a parent with AIDS or HIV infection. A parent's AIDS or positive HIV status does not in and of itself say anything about fitness as a parent or about what kind of custody arrangement would be in the best interests of the child. But in the heat of AIDS hysteria and homophobia, these basic insights may be overlooked. The courts need to be educated about AIDS and several commonly raised questions need to be addressed: Is the person's ability to care for a child impaired as a result of AIDS or positive HIV status? Is the child in danger of being infected? How will the experience of a parent's decline and death affect a child, and in what circumstances can that best be dealt with? And, as with other homosexual custody cases, will the child be stigmatized, and can this be a basis for custody determination?

The impact of any illness or disability on a parent's capacity to take care of a child must be assessed on a case-by-case basis; it can't be ascertained simply by abstractly considering the disease or injury. Since the physical condition of those with AIDS varies tremendously, it is even more crucial that a person be individually assessed by a qualified physician, familiar with the manifestations and disease course of AIDS, before any conclusions about parenting abilities are reached. In Elliot's case, the lower court's ignorance about AIDS was exacerbated rather than ameliorated by the social worker's inaccurate testimony about AIDS dementia. At Elliot's appeal, his attorneys argued this point, and medical testimony corroborated the fact that his parenting abilities were not in fact impaired by his physical condition, particularly since he'd responded well to AZT and was working less outside the home.

To address AIDS hysteria as it may appear in a custody case, it is crucial to refute the idea that children are at risk of infection by their parents. Numerous studies have documented that HIV is transmitted through exchange of bodily fluids—primarily blood, semen, and vaginal secretions. Studies of families of AIDS patients demonstrate that the level of intimate contact involved in sharing a household does not pose risk of exposure. In Elliot's case, the fear that he could infect his son was not raised overtly in court. But such fears have figured in other cases. For instance, in a 1988 Indiana case involving an HIV-infected father and a mother who was clearly unfit owing to severe ongoing drug abuse, the judge's prejudices and hysteria regarding AIDS overrode all other considerations. He denied the father both custody and visitation, stating "even if there is a one percent chance that this child is going to contract it from him, I'm not going to expose her to it." Fortunately, on appeal this decision was overruled, and the higher court recognized that prejudice had led to abuse of judicial discretion. The appellate decision established a local precedent against custody denial based *per se* on a parent's positive HIV status.

One strategy used by Karen's attorneys to argue that Elliot should not maintain joint custody was to claim it would be traumatic for Mark to be exposed to his father's physical deterioration over the years. Though this issue is commonly raised in AIDS custody cases, mental-health experts and psychological literature are very clear that children whose parents are terminally ill are far more traumatized by being separated from those parents than by maintaining contact. In fact, an ongoing relationship between parent and child throughout the illness facilitates a healthier grieving process in the long run.

As with other lesbian and gay custody issues, attorneys may argue that granting custody to a parent with AIDS or HIV will cause the child to be stigmatized. The argument against this line of reasoning in AIDS custody cases is the same as in other situations: As the *Palmore* v. *Sidoti* ruling established, fear of stigmatization is not a sound basis on which to deny custody.

During Elliott's appeal the judge listened to these arguments and counterarguments, and interviewed Mark about his wishes. She concluded that Karen and Elliot should return to the joint physical custody arrangement they had prior to Elliot's diagnosis. She saw Elliot as "able to care for [Mark's] physical needs" and Mark as "entitled to continue to receive the obvious benefits he has enjoyed thus far by spending substantial time with both parents in a normal day-to-day setting, rather than seeing his father only on weekends." The judge recognized that "this is particularly important now when the child's desire to do so is unequivocal and when at some point in the future it may no longer be possible because of his father's health."

Elliot's case ultimately turned out well, but that is not the situation for many when AIDS or HIV become custody issues. Hysteria and ignorance pose formidable challenges to those advocating for lesbian and gay parents in the courts, especially because this is a relatively new experience both for society and for the law.

Custody Disputes and Constitutional Rights

From an ethical standpoint, the only concern that should govern decisions about children's lives is the fulfillment of those children's needs. In legal terms this perspective is captured by the best-interests-of-the-child standard. However, despite the best-interests guidelines, all too often family-law decisions ignore children's interests in favor of parental rights. We have recently seen this in the overturning of adoptions even after children have formed crucial connections to their adoptive parents. These cases are tragic because it is the child's rights, not the parent's, that should be paramount. In all custody cases, both legal and ethical guidelines point to consideration of children's best interests over and above any concerns about parental rights. Thus the most powerful arguments for lesbian and gay parents maintaining their relationships with their children focus on children's well-being. Legally as well as morally, the question of lesbian and gay parents' rights is secondary. However, in these cases, the best interests of the children are not in opposition to parental rights; in fact, negative custody rulings simultaneously undercut parents' civil rights and children's emotional well-being. When courts don't employ a nexus or detriment standard, not only are the best interests of the child inadequately considered but the constitutional rights of the parents are seriously violated. The questions surrounding parents' civil rights and children's well-being thus converge in lesbian and gay custody battles.

Both *per se* decisions and those based on unproven presumptions of harm deny parents the constitutional right of due process. They lose custody of their children without the opportunity for a meaningful hearing. Due process is clearly violated whenever decisions are based on irrebutable presumptions, as for example the idea that lesbianism *per se* constitutes parental unfitness. But due process is also violated when the burden of proof is shifted from the state to the parent, and when the reasoning behind custody denials is not supported by clearly documented evidence of harm. This is the situation in many lesbian and gay custody hearings where parents have to justify themselves in response to unsupported allegations of detriment. The U.S. Supreme Court has established that individuals cannot be deprived of significant private interests, including custody, without due process. The individual's interests can be superceded only by a compelling state interest that clearly necessitates the action. The relevant state interest in these cases is the best-interests-of-the-child standard. However, it cannot be demonstrated that that interest is met by denying custody to lesbian or gay parents. In fact, the evidence clearly establishes that parents' sexual orientation in itself is irrelevant to children's well-being.

Along these lines, proceedings that lack a detriment standard violate the rights of lesbian and gay parents to equal protection under the Fourteenth Amendment. Essentially, the law states that when the state utilizes a "suspect" classification, its actions must bear up under "strict scrutiny"—that is, as stated above, any abridgment of individual rights must be demonstrably necessitated by a compelling state interest. Classifications such as race, religion, nationality, and alienage have all been deemed "suspect" by the Supreme Court; "quasi-suspect" classes include gender and illegitimacy. The purpose of applying "strict" or "intermediate" scrutiny (in the case of "quasi-suspect" classes) is to ensure that discrimination does not influence legal decisions. Denying custody to lesbian and gay parents because of their sexual orientation would not hold up under "strict" or "intermediate scrutiny" because the state cannot demonstrate that its compelling interest (the best-interests-of-the-child standard) is met by such denials. Applying equal-protection principles requires strict adherence to a true nexus or detriment standard.

Equal protection has been a difficult area for lesbians and gay men. To date, homosexuality has not been recognized as either a "suspect" or "quasi-suspect" class. The legal criteria for such classifications are: (1) a history of discrimination, based on (2) an immutable characteristic, that (3) bears no relationship to the ability to contribute to society. The major sticking point for lesbians and gay men has been the question of whether homosexuality is an immutable characteristic—that is, essentially beyond a person's control. There is no definitive understanding of the origins of homosexuality. It appears to be a complex phenomenon that cannot be reduced to the status of a biological, inborn trait. However, several scholars argue that this narrow use of "immutability" in fact does not hold up for other "suspect" classifications, such as religion, and that the more salient feature of the characteristic in question is how central it is to the individual's identity and being. Under this set of criteria, homosexuality would undoubtedly qualify as a "suspect" or "quasi-suspect" classification. Another potential approach to equal protection for lesbians and gay men is to argue that custody denials are essentially premised on gender discrimination—that is to say, the basis for the decisions is the gender of the parent's partner. Since the courts recognize gender as a "quasi-suspect" classification, this approach bypasses the judicial reluctance to acknowledge homosexuality itself as a "suspect" or "quasi-suspect" classification. However, these arguments have yet to be legally recognized.

In many custody decisions, lesbian and gay parents find that their First Amendment rights such as freedom of association and freedom of speech are also violated. This is blatant in decisions that impose contingencies on lesbian or gay parents, such as restricting their political activity and degree of openness, or forbidding them to live with same-sex partners. Arguments that children should not be exposed to parents' deviant lifestyles similarly violate these protected rights; the government is not supposed to have the power to restrict such expression.

The religious base of homophobia in our culture is evident both historically and often explicitly in legal discussions of homosexuality, such as the language of the sodomy statutes. The First Amendment requirement that the state neither prohibit nor advance any particular religious theory is violated when lesbian and gay custody denials are influenced either directly or indirectly by religious beliefs. Essentially, "Americans are guaranteed both freedom of and freedom from religion." The legal support of homophobia abridges that basic right.

While the right to privacy is not explicitly guaranteed in the Constitution, the Supreme Court has recognized it in many contexts. This right is violated when someone even inquires about a parent's sexual orientation in the absence of an established nexus between it and harm to the child.

Sometimes judges grapple with concern about fundamental rights of parents but nevertheless impose grave restrictions on them without establishing a connection between their homosexuality and harm to the children. In these instances the power of homophobia overrides the most basic principles of our judicial system. In 1974, a gay father who had been granted severely restricted visitation rights sought redress and claimed that the Constitution prohibited restrictions on the basis of his homosexuality. The New Jersey court hearing the appeal agreed with this assertion, stating:

> Fundamental rights of parents may not be denied, limited or restricted on the basis of sexual orientation, *per se.* The right of a parent, including a homosexual parent, to the companionship and care of his or her child, insofar as it is for the best interest of the child, is a fundamental right protected by the First, Ninth and Fourteenth Amendments to the Constitution. That right may not be restricted without a showing that the parent's activities may tend to impair the emotional or physical health of the child.

However, as Hunter and Polikoff described, the judge went on to examine "the father's involvement in gay rights activities and the fact that his children had accompanied him to protest marches, meetings, and social gatherings. . . . The judge noted 'The factors which enter into consideration must be more inclusive than the threat of mere physical harm. We are dealing . . . with a most sensitive issue which holds the possibility of inflicting severe mental anguish and detriment on three innocent children.' " Without explaining what anguish and detriment the children would experience, the judge awarded restricted visitation consisting of alternate-week daytime visits and three weeks of visitation during the summer only at some place other than his home, during which time, according to Hunter and Polikoff, "he was ordered not to sleep with anyone other than a lawful spouse nor to involve the children in any homosexual-related activities or publicity nor to see his male companion in the presence of his children."

In general, legal arguments based on constitutional rights have not been widely recognized in custody proceedings, which emphasize the best interests of the child over any concerns about parents' rights. However, some judges have attended to these issues explicitly. One judge in a 1973 case of a lesbian mother who lost custody eloquently expressed the lone dissenting opinion:

> Where neglect, abuse, or mistreatment in some manner is absent, the state has no right to inquire into what a parent teaches [her] child, or with whom a parent allows [her] child to associate, or the type of environment a parent permits [her] child to inhabit. These are fundamental family rights, protected by the Common Law and our Bill of Rights, free from government intrusion. Freedom to think, teach, and express; freedom of association with other persons or classes of persons with varying degrees of morality and philosophy; freedom to inhabit a chosen cultural environment; and freedom to adopt a lifestyle that may not have the approval of the majority; all of these . . . freedoms exist even more emphatically within the family or the parent-child relationship.
>
> Within this relationship the family or the parent adopts a moral standard for the members' conduct and associations, and the state cannot intrude upon or disrupt this relationship by asserting a different moral standard, conceived by judges, that must be adhered to.

This judge pointedly recognizes that homophobic custody denials encompass both the incorrect assessment of children's needs and the abridgment of parents' civil rights. The constitutional issues that lesbian and gay custody battles touch upon are significant. In this area, the link between homophobia and the state's undue interference in the private lives of citizens is crystal-clear. The question should not be whether particular judges—or mainstream society, for that matter—approve of lesbians and gay men raising children. When cases are decided on that basis, we are well on the road to having Big Brother determine the nature of our intimate lives.

Where We Are Now

About two decades have passed since lesbian and gay parents first appeared in the courts. While much has changed, there is still a long way to go. We are like runners at the beginning of a long race, glancing briefly over our shoulders to see how far we've come. We must remember that the road ahead is much longer than the distance we've covered.

When I began my research on the legal status of lesbian and gay parents, I naïvely assumed that the custody losses and visitation restrictions I've described were largely a thing of the past. Now I recognize that assumption as a wish, rather than a fact. At this writing, five states still have *per se* precedents that guide all lesbian and gay custody rulings. On the other hand, several states have nexus or detriment precedents, and among many jurisdictions without precedents there is a trend toward this standard. However, throughout the country there continues to be difficulty dissuading courts from approaches that claim nexus while in fact being satisfied with no real evidence of harm. The presumption-of-harm standard continues to result in visitation restrictions, custody awards contingent on parents staying closeted, and outright custody loss.

Although there is now a substantial body of research demonstrating that children reared by lesbians and gay men are indistinguishable from those in heterosexual homes with respect to psychological adjustment, myths abound. These myths need to be dismantled on a case-by-case basis by educating the courts in the realities of lesbian and gay life.

Maria Gil de Lamadrid, an advocate for lesbian and gay parents, had this to say: "In the early 1970s no states had established standards or there was an automatic presumption against lesbian and gay parents. That has changed and we continue to chip away. Compared to fifteen years ago, when the Lesbian Rights Project was founded, we now receive, at minimum, lip service from most courts in recognizing there can't be a presumption of harm. It reminds me of racial discrimination in that thirty years ago employers had no problem being blatant, whereas now it's often more subtle. With these custody cases it's similar in that there's an official recognition that maybe this bias is not proper, but courts continue to find ways of finding harm to the child that are based almost entirely on stereotype."

As an example, Gil de Lamadrid told of a case recently decided in Michigan, in which a lesbian mother whose custody was being challenged on that basis ended up with a decision that hinged on her dissolving the household she'd formed with her lover. The court did not directly specify that the decision was made because the mother was a lesbian; as Gil de Lamadrid pointed out, "they didn't dare say it." However, homophobia was clearly evident in the hearing. Expert witnesses, including psychiatrists and psychologists, testified for both sides. The psychiatrist testifying on behalf of the mother had professional expertise with families headed by lesbians and gay men. The father's witnesses did not. Yet the testimony of the impressively credentialed psychiatrist was discredited by the court on the grounds that he was an "advocate" because he himself was gay. It did not occur to the court that the heterosexual experts were "advocates" of heterosexual parenthood.

The antihomosexual bias of the American justice system continues to etch itself on the lives of people like Minnie Bruce Pratt and her sons. But there are many kinds of victories. Over the years Minnie Bruce and her children forged bonds that no law could touch. And Minnie Bruce, having grappled with the push toward silence, finally told her story: "I don't think I would have started writing again if I hadn't come out. I think that gave me the energy and centeredness that I needed. I also think that my writing was fueled by the pain and anger of what I went through. I really feel that I wrote to save my life and to keep my sanity. It took me a while to get to not being closeted in terms of my work, but I was always pushing toward a place where I wouldn't have to hide myself—where I could talk about myself and write about my life. Ultimately, it became *Crime Against Nature*, which was a wonderful experience for me; the boys read it in manuscript form. I felt as if I had set aside my victimization, and I have gotten tremendously rewarded for it in a way that I never ever would have thought could happen. It's so contradictory, but it's a message for me. My whole life with my children has been a very positive message. If you hang on, if you love them, if you don't lie to them, if you tell them the truth, if you stay faithful to yourself, then you will get this reward in the end: the love of your children for yourself as yourself." In 1989 Minnie Bruce Pratt was awarded the distinguished Lamont Poetry Selection by the Academy of American Poets for her book of poetry entitled *Crime Against Nature*, a chronicle of the loss of her sons—who proudly accompanied her to the award ceremony.

Every homophobic statement quoted in this chapter is matched by a corresponding profound loss for both parents and children. And beyond that, there is a loss for all of us—a diminished sense of possibility that comes when people fail to hear beyond their prejudices. I am reminded of something Ben, Minnie Bruce's younger son, told me: "People can make laws discriminating against lesbian and gay parents because they've never experienced it—they've never had that eye-opening experience of what it means to be something that's never talked about or mentioned in a public school or on television. It's made me attuned to what isn't said and isn't done. I recognize situations that don't allow people to speak. Since I realize the domination and tyranny of those moments when I left things unsaid, I give other people the opportunity to speak—it's imperative."

· 4 ·

Save Our Children

Foster Care and Adoption Struggles

Each of us has many coming-out stories—tale upon tale of epiphany, rebellion, courage, transformation. One of mine begins in innocence. I was seventeen, shy and studious but deeply committed to adventure. That year I avidly watched every move of the one lesbian couple I knew. They seemed so strong, so clear in themselves. I studied them because I knew—had always known—that I loved women. What I didn't know yet was that I could have the life I wanted, that I could reach for what made me happy.

After months of mulling it over, my roommate, Beth, and I sat across the breakfast table and shyly asked each other, "Do you want to try it?"—acknowledging our curiosity, our hunger for the experience. We knew we weren't in love, but affection filled the air between us and we longed to touch. So one awkward night I waited while she showered, then we wordlessly ascended the stairs to her room. I remember the slippery moistness of her body, her hair still damp from the shower, the smell of lemon soap. Neither of us knew what to do. The precise image of our fumbling has not stayed with me, but I will always remember the kiss.

There are moments when you recognize that you will never be

the same—when you feel the jolt of all your cells transforming in an instant, your whole being changing form like ice suddenly seared into liquid. That is what happened when Beth and I kissed. Afterward I lay in the darkness trying to ground myself in this new place. It was the first time I'd kissed someone because I wanted to—the first time I understood that sex could be what you choose, not just what you give in to. Once I knew that, there was no turning back. What I will always remember about the spring of 1977 is careening through the streets of Brooklyn, perched precariously on the handlebars of Beth's bicycle, celebrating the freedom of that kiss.

In 1977 Anita Bryant campaigned particularly vehemently against lesbians and gay men, with the slogan "Save Our Children." So while I was exuberantly exploring my new-found capacities to love, to rejoice in my sexuality, and most of all, to live my life with integrity, Bryant was trying to save children from the likes of me. Or perhaps, while I was a minor, she was trying to save me from the likes of those whose guidance and affirmation were my lifelines. Give or take a year, it made little difference in the end. The world I came out into was ablaze with high-pitched battles between gay activists and homophobes.

In the 1970s the efforts of lesbian and gay activists led to the adoption of civil rights ordinances in many U.S. cities and municipalities. Essentially, these laws banned discrimination against homosexuals in housing and employment. In 1977, Dade County, Florida, became the first Southern region to enact such a bill. But within five weeks of its passage, Bryant's Save Our Children group had collected 65,000 signatures protesting the new law—well beyond the 10,000 needed to force a referendum on the issue. Referring to homosexuals as "human garbage," she criticized the bill as an attempt to "legitimize homosexuals and their recruitment of our children." Appealing especially to fundamentalists who carried out much of the work, her campaign propounded an image of lesbians and gay men not only as sinners but as a corrosive force in society that would inevitably destroy the family.

Bryant's rhetoric pitted lesbians and gay men against children.

For her, homosexuals were either child molesters or obsessed with recruiting children into their ranks. The fact that the overwhelming majority of child molesters are heterosexual men was ignored, as was the basic humanity of homosexuals. Children, in turn, were defined as exclusively heterosexual and necessarily embedded in the "traditional family." On June 7, 1977, voters overturned the Dade County gay rights ordinance. The very next day, Governor Askew signed laws barring same-sex marriage and prohibiting lesbians and gay men from adopting children. Florida thus became the first state to enact legislation explicitly banning gay adoption.

Anita Bryant's campaign marked the beginning of a strong backlash to gay rights throughout the nation. During the next year lesbian and gay activists put forth proposals to ban discrimination in many cities including San Francisco, Hartford, Baltimore, and New York. But at the same time, many existing ordinances were repealed, including those in St. Paul, Wichita, Seattle, and Eugene.

On the heels of the Dade County repeal, in a move calculated to boost his upcoming campaign for governor, California senator John Briggs announced his plan to ban gay teachers from public schools throughout the state. Again, the most virulent homophobia was expressed by pitting lesbians and gay men against children. Pairing the proposal with one calling for a stronger death-penalty statute, Briggs's organization, the California Defend Our Children Committee, declared "You can act right now to help protect your family from vicious killers and defend your children from homosexual teachers." Briggs maintained that children were the central battleground for homosexuals. "There are all kinds of organizations to abuse your children," he pronounced. "Pornographers want your children. Dope addicts want your children. Homosexuals want your children. . . . They don't have any children of their own. If they don't recruit children or very young people, they'd all die away. They have no means of replenishing. That's why they want to be teachers and be equal status and have those people serve as role models and encourage people to join them." Briggs, too, got enormous support and was able to get the bill on to the November 1978 ballot.

There was intense struggle regarding lesbians and gay men throughout the nation, but events in California during 1978 most clearly illustrated the dimensions of it. In January of that year Harvey Milk assumed his post on the San Francisco Board of Supervisors, becoming the city's first openly gay elected official. It was a heady time for lesbians and gay men in the area, with much progress in sight. Yet at the same time there appeared to be growing support for the Briggs Initiative, with polls predicting passage by a large number. As in Dade County the year before, gay activists had a tough battle on their hands, but this time they won. On November 8, as a result of massive organizing efforts, the initiative was defeated by a wide margin.

Just two weeks later, Harvey Milk was assassinated along with Mayor George Moscone by Dan White, a supervisor who stood for "traditional values" and whose district was the only one in San Francisco to support the Briggs Initiative. White was distraught over Moscone's failure to reappoint him after he had resigned from the board, and he was enraged by Milk's role in that decision. As a former police officer, White was supported by the police department, and tensions between homosexuals and the police were high following the killings. Despite the fact that White had pumped several bullets into Mayor Moscone, then carefully reloaded his gun and hunted down Milk, he was convicted only on two counts of voluntary manslaughter, with a maximum sentence of five to seven years in prison. The verdict prompted riots throughout the city. San Francisco's lesbians and gay men were galvanized into action. As Milk himself had recognized, the backlash did more to place lesbian and gay rights in the forefront of the nation's consciousness than anything else. Faced with multiple death threats during his political career, Milk, anticipating his own murder, declared, "If a bullet should enter my brain, let that bullet destroy every closet door."

There are many important lessons to be gleaned from the events of the late 1970s. It is no coincidence that the most intense homophobic attacks portray lesbians and gay men as being against children. Though these struggles occur on local levels, the rhetoric

resonates with what seems to be a national collective consciousness, with lesbians and gay men on one side of a line and children
and families on the other. At its most extreme, the idealization of
the traditional family is paired with the demonization of lesbians
and gay men—evil stalkers of children out to recruit the world and
thus destroy society. But one doesn't have to be a fundamentalist
to believe on some level that homosexuals and children don't mix.
Many people of liberal leanings readily express the sense that children belong in traditional families and should not have homosexuals as parents or role models. The myth remains that homosexuals
are pedophiles despite overwhelming evidence to the contrary.
Lesbian and gay parenting cannot be understood without seeing it
in this social context.

One striking dimension of the Bryant and Briggs campaigns is
the extent to which society's deep homophobia can be easily har-
nessed by zealots. The battles that ensue may be long or short-
lived, but in either case they often leave lasting damage. Bryant's
campaign faded, but the Florida ban on adoption remains a force in
the life of the state.

The struggles that came to the fore during the 1970s were characterized by intense feelings on both sides and by repetitive steps
forward and backward. In this case, the adage "history repeats
itself" is apt. The same battles recur, and therefore the work is
ongoing.

The Massachusetts Foster-Care Battle

In 1985, Dan White committed suicide, in a sense closing the book
on the Moscone-Milk assassinations. But that same year, events
occurred in Massachusetts that bore an uncanny resemblance to the
Bryant campaign in Florida. Once again a community was captivated by the ideological pitting of lesbians and gay men against
children. And once again, a single individual was at the core of
homophobic hysteria. It all began when a gay couple acted on one
of the most profound human desires: a wish to be parents.

When Don Babets came home from work that Wednesday he

opened the door on a scene that filled him with pleasure. David Jean, who loved applying his nutritionist training to his family, was cutting vegetables for dinner. Three-year-old Richard was sitting at the table playing with a plastic penguin they'd bought him at the aquarium the weekend before. Twenty-two-month-old John was nestled by David's feet, petting the rabbit they'd gotten at Easter.

Don had never been certain they'd reach this point. He'd always wanted children, but didn't know how it would come about since he was gay. David had given up on the idea when he came out, assuming that childlessness was the price he had to pay. But during their nine years together it became clear that they wanted their family to include children, and gradually they worked toward making that happen. They lived in the inner city and knew from daily experience that there were many children in Boston who lacked basic nurturance and support. Hearing about the shortage of foster-care homes on a radio advertisement, they decided to inquire about whether they could apply as gay men. Through informal networks, they found out that it was possible. After filling out the thirty-nine-page questionnaire, they spent six weeks in training, underwent an extensive home study, and waited. Don was not one to leave his dreams in the hands of fate—or even worse, a recalcitrant bureaucracy—so he called the Department of Social Services (DSS) weekly, asking where their case was, each time making sure it got moved along to the next level. It was almost a year before they were approved, and then only after review by the department commissioner. Don and David prepared their household for the arrival of a child. Then they waited some more. They were official foster parents, but there were no children in their home. The radio continued to describe the shortage of available caretakers. So Don got on the phone again, this time asking where the children were. Finally the call came from the DSS. There were two little boys who were being removed from their mother owing to neglect. Don and David had expected only one child, but they didn't hesitate to welcome both.

Like all new parents, when the boys arrived Don and David were overwhelmed with countless details, each demanding immediate attention. There were diapers and toys to purchase, meals to prepare, schedules to coordinate. But most pressing of all, there were two very small, frightened children standing before them, needing to be loved. On the first night, the challenge was made clear. No sooner had Don picked John up than Richard came charging at them, hitting John with a force that practically knocked him across the room. The next day, Don bought a He-man punching bag for Richard, but it would be weeks of work before he'd come to prefer it to hitting his little brother.

In fact, it was on that particular Wednesday night, two weeks later, that for the first time Richard, about to hit John, paused, looked at Don, said "He-man" and ran to the punching bag instead. Don and David beamed with pride. The glance that passed between them said it all. They loved caring together for these children more than they'd ever imagined. When they tucked them into bed that night, none of them had an inkling of the disaster that would arrive on their doorstep along with the morning paper.

On Thursday, May 8, 1985, on the front page of the Metro section of the *Boston Globe*, there was an article entitled "Some Oppose Foster Placement with Gay Couple." The article said that neighbors disapproved of the two little boys being placed with an openly gay couple. Many close to the family were immediately angered by the skewed reporting. Supportive neighbors who had also been interviewed were given short shrift, while those quoted more substantially had never met the family.

Though its tone caught Don and David off guard, the fact of the article was not a total surprise. Since rumors of the article had been in the air days before, the Department of Social Services, anticipating controversy, had contacted the children's mother and asked her to sign an agreement for her sons' placement with Don and David, knowing they were an openly gay couple. She did so willingly, since she had been impressed by the care the boys were receiving in their home. That Thursday morning, the DSS called Don and David and once again reassured them that the placement was secure.

It has never been officially clear what transpired between the

DSS and the administration of Governor Michael Dukakis, but by two o'clock that afternoon, social workers arrived to take Richard and John to another home. In a statement to the press, the Department of Social Services labeled the removal as an effort to protect the children from publicity. However, since the young children had little concept of what the *Boston Globe* was, much less what it said, and the abrupt move was clearly traumatic for them, this statement seemed to many a lame excuse for what had in fact been a political decision high up in the administration. The events of the next several years would bear out that interpretation.

Neither Don and David nor the children had time to prepare for their departure. David picked Richard up at day care and told him he would be going to a new home. Richard didn't seem to comprehend the situation, asking repeatedly "Mommy all better?" While the social workers waited in the living room, David went into John's room to get him ready. Pained by the prospect of a final good-bye, he lingered over his crib, softly talking with him for the last time. He was in the room so long that the social workers came in after him. When they left the house the children were crying and confused. It was the second time in two weeks that they were abruptly uprooted and whisked off to an unfamiliar place. As the car pulled away, John yelled, "Where we going?"

The next day, Governor Dukakis ordered a review of foster-care procedures and establishment of a policy on the placement of children in gay households. The existing guidelines evaluated caretakers on the basis of their capacity to provide "safe, nurturing and stable family environments" along with basic living needs. Excluded were people with "criminal records, or physical, mental, or emotional impairments affecting those capacities." There was no explicit reference to sexual orientation in the guidelines, and the Social Services Commissioner, Maria Matava, pointed out that the state could not "discriminate based on anything." However, once the media focused on Don and David, the absence of a clearly stated policy on gay foster parents became a heated issue. Caught between the obvious discrimination inherent in an exclusionary policy and the homophobic hysteria regarding the children's placement, the Department of Social Services and the Dukakis administration initially framed the policy review as not "shutting gays out of the foster care system." In the months and years to come, this absurd denial of discrimination, combined with intense homophobia, would increasingly characterize the administration's position.

The day after Dukakis called for a policy review, Don and David filed a challenge to the DSS's decision to remove the children from their home. They felt shocked and betrayed. They had applied as an openly gay couple, and after long and rigorous scrutiny, they had been approved by the very top level of the department. They had embraced their role as foster parents with conscientious enthusiasm. Quite suddenly, the department and the governor had pulled the rug out from under them and the boys. David described the aftermath: "Any time you get a new addition to your family it's an upheaval. Everybody's finding their niche and you're trying to deal with these children and give them what they need. They don't speak clearly—they have major speech problems—so that's taking all your concentration and energy. We wanted to do a really good job. Then Dukakis just reaches his hand into our house. I felt really violated and trampled on. I kept saying to myself, 'I shouldn't have done this,' blaming myself—then on the other hand saying, 'I didn't do anything wrong. In fact, I was doing good.' " There was absolutely no question that they would fight this decision all the way.

The *Globe* article touched off a chain reaction that quickly led to explosive public debate, highly significant moves by the state, and prolonged legal and political struggles. It was as though someone had carelessly discarded a lit cigarette in a draught-ridden, windswept forest. The blaze would continue for years to come.

Media coverage was intense and constant. The Gay and Lesbian Advocacy and Defense and the Massachusetts Civil Liberties Union publicly criticized the Department of Social Services' removal of the children as discriminatory and in violation of the 1964 Civil Rights Act. The Unitarian Church characterized the removal as a grievous error that both denigrated Don and David and ignored the needs of the children they had cared for so well. On the other hand, Archbishop Bernard Law declared the Catholic Church's position to be that children should be placed only with married couples. Juvenile Court Chief Justice Francis Poltrast said that he would not place foster children with gay men because of the risk of abuse. Two state representatives called for a legislative review of the existing policies, and State Senator David Locke proposed a resolution that would require the DSS to "place children in need of foster care exclusively in the care of those persons whose sexual orientation presents no threat to the well-being of the child."

No one was more surprised by the extent of public furor than Don and David. By nature private people, they were suddenly thrust into the media's spotlight. Though both men had long since come out to their families, the media attention forced them and their relatives to deal with their homosexuality in entirely new ways. David's mother was suddenly faced with neighbors and friends who would not speak to her in the grocery store. Don, drawing on his hard-earned wisdom, told her, "Well, Mom, now you'll learn who your real friends are."

Over the next two weeks, Human Services Secretary Philip Johnston conducted a review of foster-care policies throughout the nation. Foster care, like other aspects of family law, is governed by statutes that vary from state to state. At the time of the review, only two states—New York and New Mexico—had clearly defined policies regarding foster-care placements in gay households, and those policies explicitly prohibited discrimination on the basis of sexual orientation. Though Florida had a law against gay adoption, it had no explicit policy prohibiting foster-care placements. Officials in states without clear policies differed on whether such placements were acceptable. A New Jersey official noted that sexual orientation was not considered an issue in foster placements there and that, unlike Massachusetts, the state had not reneged on placements with gay couples in the face of negative media attention.

As the review progressed, another strand of the homophobic hysteria unleashed by the *Globe* article emerged on May 23. The Massachusetts House voted 112 to 28 on an amendment to the state budget that explicitly defined homosexuality as a threat to children's psychological and physical well-being, and ordered the Department of Social Services not to place any children in the care of lesbians or gay men. The amendment's language was broad, restricting not only foster care but also adoption, guardianship, respite care, and family day care. On the heels of this vote, though he denied any connection, Philip Johnston abruptly announced that he would reveal the administration's new foster-care policy.

Facing a standing-room-only crowd, Johnston put forth the new policy: "This administration believes that foster children are served best when placed in traditional family settings—that is with relatives or in families with married couples, preferably with parenting experience and with time available to care for foster children. In exceptional circumstances, it may be necessary to place a child in a non-traditional home—that is with an unmarried couple or with a single person. Any such placement will henceforth require the prior written approval of the Commissioner. No placement in a non-traditional setting will be made, however, unless it can be clearly demonstrated that there is no traditional family setting available or likely to be available for the child in question." Johnston was, in effect, announcing a hierarchy for foster-care placements. No matter what the other variables were, married couples were to be given preference. Those with parenting experience would be chosen over those without. However, married couples with *no* parenting experience would be preferred over unmarried couples or single people with parenting experience. Furthermore, while prospective foster parents had not been queried about their sexual orientation, now it would be a mandatory question posed not only to new applicants but also to those already approved. Anticipating public reaction, Johnston made a point of saying that there would be no "witch hunt." He declared that homosexuality would not automatically preclude foster-parent status, but that lesbian and gay applicants would require approval from the commissioner. Though this wasn't an absolute categorical restriction, it was generally understood that openly gay people would not be approved. Indeed, this was borne out over time. At this point, Johnston clearly declared that placements with homosexuals were "highly unlikely." He also made it clear that under the new guidelines Don and David would not have been approved as foster parents.

During Johnston's speech there were audible gasps in the audience and many spoke out in opposition. Despite the extent of the administration's homophobia, many had expected that, after careful consideration of the issues, a nondiscriminatory policy would prevail. The policy review had included discussion with child-welfare advocates and clinicians with expertise in child development, who strongly supported gay foster parents. The feedback given to the administration was overwhelmingly that sexual orientation of caregivers was irrelevant to the psychological and physical well-being of children, and that the existing policy of considering the specific needs of each child and the caretaking and nurturing abilities of potential foster parents was the best way to ensure meeting the needs of children in the foster-care system. Taking up the issue of sexual abuse, the child-welfare professionals made clear the fact that offenders are predominantly heterosexual men. There was a 25 percent shortage of available foster-care placements; if lesbians and gay men were to be ruled out, the pool of competent and caring foster parents would be even further reduced.

Immediately following the press conference a group of about thirty people walked directly across the street to the Unitarian Church's basement to figure out how to oppose the new policy. At that moment the Gay and Lesbian Defense Committee was born. It was the Friday of Memorial Day weekend: by the following Monday, the Gay and Lesbian Defense Committee held a press conference of its own on the steps of the capitol, where it announced plans for a protest demonstration to occur the next day. Three thousand people participated in the demonstration.

Lesbians and gay men were not the only ones enraged by the policy statement. The language of the policy clearly denigrated all who did not fit the *Ozzie and Harriet* image it so revered. A unique opportunity for coalition thus presented itself. Single heterosexual women who were (or wanted to be) foster mothers were almost as hurt by the policy as lesbians and gay men. Several African-American leaders responded with fury to the administration's devaluing of family structures that were central and positive features of many people's lives. Social-service providers and clinicians were horrified by the implications the policy had for children in the foster-care system. Not only would a significant number of highly qualified parents be excluded from the already inadequate pool of available caretakers, but by instituting a rigid hierarchy the policy made it impossible for social workers to consider, on a case-by-case basis, the individual needs of each child. Clearly the policy reflected not only ignorance about lesbian and gay lives but, equally important, ignorance about the realities of children in the foster-care system.

Nowhere were the fallacies of the new policy more evident than in the experiences of Richard and John. Their mother had approved of their original placement, and Don and David had been prepared to keep them until she was ready to have them return to her. Instead of that, over the course of the next several months they were moved through three more foster-care placements. In the last one there was an allegation that they were sexually abused. Many believe that when they were returned to their mother at the end of the year, it was not because she was more able to parent them, but because the public focus on their status made them a liability to the Department of Social Services. Moreover, they had suffered so much in foster care that returning them to her seemed better for them than remaining in the system, regardless of how ready she was to receive them.

In an unprecedented moment of consensus, the three disciplines of social workers, psychologists, and psychiatrists came together to officially denounce the policy. In addition to the Massachusetts chapters of the National Association for Social Workers, the American Psychological Association, and the American Psychiatric Association, organizations such as the Massachusetts Society for Prevention of Cruelty to Children and the Massachusetts Office for Children quickly spoke out against the policy. Nonetheless, Governor Dukakis declared that the "real majority of people in this state and across the country" shared his view that a traditional family is the "best possible for a youngster, any youngster." One of the more pointed moments of protest was a Father's Day march to the governor's house. A week later, demonstrators carrying a huge replica of a 51-A, the form used to report abuse to the Department of Social Services, symbolically filed child abuse and neglect charges against Dukakis.

Lesbians and gay men in the area were deeply shaken by the events stemming from the *Globe* article. People felt attacked at their very core in new ways. Awareness of the depth of society's homophobia did not inoculate anyone from the horror of such obvious denigration. Lesbians and gay men were publicly declared inferior to heterosexuals with respect to their lives as parents or potential parents, their work with children, and ultimately their very being. The policy, the moves by the state house and senate, and the preponderance of homophobic newspaper editorials struck at the entire spectrum of lesbians and gay men. Many divisions usually apparent within lesbian and gay communities dissolved as those from all walks of life struggled to respond to the attack. Gay men joined with lesbians to address issues so often previously seen as primarily women's concerns. Present at any given protest were people with a range of issues: those who had no interest in childrearing but recoiled from the homophobic torrent, those who were fearful about their wish to adopt children, parents grappling with coming out to their children, and teachers who felt their life's work was under siege. As one protester noted, "We understood that it was the most profound attack on our value. It was basically saying 'You are fundamentally less than.' We had to break it. It was not something we could live with."

As so often happens in America's social debates, the creation of the new policy put lesbian and gay dignity in opposition to the ostensible needs of children. Policy endorsers pointed out that foster parenting was not a "right" and that the state's primary obligation was to meet the needs of children; hence, accusations of discrimination shouldn't apply. Those opposed to the policy presented powerful arguments dismantling this false dichotomy of children's needs versus lesbian and gay rights. Both the grassroots organizing and the legal battle continually drew on assertions that the best interests of the children were not served by the policy, and, in addition, the policy was discriminatory.

It became increasingly clear that Governor Dukakis was at the center of the policy change. Though Department of Social Services commissioner Maria Matava originally told the press that she alone had made the decision to remove the children from Don and David, there were several reports that the orders came directly from Governor Dukakis. Furthermore, it was widely believed that most DSS workers at all levels were opposed to the policy they were required to enforce. In fact, the National Association of Social Workers (NASW) pointed out that the policy entailed a breach of ethics for social workers, whose professional oath included refraining from discriminatory practices.

Many felt particularly betrayed by the governor. Here was a liberal espousing homophobic rhetoric many expected to hear only from conservatives. Only after protesters spent the night at the statehouse did Dukakis agree to a meeting. Don and David were joined by fourteen protesters in the governor's chambers. The dean of the Simmons School of Social Work presented findings from her review of the clinical literature showing that the only way children reared in lesbian and gay households differed from those in heterosexual homes was that they tended to be more tolerant of homosexuality. Dukakis pressed her, saying that if all things were equal and she had to place a child in either a gay household or a traditional family, she would surely choose the latter, wouldn't she? She told him that wasn't the case at all. Boston School Committeewoman Jean McGuire, an African American, scolded him for the bigotry inherent in his view of nontraditional families. But perhaps most powerful of all, a seven-year-old girl who had previously met the governor at a school award ceremony said quite simply, "Why are you saying these terrible things about my daddy?" Dukakis remained resolute. While many observers felt his creation and unwavering support of the policy stemmed from political expediency, others saw it as a reflection of deeply held personal values. Whatever his motivation was, he dug in his heels and would not be moved, even as protests intensified during the next year.

Responding to widespread criticism that the policy had been hastily drawn up, the administration appointed another commission and scheduled hearings to review the issues more thoroughly. Again, despite the lack of support for the policy evident in the hearings, the administration stubbornly refused to yield. At the end of the year, Don and David were confronted with the ultimate irony. Don, who worked for the state in the Fair Housing Commission, received a card, cheerfully decorated with a photograph of Dukakis and his family. He opened it to read the message "Merry Christmas and Best Wishes for the New Year." By January 1986, just after the new policy had officially gone into effect, the Gay and Lesbian Advocacy and Defense group and the Civil Liberties Union of Massachusetts filed a lawsuit. A single woman who'd been a foster parent for thirteen years refused to answer the question about sexual orientation; she joined Don and David in the suit.

During the next several years, people's lives were profoundly upset by the policy. Though it was officially limited to foster-care placements, the policy affected adoption in several ways. Public adoption—that which occurs through state agencies—was essentially eliminated for lesbians and gay men because such adoptions require initial approval at the foster-care level. Furthermore, all but two private adoption agencies in the Massachusetts area refused to consider lesbians or gay men and were leery of single people. Those in the process of adopting or considering adoption were extremely vulnerable. There were also a number of lesbian foster parents who remained closeted, at least in their official relation to the Department of Social Services. Many lived in fear of being reported by neighbors or school personnel. Though the administration had denied conducting a "witch hunt," the resemblance to McCarthyism was strong. The policy carried with it a powerful push toward the closet. Yet opponents knew the most forceful response was to come out with a vengeance. Many could not afford to do so when it meant risking the loss of their children. On the other hand, there were people who might otherwise have been adopting children, but would not choose to pass as straight.

The policy enactment was rife with absurdity. One widely circulated rumor concerned a DSS worker who posed the sexual-orientation question to a nun. When she replied that she was celibate, the worker, undaunted and faced with the task of completing a mandatory question that required one of only two answers, pressed on: "Yes but if you weren't, which way would you be?"

The Gay and Lesbian Defense Committee protested in several ways. Recognizing the dangers of the closet, they organized "visibility campaigns," whereby groups of thirty to fifty lesbians and gay men would appear in "straight" places such as bowling alleys and happy hours, essentially declaring, "We're here to let you know we've always been here." They also ran the Foster Equality campaign, at one point sending out ten thousand stickers for people to wear throughout the state on the same day. When Governor Dukakis announced his presidential candidacy, the Gay and Lesbian Defense Committee formed "DukeWatch," a national network that followed him along his campaign trail, demonstrating and distributing tens of thousands of pamphlets about his actions. The energy sparked by the administration's moves fueled over three years of intense activism. There was now a public forum for questioning the state's mode of defining a family. Lesbians and gay men were declaring themselves as subjects, not victims—saying very clearly that they were proud of who they were.

The lawsuit dragged on for five years. It was not until a court date was imminent that the state agreed to a settlement. In 1990 the policy was finally rescinded. The new and current policy now has a hierarchy that hinges on parenting experience rather than marital status. Both married and unmarried people who have parenting experience may be approved without review at higher levels, while all those who lack parenting experience need such review. The question about sexual orientation remained in effect for some time after the policy was rescinded, but it too is now gone. Repercussions continue from the five years that the discriminatory policy was in effect. Though discrimination against homosexuals is not written into policy, potential applicants are often unclear how the process actually works, and the memory of these past years lingers on.

Save Our Children

New Hampshire Follows Suit

When the Massachusetts foster-care policy was first announced in 1985, the administration expressed hope that it could be used as a model for other states. By and large, that did not occur, with one exception. In 1986, New Hampshire State Representative Mildred Ingram pushed to establish a bill prohibiting homosexuals from adopting children, becoming foster parents, or operating day-care facilities. With remarkable resemblance to the Massachusetts scenario, the press once again played a pivotal role. The bill died when it was first introduced, but representative Ingram tried again the next year. This time the *Manchester Union Leader* took up the cause, printing dozens of homophobic editorials and specifically targeting members of the House who didn't support the bill. The floor debate within the House was marked by inflammatory depictions of homosexuality, describing gay men as feces-consuming barbarians out to recruit the state's children.

Meanwhile, as in Massachusetts, reality was obscured by hysteria. Shortly before the bill was first introduced, a gay couple had been specifically recruited by the New Hampshire Department of Social Services and asked to take in a very troubled teenage boy, a chronic runaway who'd had many brushes with the law and been unmanageable in previous foster placements. The Department of Social Services contacted this couple because of its past success in running a group home for teenagers with similar difficulties. The couple took the boy in and endured a rough adjustment period. Eventually he warmed up to them; remaining in their care for three years, he was able to use their support and discipline as a motivating force in his life. The couple became ineligible to be foster parents upon passage of the bill in 1987.

On that occasion Mildred Ingram said, "I'm not against homosexuals. They are adult people. They made their own choice and the only one they have to answer to is their maker. They can go on their merry way to hell if they want to. I just want them to keep their filthy paws off the children." The New Hampshire ruling remains in effect.

In July 1991, the editorial section of the *Boston Globe* contained
the thoughts of Betsy Janeway, a New Hampshire mother of five.

> Now that summer is here I can picture children run-
> ning through the pasture to go swimming in the river.
> I see them cuddling small animals in the barnyard,
> and making tunnels in the sweet, new-mown hay. I
> hear children's voices filling this 200-year-old farm-
> house. . . .
>
> Ah, to be a foster parent in New Hampshire, where
> the need is so great. My husband and I meet all the
> qualifications so well—all but one. We have the edu-
> cation, the space, the experience, the income. We
> were not abused as children; we did not abuse our
> own five children. We do not believe in harsh meth-
> ods of punishment for children.
>
> We have the requisite amount of bedrooms and bath-
> rooms, and good schools. Our children are all college-
> educated, worthy, hard-working citizens, yet our
> application was denied. It was denied because we
> have a gay son and two straight sons, a lesbian daugh-
> ter and a straight daughter. So as I sat at our kitchen
> table filling in the multi-paged application, I reached
> that incredibly awful question and felt myself begin to
> hurt inside. "Are there any homosexuals in your fam-
> ily?" You bet there are!
>
> Yes, two children, I wrote on the dotted line. I fin-
> ished the application, feeling sick, and mailed it. I
> heard nothing for months until one day I telephoned.
> After a few hours, a social worker phoned to say my
> application had been denied.
>
> It's the law, I was told. If I had been able to assure
> him that my gay son or lesbian daughter would never
> come home to live or for an extended visit, then per-

haps we might have made it, but there is no way I would close my house to my children.

And that's the story of one family in New Hampshire who won't be having foster children come to live with them. . . .

The Florida Adoption Ban Revisited

The Florida ban on gay adoption remained on the books unchallenged for fourteen years after Anita Bryant's crusade. There was talk in the legislature about rescinding it, but the talk went nowhere. During the 1980s, lesbians and gay men throughout the nation were becoming parents in record numbers, so it was only a matter of time before someone in Florida came head-to-head with the ruling. Perhaps less predictable was the fact that Ed Seebol would be that person.

Ed was born and raised in the Flatbush section of Brooklyn. He comes from a hard-working family who kept a kosher home and attended temple regularly. Before his seventh birthday, Ed's mother was killed when a gas stove exploded while the family was on vacation. His grandmother and maternal aunt moved into the home shared by Ed, his older sister, and their father. Ed recalls little of the years before the accident. What he remembers most about his childhood is his aunt's love and nurturance.

Ed knew early on that he was attracted to men. At City College of New York he quietly established his life as a gay man. By nature, he was a shy and reserved person, not one to share the details of his personal life with many. Being gay in a homophobic world accentuated that tendency; Ed mostly kept to himself. After college he worked for several years at IBM, maintaining the double life common to many lesbians and gay men—known little by his co-workers during the day, but involved with a small circle of friends by night.

In 1969, after years of the New York City grind, Ed took stock. He would never get wealthy this way and there was little pleasure for him in the corporate life. So he pulled up roots and moved to Key West, Florida. For Ed, Key West was a haven—a quiet and beautiful area where gay men were accepted. He quickly settled into a comfortable life. Over the years he established a gay guest house, founded the Gay Business Guild, and traveled around the country on trips organized according to a new theme each year—all the national parks one year, ghosttowns the next.

By the mid 1980s, AIDS had hit the Key West community very hard. Ed knew many men who'd become ill or died. He became increasingly involved in AIDS education work, and eventually became the director of AIDS Help. During this time changes were stirring inside him. No longer content to simply enjoy his own life, Ed felt an increasing need to "pay back" his aunt's gift to him. His AIDS work also left him longing to see, as the fruits of his labor, not just an easeful death but a flourishing life. In short, Ed wanted to be a father. His discovery of this while in his late forties led him to reject the idea of fathering a child biologically, and he assumed that as a single man, let alone a gay man, he would be ineligible to adopt.

Then one day while browsing through the local paper, he came upon an article about a young boy with special needs awaiting adoption. A social worker suggested the boy might do well with a single father. At that moment, the possibility that he could adopt clicked.

In an effort to gain some experience with children, Ed became a guardian ad litem for the state of Florida. His job was to look out for the interests of children involved in the court system. During his years doing this work, Ed came to know abused children, children in foster care, children in the midst of wrenching divorces. But most of all, he came to know himself in a new way. He thought deeply about the kind of parent he would be, and the kind of child he could nurture. Because of his age, Ed felt adopting a very young child was not a good idea. He decided he wanted to adopt a special-needs child—perhaps one who was slightly retarded and would need stable care over the long haul. He believed that "You can take someone and with one-on-one love and understanding—by being there as a support—you can get the best out of that person. That would be rewarding for me, and also a way to pay back what I received from my aunt." In Florida at the time of Ed's decision there were approximately eleven hundred children on the waiting lists of public agencies alone. Of those, the special-needs children would have the most difficulty finding homes.

In 1989, Ed filed an application with the state of Florida to adopt a child. Shortly after sending it in, he received a phone call from a social worker who asked him if he'd read all the material. Had he read the part about who was ineligible? Ed recalled the sentence about those with criminal records and homosexuals. When the worker told him his application was denied, Ed asked for an explanation in writing. What arrived in the mail was a simple and blunt statement: the only reason for the denial of his application was his sexual orientation.

Ed didn't see himself as a crusader. He'd led a quiet life, and tended not to like the front lines. What he wanted was a child, not a political struggle. But he knew that this was wrong and he wasn't going to let it go by without a fight. "If you could prove that homosexuals make bad parents and heterosexuals make good ones, I'd support this law. But it doesn't work that way. Every child I've worked with was abused by heterosexual parents. It's just wrong to say I'm not qualified." A friend hooked him up with the American Civil Liberties Union (ACLU), and the challenge was under way.

The ACLU has not always considered discrimination based on sexual orientation to fall under the category of civil-liberties violations that they, as an organization, are committed to battling. As late as 1957 the national board of directors issued a policy statement upholding the constitutionality of sodomy statutes and federal regulations denying employment to lesbians and gay men. In fact, the history of the ACLU's endorsement of lesbian and gay rights on a broad level is relatively brief, having taken hold in the mid-1960s only after protracted internal debate. Struggle takes place at many levels—in the hearts of individuals, in the ranks of organizations, in courtrooms and legislatures. Sometimes a few of these factors line up and change occurs.

In March 1991, Judge M. Ignatius Lester, a relatively conservative judge from the "old school," listened to arguments concerning the Florida adoption ban and Ed Seebol's denied application. Then he decided, in agreement with the ACLU, that the law violated Seebol's constitutionally protected rights of privacy, due process, and equal protection. The law was thus struck down in Monroe County and Ed became officially eligible to adopt. The decision allowed Ed to proceed, but his search for a child was long and difficult. Despite having the law on his side, Ed had little success with the Florida adoption agencies. Finally, two years after his legal victory, Ed adopted a child from another state. Shortly after the Monroe County decision a gay couple in Sarasota took up the struggle in their county. There are thirty-nine counties in the state of Florida, so it will most likely be a long battle.

A Place to Belong

I set out to visit Don and David on a beautiful, warm morning in May exactly seven years after the day the *Boston Globe* article hit the stands. Don and David had moved to the country shortly after the foster-care debacle. For a while after the removal of Richard and John, they had no children to care for. Eventually they briefly took in some children through informal arrangements, not involving the state. When the policy was rescinded they once again became eligible to be foster parents. About a year ago, they agreed to take on the care of several siblings ranging from infancy to school age. Now they are in the process of adopting them. The children come from an extremely violent household, where they were literally tortured. When they first arrived they were abusive both to themselves and to each other, and they had a hard time functioning in school. They are doing quite well now, getting along with teachers and friends. David spends time each week showing their classmates how to work with computers. The children's teachers have all been to the house for dinner and are very supportive.

Before we got to talking we wandered over to the goats, which are the baby's favorite animals. He takes great delight in watching them. The older children played in the yard, one wearing an Indian headdress. As we sat in the kitchen, they popped their heads in one by one, wide-eyed and curious.

I asked Don and David about their lives as parents. "When I was growing up it was a pretty strict household and I was always told what to do," David said. "So I look back on that stuff and I say 'give me a break—there's another way to live.' I kind of watch out for that. I tend to be more flexible than Don, who's stricter. There's so many things to keep in mind—so many mistakes you try not to make. You're not gonna get them all, that's for sure. What we both insist on is that they treat us with respect, and we treat them with respect, and they treat each other with respect. So that's an ongoing theme that we're teaching them and it seems to be the bottom line."

Don said, "There are days when there are no goodies and days when you walk in and, my God, the house is abrim with them. Every day is a challenge. There's times when you don't see results, but there's days when you do. Then there are days when it just happens and you say, 'Oh what did I do? How come I'm on this lovely cloud?' We're on a cloud now—we've just turned a corner where they know the past is still there but it's past—they're not going back to that. They don't have to worry about being abused. So now we can deal with the issues because they have this sense of family. From day one, when they were asked to draw pictures of their family at school, they drew each other and us. So the seed was there and now they can start to deal with who they are and who we are as people."

Don says the oldest asks things like, "What are gay people?" and he replies, "Like Poppy and me." On Martin Luther King Day they talk with the children about how Martin Luther King, Jr. wanted equality for all people. They describe the many forms that families come in. They call all this the ABCs.

When I asked about their hopes for this family, David said, "I want to keep some kids out of the mess the world is in. So when I see them taking care of themselves, things that we taught them, that's my biggest reward emotionally. They used to hurt themselves when they were upset. Now with our help, they don't do that. They can talk about it instead." Don added, "Once they're adopted we'll look for a larger farm—show them another way of life." Then, nodding toward the baby nestling in David's arms, he said, "And I want that one to be the first president of the United States to be raised by gay men." Laughing, I asked, "Can I quote you on that?" "Sure," Don answered. Then, as though suddenly seeing that first *Globe* headline, he added, "Just don't mention his name."

On the way home my thoughts are of Julie, a ten-year-old girl I used to work with. Julie often brought her photo albums to therapy. They were filled with pictures from six out of the too-numerous-to-count foster homes she'd lived in over the years. What she wanted more than anything else was a family—a place to belong. To all of us who knew the system, it seemed she was unlikely ever to have that. This quite delightful little girl was too old, too dark-skinned, and too sad to get a permanent home. When I last saw her she was living in an institution.

I recall Ed's wish to show a child the country as he's seen it over the years. I think of his garden apartment and the room that was waiting to be occupied—a place to belong. I think of the rows and rows of children's faces staring out from his adoption catalogue, and I take some comfort in knowing that one finally found his way to that room.

Then the hand shadows come to me. When I was a child, my sister and I would put on shows as we were falling asleep at night. Using a small night-light, we'd project giant witches, man-eating alligators, and tiny, beleaguered creatures against the wall across from our bunk beds. The trick was to make the characters look as little like hands as possible. On nights when we'd done a particularly good job, the shadows, having taken on a life of their own, stayed with me long after our hands were at rest and my sister had fallen asleep. On those nights my ability to see in shadows a world of my own making took over. Suddenly the shadows cast by the tree swaying outside my window, the edge of the dresser, and the point of the bedpost became truly terrifying. In such moments there was only one solution. As frightened as I was of getting out of bed and walking through the perilous darkness, I had to summon my courage to go turn on the light. One good hard look at my hands, the tree, the dresser, and the bedpost was enough to banish the menacing shadows. Perhaps that's where my propensity for turning on lights began.

But now I'm grappling with a new problem: what to do when you realize that you are the swaying tree—when it is your own shadow that terrifies and enrages others. How do you carry on your life, aware of the distorted shadows you cast, suffering the blows of the fear they inspire, all the while searching for a hidden light switch?

As I pull into the driveway I think about Julie, Richard, John, Ed, Don, and David. But most of all I contemplate the shadows they cast.

· 5 ·

Choosing Children

Biological Parenting

There is a certain distortion that occurs when we look back at the past through the lens of the present. When what once seemed impossible has become reality, it is easy to forget the groping in the dark along an untrodden and sometimes treacherous path. It was with this in mind that in March 1988 I read the clipping a friend had sent me from the *Hartford Advocate*. Underneath the headline "The Lesbian Baby Boom," it said "Even Geraldo's covered it—but the women who are doing it say it's no big deal." Almost a decade had passed since I first dared to ask myself if I, a lesbian, could choose to have children. Now as I read the words "No big deal" I flashed back to those sleepless nights clouded with confusion, shame, trepidation, grief, and longing.

One's perspective on the lesbian baby boom is clearly a matter of whom you talk to. When I finally broke through my isolation and began to speak to lesbians who had chosen to raise children, some—like the women described in the *Hartford Advocate*—told me they had never viewed their desire for parenthood as incompatible with their lesbianism. Andrea, a mother of two, said, "I always knew that I was going to be a mother, and being a lesbian never felt like

I was making a choice not to have children. That probably had a lot to do with the fact that I came out during the seventies, amid a sense of all sorts of opportunities for women." Yet Andrea's ease with her status as lesbian mother was only one story. There were many other lesbians who had come to be mothers only after significant personal struggle. It is no wonder that I found myself drawn to their descriptions of arduous journeys. Susan lived years of ambivalence about her sexuality, not because she was uncertain of whom she loved but because she believed that choosing a woman meant giving up her lifelong dream of being a parent. Esther talked of being suddenly overcome by grief on an otherwise ordinary evening as she watched her lover washing her hair, when she recognized for the first time a yearning she could not imagine would ever come to fruition: to raise a child with this person she loved so deeply.

If we were indeed in the midst of a lesbian baby boom, then it *was* a big deal, for it was a painful and often lonely journey past grief that had brought us here.

Somewhere along the way these lesbians stopped assuming they couldn't be parents and began figuring out how to bring children into their lives. As I listened to their tales of transformation, each marked by a unique moment of revelation, the "boom" seemed the social equivalent of spontaneous combustion. So many lesbians struggled to become parents at precisely the same historical moment, yet each experienced herself as unique and alone. Of course, no one was as alone as she might have felt, and the movement certainly hadn't appeared out of the blue. Many social forces had laid the groundwork for its emergence.

As women influenced by second-wave feminism questioned their roles in the traditional family, they discovered possibility where before there had been only closed doors. Raising children without being married emerged as a potentially positive decision, not an unwanted circumstance. It is no accident that the rise of lesbian parenting has coincided with the burgeoning of single heterosexual women choosing to have children. The idea that women could shape their intimate lives according to their own standards and values rather than conform to constricting social norms was powerful in its own right. But the feminist movement was significant beyond the realm of ideas. On a very practical level, women's fight for control over their reproductive capacities created a context in which the choice to bear a child was as significantly opened up as the choice not to bear one; abortion rights and access to reproductive technology such as donor insemination are flip sides of the same coin.

The gay rights movement also contributed greatly to the parenting boom, enabling people to take a less fearful, more assertive stance toward society and yielding more visible communities, with the support and social dialogue that implies. From that supportive base, many began to define the kinds of lives they wanted to live, and to pursue their wish to be parents.

Perhaps most significant of all to what has became known in some circles as the choosing children movement, were the lesbian and gay parents who'd come out of heterosexual marriages. They had stepped out of the shadows, transforming the notion of lesbian and gay parents from a contradiction in terms to a visible reality that society had to contend with.

The fact that in our society women tend more than men to be intensely involved with raising children was reflected in the choosing children movement, just as it had been in the battles of parents coming out of heterosexual marriages. During the late 1970s, the first signs of lesbians choosing to have children were evident. By the mid-1980s, the trend had expanded from its initial West Coast and urban-center origins to throughout the nation. It was not until the late 1980s that a similar movement, smaller in scope, emerged among gay men. Though gay men's efforts overlap in some ways with lesbian endeavors, they are also distinctive. Often societal taboos against homosexuals more strongly burden gay men. And homosexuality aside, the notion of men as primary nurturing parental figures is ill defined in our culture. Many gay men seeking to become fathers, and perhaps to raise children without significant female input, feel out of place simply by virtue of their gender.

Initially, gay men participated in the lesbian baby boom as fathers sought by lesbians who chose to bear children. The advent of

AIDS profoundly curtailed the move toward joint parenting arrangements. But in many communities it also brought gay men and lesbians together; and in more recent years, with growing consciousness about HIV prevention and testing available, joint parenting arrangements seem to be on the rise again.

Taking on secondary parenting roles in families headed by lesbians does suit some gay men, but others want, as do their lesbian counterparts, to have a more intensive, primary parental relationship. Increasingly, gay men are choosing to become parents through adoption, surrogacy, or joint parenting arrangements.

Within a decade, the unimaginable became commonplace. This remarkable shift occurred against a backdrop of skepticism and hostility. Society remained fixed on the question of whether homosexuals should be allowed to raise children, even as they were becoming parents in record numbers. The fierce debates that began in the early 1970s only continued as openly gay men and women chose parenthood. By the mid-1980s, a multitude of new controversies clamored for attention. Lesbian and gay parents had pushed Americans to look more closely than ever before at a deceptively simple question: What is a family? If the family is not defined by heterosexual procreative union, then what indeed is it? Perhaps it was the fear of this very question that underlay the hostility toward lesbian and gay parents to begin with. If the capacity to have and raise children does not distinguish heterosexuals from homosexuals, then what does?

In a recent *New York Times* book review, Margaret O'Brien Steinfels posed the following question: Does a married heterosexual couple's "capacity to have children [represent] a differentiating quality in heterosexual relationships?" According to Steinfels:

> Our legislatures and our religious faiths may come up with new ways to regulate or recognize erotically bound relationships beyond the traditional form of marriage: the state may devise practical solutions to problems like insurance and shared property, and religious bodies may try to encourage lasting and

exclusive intimacy in a monogamous setting. Nonetheless society has a legitimate interest in privileging those heterosexual unions that are oriented toward the generation and rearing of children. That, at any rate, is the widely held conviction that remains to be debated. . . ."

Steinfels's suggestion that heterosexual unions are uniquely bound to childrearing rings false at this historical moment. Heterosexual procreation is only one of many means of family making. This is underscored not only by the fact that lesbian and gay unions can include childrearing but also because heterosexual unions often do not. Many heterosexual couples choose not to raise children, and many others, despite their heterosexuality, cannot procreate. Divorce, adoption, and reproductive technology mean that children often aren't raised by their birth parents, and likewise many parents aren't genetically connected to their kids. Steinfels's query embodies a myth our society clings to despite its distance from reality: that heterosexual unions, by virtue of their potential link to procreation, are somehow necessary to the survival of the species and therefore morally superior. Lesbians and gay men choosing to parent are not unique in challenging this myth, but they do so most explicitly, often sparking heated backlash.

During his 1992 campaign for reelection, George Bush said that "children should have the benefit of being born into a family with a mother and a father," thus citing the number and gender of parents as a pivotal aspect of optimal family life and implicitly privileging biological connection between parents and children by the phrase "born into." In short, he held up as the ideal the traditional family, characterized by heterosexual procreative unions and legal sanction.

Eight-year-old Danielle, the daughter of lesbian and gay parents, vehemently disagreed. "I have two moms and two dads," she said. "A family is people who all love each other, care for each other, help out and understand each other."

In defining the ideal family, Bush emphasized structural characteristics while Danielle, in contrast, highlighted emotions and relationships. Their disagreement aptly reflects this moment in American society: the tension between idealization of the traditional family and the reality of families that don't fit that mold is strongly emerging as a key issue of our times. As lesbians and gay men choose to raise children, the many different kinds of families they create reveal the inadequacy of a definition of family that rests on one particular structure. Increasingly, our society must heed Danielle's idea that family is defined by the quality of relationships, which can exist in many forms.

Donor Insemination: A Mimicry of Procreative Union

In 1884, according to one of the earliest accounts of donor insemination in America, a woman lay unconscious on an examining table while, without her knowledge much less her consent, a doctor inseminated her with sperm from the "handsomest medical student" in his class. It was only after the insemination that the doctor informed the woman's infertile husband, who, pleased by the news, asked that his wife never be told what had occurred. The insemination resulted in the birth of a baby boy, who, presumably along with his mother, wasn't informed of the circumstances of his conception. A little over a century later, though women who are inseminated are neither unconscious nor uninformed, much of this early account remains salient. Donor insemination has evolved as a medically controlled practice, largely restricted to infertile heterosexual couples and shrouded in secrecy. Where then do lesbians fit in?

In the beginning of its use in this country, donor insemination was seen solely as a solution to infertility among married heterosexual couples. As such, donor insemination practices were structured to produce families that mimicked in every way possible the traditional heterosexual family. Both medical practitioners and the law geared donor insemination toward creating families that looked like, and had the legal status of, a family consisting of a married man and woman and their biological offspring.

This attempt to mimic the traditional heterosexual family included an effort to hide the very fact that donor insemination was used. The appearance of a biological connection was painstakingly constructed by matching the donor's physical traits with the husband's. By and large, the fact that a child had been conceived through donor insemination was rarely disclosed within families and was barely discussed in the larger cultural arena. In one major text of the 1960s, a doctor noted that one of the advantages of donor insemination, as compared to adoption, was that its use need never be revealed. He further suggested that screening criteria for couples receiving donor insemination include an assessment of how well they could keep a secret. Now, thirty years later, donor characteristics are still most often matched to that of the husband and secrecy continues.

The effort to hide the use of donor insemination parallels past approaches to adoption. There, too, great pains were taken to match the physical characteristics of children with those of their adoptive parents, and adoption was held as a secret around which much anxiety revolved. More recently, adoption practices have shifted: there is much less emphasis on matching physical characteristics, and experts encourage parents to speak openly about adoption, with the idea that talking to children about their origins from an early age is key to their overall well-being. Unlike earlier practices, this way values honesty in family life over the appearance of a biological family unit. Along with more honesty within adoptive families has come more open discussion of adoption in society. While much thinking about adoption continues to reflect a cultural bias that elevates biological families over all others, adoption practices have begun to move beyond this ideology by coming out of the closet. In contrast, the secrecy surrounding donor insemination points up the continuing emphasis on the appearance of a biological family unit.

The painstaking attention to appearance and the secrecy surrounding donor insemination stem from an insidious ideology: heterosexual procreation is the ideal basis of a family, one which if not achieved in actuality should at least be aspired to in appearance. With this as an undercurrent, donor insemination is characterized by a contradictory view of genetics. On the one hand, the practice distinguishes genetic and social parent roles, relegating genetics to an inconsequential position by severing all ties between donors and their offspring, and by recognizing those who take on the social role of parenthood as fathers of those children. On the other hand, hiding the fact that this process has occurred reveals an almost superstitious belief in the power of genetics. The implication is that biological connection is such a crucial aspect of parenting that its absence is shameful and should be hidden. The social role of a nonbiological parent is not highly valued in its own right, and instead must be bolstered by the illusion of a genetic connection. In this pervasive view, a "real" parent is the biological parent. If you have to, donor insemination is okay to do, but it's not okay to talk about.

The Legal Constructions of Family in Donor Insemination Practices

As with the secrecy and matching practices, the laws surrounding donor insemination reinforce efforts to make these families look like the standard nuclear model. Children conceived through donor insemination in the context of a heterosexual marriage are deemed the legal children of the recipient and her husband. Donors, on the other hand, waive all parental rights and responsibilities. The complex reality of such families—that there are both a biological and a social father involved—is set aside in favor of a simpler one. Severing the donor tie and sanctioning the husband's parental relationship serve the purpose of delineating one—and only one—father.

As donor insemination was more widely practiced in this country, legal parameters developed that, like the practices themselves, value the traditional family over all others. Among the first legal questions posed about donor insemination was whether it constituted adultery and, along with that, whether the child so conceived was "illegitimate." As the courts decided these initial cases they exhibited a strong conviction that children need to be "legitimate"—that is, to have fathers. From this premise the law constructed the husbands of inseminated women as the legal fathers of the resulting children. Father status thus hinged on marriage—that is, children were considered to be the "issue of the marriage." This was automatic, with no mediating process such as adoption needed to complete the arrangement. Initially these parameters were outlined only when disputes arose, but as the use of donor insemination grew more widespread, legislation was enacted that explicitly delineated what the courts had implicitly held all along: families that, in fact, were not created through the procreative union of a married heterosexual couple were given the legal status of this traditional unit. The state threw a safety net around the families created through donor insemination when, and only when, those families were headed by married heterosexual couples. On a state-by-state basis, the law carved out a distinction between donors and fathers: donors, in surrendering their sperm to doctors, waived parental rights and responsibilities, while the men married to inseminating women took on the legal rights and responsibilities of fatherhood.

Significantly, in many states, the donors' lack of parental status hinges on medical mediation. That is, donors who directly give sperm to women can be, and often are, legally considered parents. Thus, not only is heterosexuality a prerequisite to the legal delineation of families constituted through donor insemination but medical control of the process is built into the law. People creating families through donor insemination do so most safely—that is, with least threat to their integrity as a family unit—if they utilize medical help.

Lesbians and Single Women Seek Donor Insemination

The extent to which donor insemination practices emphasize the appearance of a procreative heterosexual union has, of course, great implications for lesbians and unmarried heterosexual women—most especially with respect to access to the technology. In conceiving through donor insemination, these women have little possibility of creating "pretend father" relationships that would obscure the fact that donor insemination has occurred. Indeed, when lesbians and single heterosexual women use donor insemination, they bring the practice out of the closet, revealing it to be a way that women can bear children in the absence of any relationship to men. It is no wonder that unmarried women, regardless of their sexual orientation, have been barred from using donor insemination, given the challenge their access poses to deeply held beliefs. To be inseminated as a single straight woman or lesbian is to boldly acknowledge that the resulting child has no father and that women can parent without input from men beyond the single contribution of genetic material. Such inseminatins also highlight the separation between social and genetic parenting roles. This last aspect is especially obvious when lesbian couples use donor insemination: a nonbiological mother, clearly not a father, becomes the child's other parent.

For many years, the medical profession would not grant unmarried women access to insemination. A study done in 1979 found that over 90 percent of doctors wouldn't inseminate unmarried women. The doctors gave several reasons for their decision, the most central being their beliefs that lesbians and single women are unfit parents and that all children need fathers. However, some doctors refused to inseminate unmarried women, not out of deep personal conviction, but because they mistakenly believed that it was illegal. Though the statutory language about donor insemination often includes mention of marriage, it does not require it. A number of doctors also feared future wrongful-life suits, assuming that children raised by lesbians or single women would ultimately be unhappy enough to sue those responsible for their existence.

In the late 1970s, into the context of medically controlled, heterosexual-marriage–oriented donor insemination practices, came single heterosexual women and lesbians wanting to have children. The technology was an obvious choice for these women, not only in its most basic sense as a source of sperm, but also as a way of forming families whose integrity would be legally protected. Many want to

establish families as couples or individuals without having to negotiate parenting responsibilities with an outside adult. Lesbians
choosing to have children are much more vulnerable than married
heterosexual couples to disputes about the boundaries of their families. Homophobia in the legal system renders them generally more
subject to custody problems. Furthermore, since lesbians are unable
to marry, and the female partners of inseminating women by and
large can't adopt the resulting children, nonbiological lesbian mothers have no protected legal parent status. In this social context, creating families through known donors poses tremendous legal risks if
those donors ever make custody claims. For lesbians, therefore, the
legal protection of a family unit created through anonymous donor
insemination is crucial.

But since access to the most legally safe source of insemination—
that is, medically controlled—was highly restricted in the early
days of the lesbian baby boom, many of the first lesbians to have
children did so on the margins of mainstream donor insemination
practices. Some women created their own alternatives. They inseminated themselves and, in an effort to protect the integrity of
their families, created their own systems of anonymity, using go-
betweens to conceal the identity of the sperm donors. However,
this means of anonymity didn't provide firm protection against the
possibility of custody disputes. In practice, the anonymity of donors would often be hard to maintain in small communities, and
legally—especially in the absence of medical mediation—an identified donor would have parental rights. Matters became more complicated with the advent of AIDS, which made this way of
inseminating a highly risky business. Ultimately, the self-created
system gave way to another approach.

Some lesbians moved in a different direction, attempting to
change the exclusionary practices themselves. During the late
1970s and early 1980s, as the feminist health-care movement grew
and women fought to gain reproductive freedom, unmarried
women made headway with demands for access to medically controlled donor insemination. The Sperm Bank of California in Oakland was established in 1982 by women running the Oakland

Feminist Women's Health Center in response to the rising number of unmarried women seeking advice about insemination. The Sperm Bank of California led the way in establishing an insemination program that didn't screen out women on the basis of sexual orientation or marital status. Currently there are several such sperm banks throughout the country, and increasingly doctors are willing to inseminate unmarried women. However, access remains restricted in certain areas, and many insurance companies will cover insemination expenses only for married women.

During the last fifteen years, lesbians choosing to be parents have been charting a course through society that began on the margins and has increasingly moved into the mainstream, yielding social changes along the way.

In the realm of donor insemination, the reciprocal influence of heterosexual, nuclear family ideology and lesbian parenthood is strikingly apparent. Lesbians choosing to have children shape their families along parameters stemming from the idealization of the traditional nuclear family, but by the same token they significantly transform many of those parameters. Donor insemination has shifted from a completely medically dominated, heterosexually defined technology to a practice that serves unmarried women, both straight and gay, and thereby yields many different sorts of families. As lesbians and single heterosexual women make more use of donor insemination, the practice itself is changing: by necessity, donor insemination is coming out of the closet. In our culture there are few stories of conception through donor insemination. Despite the fact that approximately a million Americans have been conceived this way, we continue to behave as though conception occurs only through heterosexual union. Ultimately, lesbians will write the stories of donor insemination, as they speak openly to their children about another way that people come into the world.

Choices: Known or Unknown Donors

As the doors to donor insemination opened for lesbians, a new era began. Having access to the technology is not synonymous with wanting to use it. Most lesbian mothers-to-be spend considerable

time deciding whether to do so through a known or unknown
donor. The complexity of this decision was a theme in many of my
talks with lesbian mothers. In December 1991, as I was trying to
sort through the many layers of this decision, both for myself and
in relation to this book, I decided to visit the sperm bank in Oakland. I was not prepared for the intensity of my response. Barbara
Raboy, the director, explained the process of freezing and storing
sperm as I stared at hundreds upon hundreds of specimens neatly
ordered in dozens of large metal tanks. It was about what I'd
expected to see, except for the names scribbled in marker across
the outside of the tanks and in smaller letters on the compartments
within each tank. In front of me was the Artist tank, with Fuchsia,
Chartreuse, and Amber as its subdivisions. Next to it was the
Universe tank, with Mars, Pluto, and Jupiter; and behind that, the
Landscape tank, with Rocky Mountain, Grand Canyon, and Yel-
lowstone. Barbara noticed my puzzlement and explained: "We
thought names would be more fun than a strict number and letter
filing system, so the staff take turns naming the tanks and the
subdivisions within them—it's how we locate any particular specimen—you know donor number 5003 is in the A row in the Fuschia
section of the Artist tank." I was disappointed that the tank names
had no more salient correspondence to the sperm inside, but the
knowledge freed me from the mind-boggling task of imagining
what distinguished a Rocky Mountain sperm specimen from a Jupiter one.

Instead, I began to imagine the people who dreamed up these
names: huddled among the slides and test tubes, who had been
most pleased by colors, who by mountain vistas or thoughts of
intergalactic travel? As the namers became more real to me, so too
did the men whose sperm was sequestered in the tiny vials. Several
pages listed donor characteristics—no. 2017, Dutch descent, blue
eyes, brown wavy hair, 6 feet tall, athletic student of computer
technology. If you wanted to know more about a particular donor,
there were additional sheets—medical history and some personal
information. But when all was said and done, the wish to know
would remain just that. To see these vials was to glimpse the

unknown. Throughout the country women were waiting—some whose male partners were infertile, some who were single, some who were lesbian. What they had in common was a strong yearning for children. This is what I was thinking as I looked at vial no. 2017. Then my ears rang with the voices of children, and I knew that I was standing in a place of beginnings, surrounded by mystery.

My initial puzzlement about the tank labels was a clue to my state of mind. I'd entered the sperm bank as I would a foreign country, imagining the tank names held some crucial meaning as unintelligible to me as a street sign in China. It struck me as odd that I could feel this way despite the fact that for years I'd thought about becoming a mother through this very process. Donor insemination was potentially a key element of my future, one that would involve my body and my most intimate relationships; yet simultaneously, I experienced it as a strange, foreign, and mystifying process.

I was not alone in this contradictory place. Though donor insemination has been practiced in this country for over a century, as a culture we have barely begun to grapple with the meaning it holds for us. Standing amid the vials of semen at the sperm bank, I could not help but be aware of the unique historical moment in which we are living. The very fact that I, a lesbian, could consider insemination is remarkable. Just ten years earlier I would have been shut out of any insemination program. But choices bring great complexity. Layers of thinking make up the decision about whether to become pregnant through a donor, known or unknown. How do lesbians aspiring to be mothers respond to society's constraints? What ways of forming a family will be safe in a culture that doesn't recognize our primary intimate connections? Because society as yet barely acknowledges donor insemination, an air of mysteriousness pervades the practice. How then do lesbians sort out the meanings donor insemination has for us and may have for our children?

From the language of "illegitimacy" and "bastards" to the tales of adoptees searching for their birth parents, we are inundated with ideas that a father's absence is always problematic and knowledge of our genetic roots always essential. What do we accept of these stories? What do we reject? All of this is filtered through our most intensely personal experiences and histories. Ultimately it is from these many layers that lesbians create their families. Self-consciously exploring the meaning of family, each woman writes her own story. But no one writes it alone: each family is shaped by the culture it is embedded in, and in turn, the culture is changed by these emerging families.

The Role of the State

After twelve years together, Jasmine and Barbara agreed they were ready to raise children. Other than the gender of their partners, they envisioned family life in rather traditional terms. Their household would define the boundaries of their family; as a couple, they would jointly share parenting. Jasmine saw their decision to inseminate with an unknown donor as stemming clearly from the surrounding social context.

Jasmine explains: "We were very stuck on the method of conception—a known versus an unknown donor. One of the things that happened around the time we were thinking about this question was the foster-care issue in Massachusetts. We knew women who had adopted young children through foreign adoptions, and I listened to their descriptions of the home-study process. I felt very uncomfortable with the idea that somebody was judging you, and that you in a sense had to give them this little drama that 'I'm the one who's adopting and this woman is my roommate.'

"Not only did we feel angry about the injustice of it, but we also felt frustrated by the fact that as a couple we had so much more to offer in terms of the structure of our lives than this fallacy would indicate. When the foster-care uproar happened, we were very indignant about the idea that we could be judged that way. If we had gone along with the little drama of who we were supposed to be, it wouldn't have barred us from adopting, so it was really our decision that we wanted as few external people as possible out there judging us or making decisions about our lives.

"We didn't want that interference. That spilled over into the issue of the donor. We really needed to feel in control. The thing was, we were the parents and we wanted to make the decisions as the child grew up about other adults in the child's life. It's not that we wanted to shelter the child from other people, but we certainly didn't want an obligation ready-set. So given that we wanted integrity as a family unit, we decided to go with an unknown donor."

The influence of homophobia and heterosexist constructions of the family is apparent in Jasmine's explanation for their decision to use an anonymous donor. Jasmine and Barbara shied away from adoption because they didn't want to be subjected to state scrutiny that would have failed to recognize the value of their relationship. The homophobia unleashed during the Massachusetts foster-care battle was a bitter reminder of their vulnerability. A known donor was also someone who could potentially bring the state to bear on their family life—someone who in the eyes of the law would have parental rights in contrast to the nonbiological mother. Protecting the integrity of their family unit as they defined it meant using an unknown donor.

Though all prospective lesbian parents face the same legal constraint—a definition of family that gives privilege to genetic connection and heterosexual parenting—people see the state's potential role in their lives quite differently. Unlike Jasmine and Barbara, Susan and Dana chose to have a child with a man they knew who would be involved as a parent but in a secondary role. Each had a close relationship with her own father, and they wanted the same for their children. Though concerned about how legally vulnerable the nonbiological mother would be, Susan and Dana proceeded on the assumption that they could work out a trusting relationship with the father, one which would not ultimately bring them face-to-face with the state's ill-fitting definition of family.

Susan, explaining their decision, says: "The legal line obviously is 'don't take risks, therefore don't use a known father who would then have the possibility of having rights.' I agree that that's one way to avoid the particular risk of a custody fight and control issues over the child. But I think it's one of the most personal choices in the world—anything about reproductive issues and how one wants to raise one's children are very intimate and individual, and I think you shouldn't make decisions frankly just on the legal basis.

"You should make them on your whole world view and your values and what you want for your child. Maybe the risk of a custody fight could be minimized by choosing a person carefully and by choosing a gay man rather than a person who would have the gay issue to use against you."

Jasmine and Barbara's thinking diverges from Susan and Dana's along several lines. First, the two couples position themselves very differently in relation to the state. Jasmine and Barbara are acutely focused on the threat the state poses to the integrity of their family unit. Susan and Dana, on the other hand, feel that threat less acutely because they believe that recourse to the state's definition can most likely be avoided through establishing trustworthy relationships. Marie, another lesbian who chose a known donor, explains the position:

> I don't have the kind of fears around the legal stuff that some people do. You have to pick really carefully. Obviously there are certainly men out there whom you could enter into this kind of relationship with and it would be a disaster. But I don't think it's impossible to find a situation where you can have some confidence that this guy will do what he says he'll do. I understand legally you leave yourself open. I think it would be dangerous to do this with a man who is conflicted and who's doing this because he wishes he had kids. Then, ten years down the line he might turn around and say, "I want the child."

These women are grappling with the question of whether you can create a family that defies the state's definition and feel safe that its boundaries will remain as you intended them to be. In part, the different choices lesbians make about family structure stem from different perspectives on the state's ultimate power in their lives.

What Makes a Family?

There is another important dimension to the decision of choosing between known and unknown donors: what should constitute the boundaries of a family? Many women, like Marie and her lover, Jana, choose a donor who will be known to the child but won't take on a parental role. Essentially, except for the fact that the child can know the donor, these families closely resemble families like Jasmine and Barbara's, where the women are the child's sole parents. However, often lesbians choosing known donors draw the boundaries around their families a little differently. Though frequently the men aren't primary parents, they do have a parental role. Susan and Dana created this type of family. While they define their family primarily within the bounds of their own household, their arrangement with their children's father is similar to an extended family. Though at first they were most concerned about maintaining their status as primary parents, as the family became securely established, Susan and Dana wanted the father to be more rather than less involved. They encouraged him to develop a strong relationship with the children. Susan says, "You realize that there are so many things to do. There's never enough time in a day. So additional people to help out is wonderful. We should all have bigger extended families, especially when we're all working. We've been lucky that not just our children's biological father but his choice of partners and his family have been a very rich source of additional good people in the kids' lives."

Opening boundaries in this way can be challenging, however. For a while, Dana, who was to be the nonbiological mother struggled with her lack of society-recognized parent status. "I think for a lot of Susan's pregnancy I was obsessed that this child might be born and this father would have more rights than I would. I had this image that he would never be doing the dirty work of everyday parenting. He'd show up as this knight on a white horse and get all this affection and admiration."

Susan and Dana were deeply committed to the idea that Dana was as much a mother as Susan, and Dana's feelings of doubt dissipated soon after their daughter's birth. "Once Danielle was born it was bizarre to think that. Her father is an important part of her life, but there's a whole 'nother ball game in terms of who her parents are who raise her. My fears were so far from reality. Before Danielle and I had this bond I imagined, in the naïveté of someone who's not a parent, that someone who shows up once a week could be an equal parent to someone who's with you twenty-four hours a day."

Deciding who will be part of one's family is, of course, a highly personal endeavor. The decision regarding a known or unknown donor is partly a decision about what kind of intimate relationships to create. Some are comfortable sharing parenting with people outside a romantic relationship, while others find this a complicated and unrewarding situation.

The Ties that Bind?—the Meaning of Genetic Connections

Beyond thinking about the relationships they want for themselves, lesbians choosing between known and unknown donors must consider how their choice will affect their children. As lesbians think about this, beliefs about the importance of genetic connections take center stage. These beliefs come partly from personal history and partly from ideas that dominate our culture. When women consider whether to use a known or unknown donor, complex, intense, and often conflicting feelings arise. Esther, for instance, originally tried to find a man who would be willing to be a sperm donor but maintain a minimal role in the child's life. The men she approached either wanted more involvement or were worried that they would be asked to take on more responsibility than they bargained for. Esther reconciled herself to conceiving with an anonymous donor, but her feelings about her son Ian's origins intensely color her relationship with him. She says, "I'm consumed by the connections. I look at Ian and see my grandmother's hands. He's an incredible dancer and my father was, too. I don't know if there's a dancing gene. That's why I wanted a Jewish donor. I wanted the history and culture. A known donor would have embodied more of that. Ian's relation to the donor has been a presence for me since he was born. It's hard to sort out my own sadness about my father's death and my sadness for Ian in not having that relationship."

It is hard also to separate Esther's personal history from the culture we are immersed in. As a society, we tend to emphasize intergenerational biological connections and pay scant attention to nonbiological relationships. For example, we continually hear stories about adopted children who feel an absence in their lives and need to search for their birth parents. We rarely hear about the adopted children—of whom there are also many—who don't feel a need for this contact. Hearing these stories of searches for genetic roots, many lesbians are uncomfortable with anonymous donor insemination. As Marie put it, "I don't think an anonymous donor is the best thing for a kid. I'm sure that kids conceived that way will manage and will be okay if their parents handle it levelly and matter-of-factly. But we don't really know. We haven't had a generation of kids growing up without knowing anything about half of their genetic material. What we do know about is kids who were adopted and don't have that kind of information. Most of them go through something about it whether they end up searching or not. It just makes sense to me that if you can provide a child with that basic information, then you should."

While many like Marie see children as better off with access to genetic information, even if the donor is uninvolved as a parent, a good case can be made for the opposite decision. Jenny, for instance, chose a sperm bank, in part to protect her child from possibly feeling rejected by a known but uninvolved donor. "I'd rather take responsibility for my choice to have him this way," she said. "He can be angry at me for my decision, rather than feel hurt because there's a man he can identify who doesn't behave as a father."

As important as it is for lesbians to think through their decisions, the reality all ultimately may have to come to terms with is not a singular model. Instead, we must come to recognize and appreciate pluralism: children who are loved and given opportunities to grow can thrive in many different family contexts. Knowing this, we can discard a determination of which family structure is "best" in favor of finding ways to make all the different structures work.

Gay Men Have a Different Set of Decisions

Gay men are often in the position of parenting children who are primarily raised by lesbians. This family model fits in a culture in which women are socialized toward primary childrearing and men toward a secondary role. While there are many gay men for whom this arrangement works well, there are also those who, like their lesbian counterparts, want more involvement with their children. But men do not have the same options as lesbians. There is no equivalent of donor insemination. Surrogacy comes the closest, but it is a much more biologically, ethically, legally, financially, and psychologically complex process. Similarly, gay men are considerably less likely to find women willing to be the equivalent of a known donor—that is, to have babies with whom they will be minimally involved (though on occasion people do make such arrangements). For gay men who want to be primary parents, adoption is often a more feasible option than biological parenting. Given all this, the issues faced by gay men who choose to become fathers through biological conception are quite distinct from lesbians' concerns.

Becoming a Father Through Surrogacy

Eric and Jeff were college sweethearts who came out together. Though each had imagined they would get married and have children, it was clear early on in their relationship that their futures were bound together. Jeff never gave up the idea of having children, though he didn't actively pursue it until he hit his thirties. At that point, he approached Eric with the idea of advertising for a surrogate mother. Though he thought about adoption, he wanted to have a child who was biologically connected to him. Eric was doubtful that they would find someone willing to be a surrogate. "Everything you read about surrogacy is these women who are married who have several kids, who want to give this to another couple who can't have kids—it's all portrayed in a straight, heterosexual way."

They discussed the possibility of co-parenting with lesbians, but that wasn't an appealing arrangement. Jeff says, "I wanted this to be our child—for this to be a family of three." Eric says, "We've structured a life for ourselves that we feel very comfortable with, that we like a lot, and we set the parameters for that. We don't let others set the parameters, and that's important to us. A co-parenting relationship would just be way too complicated, and too many people who we know don't approach life the way we do." Jeff adds, "Being dependent on someone else would be very frustrating." They placed an ad that specified they were two gay men wanting to raise a child. They got one response, which they pursued.

Paid surrogacy is a complicated social and personal step. It is fundamentally a financial arrangement through which a child comes into the world. The biological parameters, including a woman's efforts to conceive and nine months of carrying a child, are much more extensive than for donor insemination. For these reasons, the social and psychological issues that surround the process are complex.

One of the most troubling aspects of surrogacy is the class imbalance: Eric and Jeff wanted a child and were well off financially; Donna, who responded to their ad, did not want a child, but needed money. Eric and Jeff hoped that they could work out a friendly arrangement, one that would benefit all concerned. At first it seemed they were on their way to doing just that. An agreement was hammered out with lawyers, and the insemination and pregnancy went smoothly. In less than two years since Jeff first proposed parenting, he and Eric had a baby girl, Leah.

Eric, Jeff, and Donna were on friendly terms and had agreed on limited visitation, but this eventually became a source of strife. Jeff and Eric wanted the visits to be supervised and to occur in their home; Donna wanted to take the baby on her own. Communication broke down when Eric and Jeff refused Donna's request. There was a series of exchanges in letters, through which Jeff and Eric tried to establish ground rules for Donna's visitation. Ultimately, Donna didn't respond and contact ceased.

Despite the problems that arose, Eric feels that, "If there wasn't a whole lot of emotional baggage involved on the part of the mother, contact would be preferable. It would be easier for Leah to understand more of her background and her heritage, and who she is as a person if she had that contact, but I could be wrong."

Jeff doesn't quite agree. "I've changed my opinion. Now I feel that other than curiosity, it would be a lot easier for them to have next to no involvement with each other. We have very little in common with her mother. . . . I think those relationships where a gay man helps out two women and stays involved and all are friends are wonderful, but they're unrealistic in these circumstances. Surrogacy is just this bizarre thing where you're dealing with different financial statuses. Because there's such disparity, there's so little in common to base that kind of friendship on."

Like some women who conceive through unknown donors, Jeff is ambivalent about his wish that there be no contact between his child and her biological mother. "I do worry sometimes, like when I see people on television who've been adopted and haven't seen their biological parents, and are freaked out. But I think that doesn't have to happen—that often those people have a lot of other emotional baggage." Eric points out the different positions of gay men and lesbians. "I feel kind of envious of women who go to sperm banks. Once they make that decision, it's over. They may still agonize over not being able to provide that connection for their child, but it's done." In contrast, surrogacy often involves a process of negotiation and the formation of a relationship. As it was for Eric, Jeff, and Donna, surrogacy can be an intense and complex undertaking. What it will ultimately mean to children like Leah is yet to be seen.

As the nonbiological parent, Eric was in a vulnerable position. Like most lesbian and gay couples raising children, Eric and Jeff had to rely on mutual trust. Jeff says, "We can't conceive of ourselves breaking up. If for some unknown reason we ever did, it would have to be amicable—it's just we can't not be that way. We have a relationship where we talk and communicate better than almost anyone we know." Eric adds, "If you can't work out your differences, I believe you have no right to take this kind of adventure. Because we are trailblazing, we take the responsibility very seriously."

Legally, the surrogacy process is not complete until an adoption has occurred. In the case of heterosexual couples, the biological mother terminates her parental rights, and the spouse of the biological father adopts the child, making the couple the child's only legal parents. In their attempt to "close the circle" of the surrogacy arrangement, Jeff and Eric attempted a second-parent adoption. When Donna agreed to terminate her parental rights, it was Eric who would adopt Leah. The legal question revolved around whether he could do that without Jeff giving up his parental rights. If he had not been able to, the couple considered having Eric become the sole legal parent, as a source of balance. However, shortly before Leah's second birthday, Eric and Jeff were successful in their adoption attempt—their particular circumstances making them a first in the country. When Leah was two years old, Jeff and Eric initiated another surrogacy arrangement through which they had a son.

For the most part, access to surrogacy—like access to other alternative modes of bringing children into one's life—is much more available to heterosexual infertile couples than to gay men. However, surrogacy is much like independent adoption, with access strongly related to financial resources. Surrogacy is far less popular among gay men than donor insemination is among lesbians. Its high cost, along with the social complexity it involves, render it a less frequent approach than adoption or joint-family arrangements.

Surrogacy has been practiced since biblical times—in some informal sense, there have always been women bearing children for friends or family members. But formal, paid contracts for surrogacy arrangements first emerged in this country around 1976, and have been on the rise ever since. Though in any given case surrogacy can work well for all involved, it poses major ethical issues not just for its participants but for society as well. It involves much more than a separation between genetic and social parenting roles, since gestation and birth are processes involving not only a woman's body but also her relation to the child she bears. For the most part, these

arrangements involve large sums of money, and bring wealthy people who want children together with poor women in need of money.
Out of these issues—the psychological ramifications and the financial exchange—arise many crucial questions.

The major societal quandaries about surrogacy fall into two categories: is it baby selling? and is it exploitative of women? These
questions came most vividly to public attention in 1987, when
Mary Beth Whitehead, having given birth to the child the courts
would refer to as Baby M after signing a surrogacy contract for
William and Betsy Stern, changed her mind and wanted to keep
the baby. Was she bound by the contract she'd signed? Was the
contract, in which there was an exchange of money and an exchange of human life, legal? Was it ethical? And, most important,
who should get the child? Mary Beth Whitehead argued that the
contract was invalid; she captured the complexity of the surrogacy
issue in her statement that she'd "signed on an egg, not on a
baby." After a much publicized trial, the Sterns were awarded full
custody of the one-year-old child. However, along with that decision came a ruling that made surrogacy illegal in the state of New
Jersey, where the case had occurred.

While there is little legislation explicitly applying to surrogacy,
after the Whitehead case, seventeen states enacted some form of
applicable legislation. For the most part, these laws make surrogacy
contracts unenforceable. The legal reasoning is drawn from several
other areas of law. One argument is that a woman cannot consent
to adoption before the birth of a child, and hence cannot be bound
by a surrogacy contract drawn up at the time of conception. Another is that in every state baby selling is illegal. Here though,
much of surrogacy bypasses this idea, treating compensation not as
money in exchange for a human life but as payment for the mother's expenses or for her work in gestation—akin to rent. Some of
the laws have focused on money as the key issue, strictly forbidding any exchange other than expenses; a few states prohibit me-
diators (that is, brokers) from accepting fees. Even with the
contracts legally unenforceable, many of the problems that arise
when mothers change their minds remain unresolved. Since sur-

rogacy arrangements by and large involve men with substantial resources and women in need of money, if a child is born from such an arrangement and the surrogate changes her mind, most often a typical custody battle ensues, with the best-interests-of-the-child standard applied by the courts. Here, surrogate mothers are at a considerable disadvantage, often not well off enough to pursue a court battle. Surrogacy practices contain a major potential for the exploitation of women in desperate financial circumstances. The guidelines that minimize the risk of such exploitation include making contracts unenforceable (that is, permanently decided only after birth, as in adoption) and giving, as only New York does, the woman custody without a court battle in the event that she changes her mind.

Another Kind of Extended Family

Not all surrogacy arrangements involve a financial exchange. At the other end of the spectrum from the tradition of women as primary and men as secondary parents are the more rare arrangements of women who bear children for men to raise. Such was the case with Kevin, John, and Toni. Kevin had always wanted to be a father and had thought seriously about adopting a child, but he was ultimately discouraged by the foster-care debate in Massachusetts. He was a publicly gay man who would neither have nor want the option of passing as straight in order to adopt a child, so he worried that his chances of getting a child were minimal. Over many years, Kevin had become very close friends with Toni, a single bisexual mother. Kevin had been present at the birth of Toni's second child, and he and John were now like uncles to the children. A close-knit extended-family relation was well established by the time Toni shocked Kevin with the offer to bear a child for him and John to raise. Toni felt she could offer a child no better parents than Kevin and John. For his part, Kevin was overwhelmed by Toni's offer. "I would never have asked a woman to have a baby for me—it's way too much to ask. But I was thrilled."

John was skeptical, feeling strongly still that adopting an existing child was a better way to go. But as the foster-care battle raged, "biological parenting began to seem more appealing because of the legal protection it provided." The three carefully hammered out an agreement, one that included a clear commitment on John and Kevin's part not to challenge Toni if she changed her mind and wanted the baby. For her part, however, Toni was far more worried about the opposite occurrence; she did not want to raise another child, and wanted John and Kevin to have primary responsibility. Her involvement with now two-year-old Amber is substantial, and the group does function as an extended family, with Toni's other children clearly Amber's siblings. Though the arrangement thus bears some resemblance to the familiar family, it is also highly unusual, especially because, simultaneously to being Amber's mother, Toni is not her parent; both the power and the responsibility of parenting fall equally on John and Kevin's shoulders.

Joint Parenting—Lesbians and Gay Men Together

Arrangements such as Kevin and John's with Toni, or Susan and Dana's with their children's father, bring lesbians and gay men together to form families. Most commonly these arrangements involve a division into primary and secondary parenting centered in one household, most often the woman or women involved. These setups resemble amicable custody arrangements in cases of divorce, but they are in reality quite different because they are planned this way and from the outset fall outside of the law's definitions.

Lesbians and gay men also come together in a different family form, that of equally shared parenting. Though it has much in common with the arrangement described above, this particular version deserves separate consideration. Joint-parenting arrangements bring lesbians and gay men together in ways that push even further beyond the nuclear family model, creating an altogether new family form. Truly joint-parenting arrangements decenter family life, creating strong bonds between lesbians and gay men established around parenting itself and independent of primary erotic and romantic unions. Such was the family Barry and Adria established.

"I always say this is the longest pregnancy in the world because it took thirteen years of actively trying to become a dad 'til the time Ari was born," Barry said. He had always seen himself as someone who would have children and, though he didn't know how it would happen, that vision didn't change when he came out at age twenty-two. In his late twenties, he began to discuss the possibility of shared parenting with a heterosexual female friend. But over the course of their conversations, it became clear to Barry that the relationship wouldn't work; much as he wanted a child, he decided not to pursue that possibility.

Then he began to look into adoption as a single man, getting as far as the home-study stage. But at that point he backed away from the process. "It was not a time I wanted to invite the state into my home to scrutinize the way I lived. Also I didn't really want to raise a child alone. I really did want to have another parent."

Shortly after that, he was approached by an acquaintance. "She had had a child when she was really young and felt both trapped in her life and not able to figure out how she could get out of the trap in terms of getting more money and some skills. She had seen me interact with her son who was three at the time, and she knew I was trying to become a father and thought it was really unfair that gay men had such a hard time doing it. She offered to be a surrogate mom if I would help her get some kind of training so that she could get a better kind of job. She still wanted to be friends, and thought maybe an appropriate arrangement would be that she would relate to this child like a distant relative. We hadn't worked out the details, but it was '81 and AIDS was happening. There were no tests, and I didn't feel like I could responsibly inseminate so I decided not to do it."

With his third attempt to become a father failing to pan out, and AIDS on the horizon, Barry put the question of children on the back burner for the next four years. Once the HIV test was available and he tested negative, he decided he could continue his quest.

On New Year's Eve, 1986, Barry was introduced by a mutual

friend to Adria, a lesbian who was looking for someone with whom to raise a child. In her early adulthood, Adria had assumed she would adopt children. But as she became focused on her work and community, the idea of becoming a parent faded into the background. Unlike Barry, Adria hadn't spent years engrossed in the pursuit of parenthood. At age forty-two, her world view shifted dramatically when a close friend was diagnosed with AIDS and moved into her home. During the process of caring for him while he was dying, Adria became possessed with an intense desire to be pregnant. What had previously been a source of ambivalence and questioning became definitive. Living through her friend's illness, Adria felt, "If I can do this, I can do anything." The catch was, that Adria had been in a relationship with Marilyn for eight years and Marilyn was not keen on the idea of raising a child. Adria, for her part, wanted her child to have an involved father. This proved to be a good fit, since from Marilyn's perspective it would be more comfortable if Adria had a co-parent other than herself.

Barry describes the tumble of feelings and questions he encountered during their first meetings: "We'd been part of overlapping communities with the same kind of political history, so we knew things about each other and felt very familiar when we actually met, but we had never met before we sat down to ask questions like, 'Would you like to make a commitment for the rest of your life with this stranger and have a very intimate relationship—not sexual, but as close as you can be?' It was very awkward, like going through a series of courting behaviors—checking each other out, putting your best foot forward, and there are these flirtations going on. Our process was that we couldn't say, 'Yes, this is working, let's do it.' It was more like looking for why it wouldn't work until we could find nothing more, then saying, 'Is there any reason why we couldn't do this?' " Adria, on the other hand, immediately impressed by Barry's integrity and level of commitment to parenting, knew at their first encounter that she and Barry would become family.

During the next five months, they let each other into their lives. "It became clear that our sensibility around child-rearing was very similar even though we're very different people," Barry remembers. "Our personalities and backgrounds are very different. Starting this process at an older age, we were both clear about what we wanted and what we didn't want. We wanted to build family with each other. I think we both hoped that ideally that could happen, but if we could find someone close enough, with a similar enough world-view, we knew enough not to expect everything on our list. We introduced each other to our circle of friends, celebrated our birthdays together, gradually doing some of those kinds of family things."

A month after Barry and Adria decided to go ahead with the plan, Barry met Michael. "Here I am, not looking for a relationship, because I'm clear I want kids. You know, if a relationship happens that's fine, that can come later. And then, here's Michael to integrate into this picture. Part of his attraction to me was that I was building a family and he loves children—so we have this dynamic of Michael who is outside wanting in as much as he could, and Marilyn, who is inside wanting to have boundaries as much as she could. And there's Adria and me in the middle, trying to make this happen."

During the next two years, Barry and Adria went through a very intense period that included difficulty conceiving and four miscarriages. The process was particularly discouraging, given Adria's age. One doctor dismissed them completely, chalking up the difficulties to approaching menopause. Adria feared that Barry would abandon the effort to have a baby with her since he so badly wanted a child. But there was never any question in Barry's mind. "We were clear that we really wanted to parent together. That had already been born in this process. We were already really close friends and had this thing that was starting to cross all the traditional lines between gay men and lesbians—building the most physical, intimate relationship you can. Being in the medical part of this process, which was very unpleasant, was really one of the things that pulled us together. Those miscarriages, though I don't recommend this as a strategy, turned out to be a way to find out how you are together. Going through hard times, what we learned is that our instincts pull us together—that's how we deal with hardship. And so that brought us even closer." Barry and Adria supported each other through each episode and were very much partners in the effort. Eventually they saw a fertility specialist, who prescribed Clomid and took over the insemination process. Barry became an expert at assisting the doctor in ultrasound and follicle measuring. At age forty-four, Adria became pregnant and carried to term.

Throughout this process a complicated dynamic developed among the four adults. In many ways Adria and Barry developed a primary intimate relationship, one that had to be balanced with their respective partner relationships. It was the beginning of what was to be their particular sort of family—not a uniform, single entity but more like concentric circles, with four overlapping intimate adult relationships. Though Barry and Adria were at the center of this parenting unit, their approach was inclusive, embracing Michael and Marilyn. This was evident as they moved about the world. Barry remembers the day Adria was late for her first Lamaze class: "So in this room are all these straight couples with very pregnant women, and in walk Barry, Michael, and Marilyn, who is an Olympic athlete, with a very slender toned body—I mean, this woman is not pregnant. It's an awkward threesome. The teacher looks at us and says, "This is the birthing class." And we say, "Great, we're in the right place." Now they're really confused, and we go around the room to introduce ourselves. You have to say your name and the magic due date, so I say 'My name is Barry and I'm the father of this child that Adria, who's not here, is carrying,' and then Michael says, 'My name is Michael and I'm Barry's partner, and I'm going to help parent this child that Adria, who's not here, is carrying,' and then Marilyn, 'I'm Marilyn and I'm Adria's partner.' Their eyes are getting bigger and their mouths are falling open, and finally Adria comes, not having a clue what she was walking into."

Ari was delivered through cesarean section in 1989—Marilyn, Barry, and Michael were all present at his birth. Adria and Barry had agreed to share parenting equally. This is difficult to achieve in the context of two separate households. Each can be with Ari whenever he or she wants and also whenever he is needing one of them. Though they have free access to each other's homes, separation is a key issue in this family. From the very beginning of his life, Ari has gone back and forth between the households almost every other day. Barry and Adria also do a lot of traveling. In the first couple of months, before Ari began to travel back and forth, Barry slept at Adria's house. After that, while Adria was nursing Ari, she would come to Barry's house on the days he wasn't with her. At six months of age, Ari began to take a bottle as well, which somewhat eased the stress.

As they look toward the future, both Barry and Adria have some trepidation about their own feelings regarding separations. They are beginning to feel that Ari, now a preschooler, needs longer stretches in each household. Barry anticipates this. "It's hard for me to imagine him not being home for three days in a row. I just can't—not that I'm not totally comfortable and happy with where he is, because he's at home being loved by his wonderful mother and other parent, and nothing could please me more, but he's not home with me. I find myself wandering into his room a lot when he's not there, looking for him."

Adria has been known to appear at Barry's house in the middle of the night, needing to check in with Ari. Speculating about Ari's responses to the constant comings and goings, Adria says, "I think he suffers as any being would suffer from everything changing all the time. It's the same two houses, it's the same people, and he has everything at both places. He always has his little shopping bag and he carries his blanket with him wherever he goes. I think he'll either grow up to be a person who will only be in one place and will be kind of rigid about it because he's had enough of this, or he'll be someone who any place he hangs his hat will be his home. I think he'll have a certain kind of autonomy and confidence, because he seems to now, but I think he'll also have some issues about being left—people always come back, but they also always leave." One of the issues Barry and Adria are currently trying to address is their desire to have more time together with Ari rather than being on separate shifts.

The complexities of the four-way relationship take a lot of energy to navigate. Though decisions are essentially a matter of consensus, the family's communication about Ari is primarily channeled through Barry and Adria. In a sense, Michael and Marilyn have become the keepers of their respective couple relationships. As Adria sees it, "they watch over the intimacy of the couples—and they help each couple to separate from the other." For Marilyn, Barry's and Michael's involvements with Ari have freed her to be his parent. "The fact that she's not the only other parent besides me, the fact that there's someone else who's fifty percent responsible for him has allowed her a lot of room, to in fact be a very important parent. In our family, because she doesn't want to be a mother, there's not much competition like you'll see in some lesbian couples. And she doesn't want to be his father; there's not competition with Michael and Barry, either. She has her place with Ari. She's the only athlete among us. He's a little talking boy—he's not very athletic. She teaches him how to jump. That's where they live together, in this sort of playful world and he's very close to her."

Michael, unlike Marilyn, has much more interest in a primary parenting role, and has had to grapple with that in the context of a family unit that is clearly centered on Barry and Adria as primary parents. He and Barry think about expanding the family—through having Michael father a child. "When Ari's at our house he's there with both of us and it's fairly equal in terms of day-to-day doing things," Barry says. "Michael has stepped in as the cook. He likes to do it and he cooks for Ari all the time, so he's Ari's best cook and when he's hungry he looks to Michael. I know Michael has felt unseen and unrecognized but not by me or our family. My father, for instance, was watching Michael put Ari to bed one night and he just said 'it's so amazing—he is a father to this child.' But even though Michael gets recognition from our family and community, there's so much in this culture that in basic ways doesn't recognize his role. We try to be especially conscious of it and name it when it's happening."

As with the Lamaze class, as they move about the world this family shakes people's attitudes. Once, Ari closed a car door on his hand. In the emergency room, Barry and Michael met Adria and Ari at the hospital. Barry remembers that day vividly; "So I'm holding Ari and he's telling me the story, saying 'Daddy, I cried a little but it's okay now,' and we go together but they keep trying to separate us all. Then we get to the point of registering, and I'm holding Ari and the clerk is asking me all these questions that I'm answering while Michael and Adria stand behind me. Then the clerk says to me, 'Okay, Michael, so you're the father,' and Michael says 'No, I'm Michael and he's on my plan.' Meanwhile, Ari is pointing to me saying, 'This is the father.' So, okay, this is the father, but Michael learned that in order to get his work to pay these bills—to not raise red flags—he says he's the stepfather. And the clerk must be thinking—well, okay, this is a very friendly divorce—here's the mom, dad, stepfather, and kid. Then he asks Michael for his address. I'd already given him my address as the father and, of course, it's the same address. At this point we're all fidgeting, and Adria says, 'I bet you want to know my address next.' So we have these funny experiences, but we make it work."

Of his family life, Barry says, "It's made us all look at how we do relationships. I think our mode of operating now is basically to act out of the basic goodness that's there in all of these relationships and to let go of a lot of the petty stuff about each other that drives each of us crazy. We pick and choose what we have to deal with. It works incredibly well, and it's also complicated trying to manage these multiple needs." Looking back at his original decision to become a parent in this way, Barry says, "It's important to try to imagine every situation you can before you do something like this, 'cause it gets you thinking, but there's no way to know what the reality will be. No matter how much we talked, there was no way I could be prepared for the instant of Ari's birth, when I went from one primary relationship with Michael to three. And of course it doesn't matter what the adults decide in advance; once the child is born, their needs are going to determine—and should determine—what happens. Sometimes that can bear no relation to all these plans."

Amid all the complexity, Ari seems to thrive. He makes families out of everything, one of his favorites being clothes hangers. The blue one is always himself, and then there is a Mommy, a Daddy, a Marilyn, and a Michael. He wonders why his best friend has no Marilyn or Michael.

The Reinvented Family

Lesbian and gay parents essentially reinvent the family as a pluralistic phenomenon. They self-consciously build from the ground up a variety of family types that don't conform to the traditional structure. In so doing, they encourage society to ask, "What is a family?" The question has profound meaning in both the culture at large and the very heart of each of our intimate lives. It is like a tree trunk from which many branches extend: What is a mother, a father, a parent, a sibling? Can a child have two or more mothers or fathers? Is one more "real" by virtue of biological or legal parent status? How does society's recognition (or its absence) foster or impede parent-child relationships? To what extent does the state shape family life? To what extent can nontraditional families alter the state's definition of family?

These questions go well beyond the issue of whether families headed by lesbians and gay men should exist. There emerges a complex reciprocal tension between lesbian and gay family life on the one hand and homophobia and the idealization of the traditional family on the other. Clearly, lesbian and gay parents don't create their families in a vacuum. Their choices are shaped by the institutions that mediate family formation, most notably the legal and medical systems, and adoption agencies. Lesbian and gay parents vary with respect to how they view the state. While some let legal definitions inform their choices, others feel they can probably keep the state out of their lives by relying on trust and goodwill.

Sometimes families who've taken this route end up, to their dismay, in the courts, challenging prevailing legal thought.

However they choose to form their families, lesbians and gay men do so in the context of the idealization of the traditional model; their families are inevitably shaped by this fact. Yet at the same time, over the past decade, many changes have been wrought by lesbian and gay family formation itself—ranging from unmarried women's increased access to donor insemination to the particular challenges that lesbian and gay families bring to the law. Though our society is a long way from embracing eight-year-old Danielle's deceptively simple statement that a "family is people who all love each other, care for each other, help out, and understand each other," her words may yet prove to be our most crucial guide to the future.

· 6 ·

Who's the Real Mommy?

It is a typical Monday morning in the Shay-Markowitz household. Elizabeth Shay, late for rounds, flies back and forth between the kitchen and bedroom trying simultaneously to get the children and herself ready to leave. Lila Markowitz, whose assistant has just called in sick, rushes to open her bookstore at the same time as she frantically tries to rearrange child care for the afternoon. Three-year-old Anna has just spilled her orange juice for the third time this morning; she's been needing extra attention ever since starting a new day-care arrangement. Five-year-old Carly sits calmly, methodically eating her Cheerios one by one, seemingly oblivious to the turmoil around her.

Lila races by the table and, estimating that at the rate she is going it will take Carly another hour to finish her breakfast, tells her to forget the Cheerios and go brush her teeth. Just as Carly gets up to do this, Elizabeth peers into the kitchen and, seeing the half full bowl of Cheerios, tells her much too skinny daughter to finish her breakfast. Carly, unfazed by the contradictory orders she's grown used to, looks up at her frazzled parents and, with the mischievous grin that is her trademark, says, "Hey, who's the real mommy around here?"

It is not an easy question to answer. As Carly's teasing smile suggests, Lila and Elizabeth are, of course, both real mommies—at least in the eyes of the four people in the kitchen. But outside that kitchen other views prevail. Lila Markowitz adopted Carly as a single parent, and Elizabeth Shay similarly adopted Anna. Each child has the same last name as her adoptive mother. Elizabeth's mother recognizes only Anna as her grandchild, though Lila's parents consider both children to be family members. Carly, in her five years on this earth, has already become quite attuned to differences in the ways people view "mommy," "family," and, by extension, life itself.

Families don't exist as independent units within which intimacy unfolds unto itself. Instead, life in every family is shaped as surely by surrounding cultural discourse and institutions as it is by the idiosyncrasies of each family member. A question like "Who is the real mommy?" reflects the meeting of the world outside and the world within. The ideas that prevail in society profoundly influence how we each construct and feel about our families and our roles within them. Conversely, as individuals create new family forms and definitions, they challenge notions that the traditional family is the only "real" or viable family. Families like Carly's are thus a force for cultural change.

Existing in defiance of the parenting roles defined by gender, heterosexual procreation, and legal sanction that constitute the traditional family, lesbian and gay parents grapple with definitions of the family. In so doing they draw on cultural norms, even as they challenge and transform them.

There is tremendous diversity as to how people define their roles in families headed by lesbians and gay men. These definitions often have great practical as well as symbolic weight, significantly shaping how the work of parenting is divided, what sorts of relationships develop, and how people feel in their families and communities.

Some lesbian and gay couples raising children see themselves as

two mothers or two fathers, while others draw a distinction between one—a mother or father—and the other—a parent. This
distinction often implies a difference in relationship intensity, responsibility, and power. Still other couples draw an even sharper
distinction, viewing one adult as a mother or father and the other
in no parental role at all.

In some families headed by lesbians, the men who beget children are defined as fathers—and in that sense key family members—while in others they are seen as donors more distantly
connected to the family. While surrogacy arrangements typically
define women who bear children as neither mothers nor parents,
the arrangement Toni, Kevin, and John made is more complex.
Toni, who bore Amber for Kevin and John to raise, remains involved as extended family; she declares that while she considers
herself to be Amber's mother, she does not see herself as Amber's
parent—her way of saying that Kevin and John bear both the full
responsibility and power of parenting.

Ranging from parents who are neither mothers nor fathers to
mothers or fathers who are not parents, such examples hint at the
complexity of how roles emerge and play out in these newfangled
families. The wide variation reflects many layers of experience.
Particular roles emerge from a combination of personal desire and
ideas about the significance of biological parent-child connections
and legal parent status. While some people, for instance, place
great weight on biological and/or legal assymetries in a family,
others assiduously avoid this emphasis, instead seeing parenting as
a matter of relationships. Gender differences add to the complexity
of role delineation. Lesbians and gay men are not immune to cultural archetypes of motherhood and fatherhood—archetypes that
may shape people's visions of themselves as parents. Delineating
family boundaries and establishing relationships within those
boundaries are further complicated by each family's relationship to
extended families and communities, as well as to society as a whole.
At each of these convergencies, lesbian and gay parents grapple
with competing definitions of family and of the roles within it. The
questions "What is a real family?" and "Who is a real mother or

father?" could be asked only in a time of great social flux. They are the echoes of the traditional nuclear family reverberating in the new families lesbians and gay men invent.

The Predicaments of
Nonbiological Mothers

When Andrea was a young child, no matter what had occurred during the course of the day, the evening ritual could be counted on. As the last remnant of daylight flickered, she bathed, brushed her teeth, and put her pajamas on. Then she was ready for storytime. The children's squabbling and their parents' hurried efforts to finish work and household chores often made the path to this moment a noisy and chaotic affair. But once the moment arrived, tranquillity settled over them like a feather quilt, and it was this feeling she would carry within her for years to come as the essence of family.

Like most fathers in the neighborhood, Andrea's father worked long hours and storytime was the main contact she had with him. She would burrow into the crook of his arm and study his face as he read. Afterward she and her sisters would plead with their mother to sing them to sleep. Later, in the silence of Andrea's darkened bedroom, the echoes of her parents' voices lulled her to sleep.

Jane had no such blissful childhood memories. Typically, having fallen asleep to the sounds of fighting and awakened to a house strewn with beer cans, she would make her younger brothers breakfast, get them off to school, and do what she could to clean up before going to school herself. Only as an adult did Jane begin to envision a family that was joyful rather than deadening. Watching her niece's exuberant discovery of crawling or her nephew's steadily growing fascination with nature, she would delight in the intensity of their relationship to their surroundings and marvel at the quickness and scope of their growth. Having made an arduous journey to adulthood with little guidance, she wanted to help them see the possibility inside themselves. But it was not only what she hadn't had that she wanted to give to children. With all the strife, there were traditions in her family—moments of love that left their mark. As she braided her niece's hair, she could feel her mother's hands upon her head and hear her saying, "When I was a little girl, your grandmother used to comb my hair this way." Thus she knew well the paradox of needing both to hold on to the past and move beyond it.

Jane and Andrea brought many layers of experience to the family they created. As lovers, their decision to have children together emerged as much from the depths of their individual childhoods as it did from the sense of possibility each inspired in the other. Each woman, independently of the other, strongly yearned to be a mother. At the same time, it was their mutual love, their sense of themselves as a couple, that moved them toward parenthood. At first glance there was nothing incompatible about these separate driving forces; their individual desires to be mothers initially dovetailed with their desire to parent together as a couple. But the birth of their first child revealed tension just below the surface. Much to their surprise, they discovered that despite their decision to have children, their visions of motherhood were imbued with the idea that every family contains only one mother. Kelly's birth challenged them to reconcile these visions within the reality of a two-mother family.

Since both women wanted to experience pregnancy and child-birth, they had decided that each would bear a child. Jane would become pregnant first, since she was older and concerned about her fertility. This concern turned out to be warranted; it took a long time and several medical interventions before she conceived. Through the drawn-out planning process and Jane's infertility, parenthood became an increasingly elusive state. Kelly's much awaited arrival seemed nothing short of miraculous.

Though their overall vision of family life was one of shared parenting, initially Jane—who was nursing Kelly—took maternity leave while Andrea continued working. Their joyful awe carried Jane and Andrea smoothly through the early sleep-deprived days. It wasn't until they settled into the routine of their new lives as parents that the first hint of trouble appeared. One evening when

Kelly became unusually fussy, Andrea tried everything she could think of to comfort her—all to no avail. When Jane walked into the room, Kelly immediately calmed down. Jealousy swept over Andrea like a wave of nausea. Taking her by surprise, it jarred her into realizing that her lifelong fantasies of motherhood hadn't prepared her for this emotional configuration. She was supposed to be the reassuring presence, the one who sang her children to sleep. Standing in the kitchen watching Kelly nuzzle against Jane's breast, Andrea felt superfluous, like a loose thread dangling from an otherwise perfect dress.

In those early months, as the intensity of Kelly's attachment to Jane grew, so did Andrea's doubt that she too was Kelly's mother. Her uncertainty was magnified by relatives and friends who easily related to Jane as a new mother while scarcely acknowledging Andrea. After years of striving to create this family, Andrea suddenly felt she had no place in it. At first she reacted to this by almost forcing herself on Kelly. At moments when Kelly seemed to need Jane's presence, Andrea would try to comfort her, a strategy that invariably left everyone frustrated and distressed. Jane, for her part, was also struggling. Though sympathetic to Andrea she was increasingly angered by Andrea's intrusions into her relationship with Kelly.

After several months, with tensions running high all around, Andrea took stock. Her relationship with Jane was deteriorating and she was worried about the effect of her behavior on Kelly. Something had to shift. Their problems were multilayered, and only from recognition of each contributing force would resolution eventually emerge.

Andrea and Jane had decided to have children together, but they lived in a world that views mothers as singular, exclusively responsible for the care and well-being of their children. To complicate matters, there was a biological connection between Kelly and Jane that did not exist between Kelly and Andrea. While the experiences of pregnancy, childbirth, and nursing were an intense part of Jane's connection to Kelly, they were not part of Andrea and Kelly's relationship. At first glance it might seem that this, in and of itself, determined the family's struggle. But looking more deeply into the situation, and thinking about it in comparison with other families headed by lesbians and gay men, reveals a different story. It was not mere biological assymetry that shaped the dynamic. Rather, it was the meanings ascribed to that assymetry by both the family and society.

Though Andrea and Jane had envisioned themselves as equal parents, Jane was the primary stay-at-home parent while Andrea was out working. This arrangement seemed to follow inevitably from the biological asymmetry, but in fact it was a choice—one which many couples, both gay and straight, don't make. Some couples, by forgoing nursing or combining it with bottle feeding, share parenting during the early months or create families in which the nonnursing parent is the primary caretaker. Others initially establish arrangements like Jane's and Andrea's but alter them after children are weaned. Jane and Andrea lined up the primary and secondary parenting roles with the biological and nonbiological connections, giving the biological asymmetry an added dimension. But that was only the beginning.

In some ways, Andrea's struggle was similar to what many heterosexual fathers say about their experiences as working parents of infants at home with nursing mothers. They, too, tell stories of jealousy and of feeling excluded from the intense mother-child bond. Yet there are also obvious, and crucial, differences. Gender plays a powerful role in distinguishing lesbian co-parent experiences from those of heterosexual fathers. While both may feel painfully excluded, lesbians, as women, are more likely to be disconcerted by such feelings. Throughout her life Andrea dreamed of being a mother—the one primarily responsible for a child's care. In contrast, most men don't expect to have that sort of primary relation to a child, but fantasize instead about becoming fathers, usually a less intensive role. While this distinction is in some flux today, stories like Andrea's nonetheless suggest that the dynamics of two-women parenting may entail more competition over parenting identities than do the dynamics of heterosexual or male couples. As a woman who aspired to be a mother, Andrea wasn't emotionally prepared to be in a secondary position, alongside a nursing mother. With Jane in the primary parenting role, Andrea had difficulty defining her own motherhood.

Andrea's problems were exacerbated by her losing sight of the fact that children change over time. In just a few months Kelly's almost exclusive physical and emotional dependence on Jane would give way to different needs that Andrea could readily meet. Andrea and Kelly would have many more opportunities to develop intimate mother-child bonds of their own. Understandably, Andrea had difficulty appreciating this early on; if she had, she might have felt more optimistic about her maternal role.

Perhaps this perspective would have been more accessible to Andrea if she were not also struggling with another problem. People in the surrounding community failed to recognize Andrea as a parent, and nothing in mainstream culture supported her in that role. She was neither biologically nor legally Kelly's mother. The lack of external recognition intensified Andrea's feelings that she was not a real mother, perhaps not even Kelly's parent.

Here again there is a crucial difference between lesbian co-parents and heterosexual fathers. Whereas Andrea had no surrounding reinforcement of her parental role, heterosexual men find their identity as fathers supported by their immediate communities and society. Since the notion that there can be two mothers is a foreign one, society tends to view biological mothers as "real" and their lesbian partners as nonparents. Thus while heterosexual fathers might feel pangs of jealousy, they are less likely to experience total displacement.

Andrea, Jane, and Kelly were caught in a whirlpool of conflicting forces, and it was only when Andrea and Jane began to sort through their predicament that the waters became calm. The intense jealousy and competition of the early months faded as Andrea's feelings shifted during the first couple of years of Kelly's life. Her first step was grief; the reality was that Jane and Kelly had an intimacy that Andrea not only longed for but equated with motherhood. Andrea's relationship to Kelly did not match her childhood fantasies. In order to embrace the relationship she and Kelly could have, she had to give up that fantasy. She remembers how that change began to occur. "Over time there was a process of acceptance—as painful as it was, I started accepting that there was something between Kelly and Jane that was different and that I needed to respect. It was kind of a grieving process."

Though this acceptance was painful, it was also freeing, for Andrea was able to stop seeing the differences as evidence that she was not Kelly's mother. Paradoxically, as she gave up trying to be a mother in exactly the same way Jane was, Andrea began to develop her own mothering role. One critical dimension of this was Andrea's asserting of that role in contexts where it had previously gone unacknowledged. "I realized that there were things that were confused for me. One of the powerful issues I was dealing with was the whole way I wasn't being recognized as Kelly's mother. Kelly's mother was Jane, not me—so I felt I had to fight hard for my place. I was fighting an external battle inside the family and when I understood that it became clear what I needed to do. I began to speak more to colleagues and friends about myself as Kelly's mother. It took people a while to join that perspective. It's a foreign notion to people, when there's already a biological mother there, to have an idea that there's another mother in the picture. But gradually people started saying 'How's your daughter?', not just 'How's Kelly?' "

When Kelly was four years old, Andrea gave birth to Melissa. The children relate to both women as their mothers, yet Andrea and Jane have become more comfortable with the differences among all the relationships in the family, and with the ways each relationship changes over time. Though it harkens back to a painful struggle, now the question "Who's the real mommy?" is a memory.

My conversation with Andrea was among the first I had with lesbian mothers. In subsequent years our conversation has reverberated as I've encountered other families for whom the question "Who's the real mommy?" is pivotal. But at the same time I've met many families in which that question is barely given a second thought. What makes for these differences among lesbian parents?

A short time after my conversations with Andrea I met Susan and

Dana, the parents of eight-year-old Danielle and three-year-old Avi. Like Andrea and Jane, Susan and Dana define themselves as two mothers, jointly raising the two children Susan gave birth to. Unlike Andrea and Jane, Susan and Dana haven't experienced jealousy or competition over maternal roles. In their family, biological mother-child connections are much less laden with meaning.

From the time of Danielle's birth, Dana was the primary stay-at-home parent, an arrangement that followed naturally from the fact that Susan's job contributed more to the family income and that Dana was in transition in her own work life. Although Danielle was breastfed for more than two years, she also took a bottle from a young age, which made the parenting arrangement workable.

Though Susan and Dana didn't plan the arrangement to address the psychological aspects of their effort to be two mothers, retrospectively they feel that the arrangement helped balance things between them. It not only created a strong bond between Dana and Danielle but also led people in their extended family and surrounding community to recognize Dana as Danielle's mother from the very beginning. Before Danielle's birth, Dana worried about the significance of Susan's biological connection to Danielle, and her lack of such connection. But this worry quickly dissipated once Danielle came along, and was not even a consideration by the time Avi arrived on the scene. Being the primary caretaker for Danielle cemented Dana's role as a mother.

"I stayed home and was the housewife for three years," she recalls. "It was exclusively because of work but in retrospect I look at it as a wonderful way to equalize things—a way to balance the biological issues. I think we've been equal parents. I can't think of any place in our lives where being biologically connected or not has been an issue. There's nothing you could point to and say, aha, you're the real mother or you're not."

How could biological asymmetry be so consequential for Jane and Andrea and so irrelevant to Susan and Dana? In part the contrast is explained by the different parenting arrangements. But the experiences also reflect different belief systems. Though Jane and

Andrea embrace the idea of being two mothers, and primarily see mothering as a social rather than biological relationship, they also believe that biological mother-child ties are qualitatively unique, as Andrea suggested in her statement that she eventually came to "accept" the differences between her relation to Kelly and Jane's relation to Kelly. In contrast, Susan and Dana seem to more deeply and fully embrace the idea that mothering is a social role. They give little emotional or practical weight to biological asymmetry.

Many lesbian couples make some distinction between biological and nonbiological parenting roles. They hold the idea that the biological mother-child bond is inherently different from nonbiological mothering. As Alice, who is raising one child that she gave birth to and one that her partner bore, put it: "I have to admit that when you're pregnant and you carry a baby around in your body for nine months, you're aware of that baby, so when it comes out you still know that baby." Tanya, the nonbiological mother of four-year-old Christopher, described her view of biological asymmetry this way: "We always said, and still do, that we want to co-parent equally, and mostly we are. But we also recognized early on that the biological factor makes a difference, especially with breastfeeding. He will still, if he's hurt or something, want her and go to her. My sense is that there's a physical security he gets from her body. It's gotten progressively less as he gets older, but there is a difference."

Some lesbians bring the view of biological mothering as qualitatively distinct from nonbiological mothering into their process of creating a family. Others come to this view only after their children are born, especially during breastfeeding. Tricia, for instance, believed that she and her partner Randy would operate in an equal manner, as two women who'd been socialized to be nurturing of children. But a more traditional division of labor arose around nursing, and that in turn led to tensions between Tricia and Randy. "I was incredibly naïve. I thought because we were two women that it would be much more mutual—that it wouldn't entail someone feeling left out because they didn't get enough attention. I thought of that as more typical of heterosexual relationships, where the man might say, 'I need to get taken care of and nurtured myself.' It was really a shock and awakening for me when that happened between Randy and me."

All of these women, in contrast to Susan and Dana, created primary and secondary parenting arrangements that matched biological and nonbiological parenting roles. The intensity of the infants' dependency on their primary caretakers was synonymous with the intensity of the infants' bonds to their biological mothers. Often lesbians structuring their families in this way don't recognize the parenting arrangement as a choice—one that in and of itself creates asymmetry. Instead, they see biological asymmetries as inevitably translating into qualitatively distinct mother-child relationships.

There are many different responses lesbian parents have to the question of biological asymmetry. Some actively attempt to balance their families by each partner's giving birth. Others attempt to counterbalance the intensity of the pregnancy, childbirth, and nursing with other kinds of activities. Chris and Diane, raising a son and daughter that Chris gave birth to, were careful to establish physical rituals between Diane and each infant. She was the one who bathed them and rocked them to sleep. When the family was out together, Diane more often carried the children, as a way to undercut other people's tendencies to recognize only Chris as the mother.

These lesbians are grappling with the question, How significant, in and of itself, is the biological mother-infant bond? If it is very significant in a particular family, then what emotional meaning does the asymmetry take on? Some couples are comfortable with the asymmetry, but for others it is quite painful. In some families the asymmetrical relationships of early infancy are recognized as temporary, and indeed turn out to be so. But in others the initial differences become the basis for qualitatively distinct relationships throughout the children's lives. Asymmetry may be construed merely as a difference—both women are mothers but they mother in different ways. Or asymmetry translates more powerfully into a view that one is a more "real" mother than the other.

Beliefs about the significance of biological parent-child bonds not only may shape how people feel in their families but may play a more formative role at the beginning of family life, determining how people choose to become parents. Some couples, strongly desiring equal parenting roles and believing that biological asymmetry is likely to interfere with that, decide to adopt. Lila, describing the decision she and her partner Elizabeth made, expresses the idea that biological asymmetry would most likely skew family relationships. "Elizabeth had some concern to the extent that there was an imbalance going into it—I was so overwhelmingly enthusiastic and she was at best reluctant. To then put in the additional factor of my having the biological relationship with a child and having the experience of breastfeeding would weight the scales in the direction of my relationship to the kid. One thing we were clear about was that the children were going to be ours. It was not going to be the kind of thing where we would stay in the relationship but I would be the one to have children. That's not what we wanted, and it's not what we have."

For Elizabeth and Lila, adoption did cut through the inequality that biological parenting might have set up. But asymmetry can also occur in adoptive situations. In these instances it is not biology but cultural definitions as institutionalized in the practice of single-parent adoptions that get taken up into family life.

This was brought to my attention by Margaret and Norah, who sought therapy because of a conflict concerning their daughter, Denise. At first they described difficulties that are common in many families: they had different parenting styles and had trouble agreeing on how and when to discipline Denise. They were also at a loss as to how to handle situations in which they simply did not agree; that is, how to incorporate their different parenting styles into the family. As we explored this territory, it gradually became clear that their difficulties were exacerbated by an unspoken idea of Margaret's. In a subtle, but ongoing way, she deferred to Norah, who was Denise's legal adoptive mother. Though the explicit agreement between Margaret and Norah was one of equal parenting, Margaret carried an unarticulated but powerful notion into their family life—namely, that as the legal parent Norah's views should prevail. Norah, in fact, wished that Margaret would take more responsibility for handling problematic situations; and Margaret, in fact, wished for more autonomy as a parent, but the unspoken belief constructed Norah as a more real parent than Margaret. Once the idea was out in the open, Margaret and Norah were able to see how it operated in their family; and since it wasn't consonant with what they both wanted, their awareness helped to shift the dynamic. This struggle, like Andrea's and Jane's, reflects the fact that people often hold conflicting ideas on different levels, and that predominant cultural definitions (such as official recognition of only one parent) can be part of what lesbian and gay parents carry into the deepest recesses of their intimate relationships.

Who's the Real Daddy?

I found a wide range of lesbian-couple responses to the question "Who's the real mommy?" When I began to talk with gay fathers, I was curious how a similar question played out in their families. The question "Who is a real parent?" interweaves many layers of experience—biological versus social parenting roles, cultural recognition or lack of it, and the different expectations women and men bring to parenting. Gender is an especially important part of how lesbians and gay men experience being "real" or "not real" parents. Usually the crucial question is not simply "Who is a real parent?" but rather "Who is a real mother or father?" Our culture tends to construct women as primary parents and men as secondary. No matter what traditions lesbians and gay men challenge, our socialization toward these roles is pervasive. Though in general couples end up with primary and secondary parenting divisions for many reasons, including different personal preferences and job possibilities, traditionally these arrangements hinge on gender. Without a gender distinction to fall back on, many lesbian and gay couples share parenting more equally than their heterosexual counterparts, or are more flexible with respect to who has primary parenting responsibility over time. But whether attempting to share parenting equally or creating primary-secondary arrangements, lesbians and gay men bring their gender socialization to their family lives.

In contrast to the lesbians I interviewed, gay male couples rarely talked about biological asymmetry as a major concern or a basis for dividing parenting responsibilities. Since biological fatherhood does not involve the physical parameters of pregnancy, childbirth, and, most significantly, nursing, gay men are freer to define their parenting roles—much as adoption frees couples of either gender. But the relative lack of discussion about competition for primary parenting roles doesn't stem only from these gendered biological parameters. It is also shaped by the different expectations men and women bring to their parenting roles.

Jeff, the biological father of children he and his partner Eric are raising, says that "as a nontraditional family, we are very traditional." Since Leah's birth, Jeff has stayed home and been a full-time father. Eric, on the other hand, maintains a more traditional, secondary parent role. Unlike the majority of men in this culture, Jeff fully embraces his role as a primary parent. "I'm in a perfect situation. Basically I'm a full-time parent, and I love it. She's good company. So we're the *Leave It to Beaver* model; he's Ward Cleaver who goes off and makes money, and I stay home—June Cleaver." Eric, in contrast to many lesbian mothers in secondary parenting roles, is quite comfortable with his less intense involvement. It fits not only his expectations but the expectations of those around him: he has the role of a traditional father. Since Leah's birth, Eric's heterosexual colleagues identify with his experience; except for the gender of his spouse, it is quite similar to their own. As Jeff puts it, "he fits the traditional role of father, so it's not hard for people to identify with that. They don't expect him to be a primary caregiver to his child."

This is in sharp contrast to the experiences of some lesbians who are often expected, both by themselves and by the rest of society, to be in a primary nurturing relation to their children. It's difficult for people to deal with the idea that in some families two mothers have primary roles. And it is likewise difficult for people to recognize a woman who has a more secondary role as nonetheless a legitimate parent. Men, in contrast, can quite comfortably take on secondary parenting roles. Sharing parenting responsibilities with another fits more readily into the father roles men have been primed for.

In fact, for gay male couples, traditional gender roles may lead to the opposite struggle from the one lesbians are prone to. Craig and Jim share the duties of parenting Sean, but they have struggled over logistics. Jim has thought a lot about how being two men affects their parenting dynamic. What he describes is in marked contrast to the lesbian competition concerning primary parenting roles. Jim and Craig went through a very difficult period during the first year of Sean's life. Though they had agreed on an equal-parenting arrangement, their employment situations resulted in Jim's spending far more time with Sean, and giving up much of his work time. Though he enjoyed his time with Sean, he grew resentful. Eventually the couple hit a crisis point, which pushed them to shift to a more equal arrangement. Jim connects what happened to the fact that they are two men trying to share parenting. "Two men raising a child is different from a man and a woman raising a child, or two women raising a child. I think one negative dimension is that men are raised with the idea that to be a success in life you have to be a success in your job, and that's the primary goal in life. You're raised to have a good career, not to be a good mother. Since this is so deeply ingrained, we have a difficult juggling act. We each need to strive for success in work. That's true for many women as well, but society also says it's okay if they stay home—they can define themselves that way. That can be a pressure, too—the idea that you have to stay home and be a good mother. But for us, the problem is pressure not to stay home."

Jim's description points to the power that social norms have in lesbian and gay parents' lives. Though gender is complex, and there are many exceptions to the generalizations we make about it, comparing lesbian and gay parents nonetheless reveals some expectable patterns. When same-sex couples are trying to work out equal parenting arrangements, lesbians more often express worry about not establishing a primary emotional bond with the child, while gay men may focus more, as Jim does, on worry about the compromised work identity that a significant commitment to parenting can entail.

Every generalization has its exceptions. There are many women who don't want to be primary caretakers and many men who do. Thus among some gay male couples I did find the question of "Who's the real daddy?" to pose as much difficulty as it had for Andrea and Jane. Here again, the reason was complex. Michael, co-parenting Ari, the biological child of his partner Barry and Adria, has been prone to feeling excluded and less legitimate as a parent. This not only reflects his wish to be a primary parent to a child who in fact has four parents, but also stems from the fact that Barry and Adria are more centrally defined in the family as Ari's parents.

Competition about parenting roles is not at all evident in many lesbian couples, and can be quite pronounced for some gay male couples. At the same time as they are deeply affected by gender socialization, lesbian and gay parents tend to stretch themselves beyond the June and Ward Cleaver model. Jim points out, for instance, that neither he nor Craig can use gender to define their parenting roles. The question of who gets up in the middle of the night must be answered from within the couple, without recourse to convention. Similarly, lesbian mothers struggling to make room for another mother, or to be a mother in the face of another mother's primacy, are pushing and altering profound social and psychological limits.

Gay men and lesbians, as men and women, both challenge and carry within them, normative cultural models of gender. One of the most interesting aspects of lesbian and gay parents is that, as they struggle to integrate their internal concepts of mother and father into their lives as lesbian mothers and gay fathers, they invariably question the givens of these terms. For instance, Martha and Jessie have developed a rather traditional division of labor with respect to the daughter Jessie adopted. Martha doesn't see herself as Jackie's mother. Then, as a female parent, what is she? "In some ways you could say my role is more like a traditional father," Martha says, "in that I'm not as involved and I'm not the first-line parent, for example, dealing with day care and such things. In my family, my mother would have done all that, and my father was available but he wasn't home as much. So I've always thought of myself as more of a traditional father, but I just spent the entire weekend with Jackie and am realizing that I'm more involved than my father was." Martha begins with a traditional gender-coded image of a father, but realizes that what she is doing doesn't quite fit that model.

Similarly, Kevin, who always knew he wanted to raise a child, begins to describe his feelings in traditional gender-coded terms, but ends up commenting that the categories break down: "Wanting to raise a child, in my heart, has to do with being a human being, and not necessarily a gay human being. It's discovering something in myself that's really prior to being gay, which surprised me. It has to do with my relationship to my mother. I think of Harvey Fierstein's line in *Torch Song Trilogy*. He says to his mother, "What I wanted was your life." He wanted the lifelong relationship with a mate, he wanted to be a parent, to have children. My mom and I were very close; we had a very rich relationship as parent and child, as adult friends. It has to do with continuing on in that, in some ways tapping into women's experiences.

"I wanted to be a 'Mommy.' Even though I call myself 'Daddy,' I conceptualize myself as a mother. It comes from a woman-identified part of me that has to do with being a human being, not just a gay man, though I think being a gay man allows me to say that, allows me to be the kind of man who's able to recognize the need to be a 'Mommy'—to be a primary caretaker, have physical intimacy with a child, celebrate a child's accomplishments, be there to teach and to guide.

"When Amber was first born, we were up in the room doing the first water feeding. The bottle went into her mouth, she was very present and opened her eyes and looked up at me—it just so thoroughly overwhelmed me. Many women in my life talk about the 'instinctual experience' of nurturing maternal feelings. I wanted to tap into that. When she opened her eyes and looked at me, I was just overwhelmed. It totally blew me away during the first weeks and months. Now that she's more independent there are other kinds of experiences that I tap into—a lot of them are more daddy-like, I suspect.

"I found out after Amber was born that it's something different than either 'Mommy' or 'Daddy.' The physical closeness, the soothing voice . . . that's really what I conjure up. That back-and-forth communication that before words has to do with just looks and touches—that is the basis of all human relationships. I wanted to be that person for her."

Lesbian and gay parents both mimic and challenge traditional gender-coded parenting models. An overview of lesbian and gay parenting reflects the larger cultural pairing of women with children and men without. It is lesbians (as compared to gay fathers) who most often retain custody of their children after divorce, and lesbians who are choosing to have children in numbers that warrant headlines about the lesbian baby boom, while a much smaller percentage of gay men choose fatherhood.

By and large, when lesbians and gay men make joint family arrangements, it is lesbians who do the primary childrearing, while gay men take on traditional "Sunday father" roles. But Kevin's description suggests that despite all the ways that lesbian and gay parenting mimics the larger culture's gender-coded parenting models, there are significant challenges lesbian and gay parents pose to those models. Although they are fewer than lesbian mothers, an increasing number of gay men are choosing to be primary parents. These men challenge the notions that young children need "mothers" and that men have neither the capacity for nor interest in the daily minutiae of childrearing. Men like Kevin draw on and develop their own nurturing capacities in ways that few men in our culture do.

As lesbian and gay parents move beyond the model of a one-mother, one-father family and begin instead to define for themselves who they are as parents outside that structure, they not only highlight our culture's tendency to define parenting roles through the lens of gender—they also challenge it at its core.

Who's the Real Mommy?

A Clash of Definitions

The lack of recognition that lesbian and gay parents encounter in their surrounding communities and in the larger society often profoundly affects how they relate within their families. For both lesbians and gay men, the discrepancies between families' self-definitions and community ideas pose great challenges. Frequently, it is the surrounding community's failure to recognize a nonbiological or nonadoptive parent that most threatens the family. Well aware of this, lesbian and gay parents often actively resist definitions that don't fit their sense of themselves.

Craig and Jim, for instance, have not told anyone which of them is Sean's legal father. Jim explains: "In subtle ways, people can treat us differently even if they don't outwardly say there's a difference. Why should it be such a concern if it's something that's not going to affect them?"

Similarly, Susan and Dana resist the outside world's tendency to categorize one as a more real parent. "We made a decision early on that when people asked the question 'Who's the biological mother?' we wouldn't answer it," Dana says. "We'd change the subject or we'd say something like 'Why are you asking that?' We realized that it often was a question about who was the real mother and who deserved to be given that authority, and we didn't want to encourage that. Just two weeks ago the school principal asked me, 'Who's her real mother?' and I said, 'Well, we're both her real mothers—she lives with both of us and we both take care of her.' He said, 'Well, I have legal considerations and confidentiality issues, and who has custody of her?' I said, 'I assure you there are no custody problems—I feel free for you to call Susan and talk to her, and she's the one who gave you my phone number at work to call me.' So he said, 'I guess you're right, she was very nice.' Then he dropped it."

The fact that society doesn't recognize lesbian and gay couples as joint parents of their children can either starkly or subtly permeate those relationships. There is a major power imbalance when one parent has legal rights and responsibilities and the other has no societally recognized role. Jessie, who legally adopted Jackie, describes her feelings about this in relation to her partner, Martha: "There's absolutely no way Martha can be a legal parent. I'm waiting for the finalization to come through before we draw up the paperwork, but she will at that point be her legal guardian so that if anything were to happen to me, Martha would be Jackie's guardian. If something were to happen in our relationship, I feel deeply committed to Martha and Jackie maintaining a relationship. This is a source of worry for Martha, I think, because there's nothing we can do legally to assure this. Our lawyer said we could draw up a contract including visitation arrangements, but she also said it would be very rare for it to hold up in court."

As Jessie points out, since society sees the family in a way that doesn't match the family's self-definition, people must rely exclusively on trust in each other. "I think, though, that this is a source of great pain. I mean, Martha is drawn to tears over this. It's very frightening for her. She says, 'What if you fell in love with someone who lived in California? Then you'd move.' But in my mind, Martha has been a parent to Jackie and will always be an important person in her life."

Martha describes her position this way: "There's some background vulnerability, but do you hold back because she's not really yours? You can't do that." Here, too, the issue is not just what limits society imposes on lesbian and gay parents but also the meanings individuals ascribe to these limits. While some couples, like Susan and Dana, are able to relegate the legal inequity to an inconsequential realm, many couples have difficulty doing this.

Five-year-old Carly's mischievous question, "Hey, who's the real mommy around here?" is one that's on a lot of people's minds. It is woven into the lives of lesbian and gay parents and their children and enhanced by many layers of experience: the discrepancy between mainstream culture and families' self-definitions, gender socialization, and the meanings we give to biological connections or the lack thereof. A meeting of the old and the new, Carly's question is a way the ghost of the traditional family haunts the new families lesbians and gay men are inventing.

As they grapple with the answers to this question, lesbians and gay men sort out what they will bring with them to their new families and what they will discard. They don't have entirely free rein in this endeavor. Yet even with the enormous constraints society imposes, as lesbian and gay parents invent new family forms, they demonstrate the human capacity for change. Though lesbians and gay men bring much of the traditional family to their own families, they also work to change themselves; in turn, they bring these changes to society. In the end, our families will be what we make them.

· 7 ·

A Rose by Any
Other Name

We walked down the path to the well-house, attracted by the fragrance of the honeysuckle with which it was covered. Someone was drawing water and my teacher placed my hand under the spout. As the cool stream gushed over one hand she spelled into the other the word "water," first slowly, then rapidly. I stood still, my whole attention fixed upon the motions of her fingers. Suddenly I felt a misty consciousness as of something forgotten—a thrill of returning thought; and somehow the mystery of language was revealed to me. I knew then that "w-a-t-e-r" meant the wonderful cool something that was flowing over my hand. That living word awakened my soul, gave it light, hope, joy, set it free! There were barriers still, it is true, but barriers that could in time be swept away.

I left the well-house eager to learn. Everything had a name, and each name gave birth to a new thought. As we returned to the house every object I touched seemed to quiver with life. That was because I saw everything with the strange, new sight that had come to me. . . .

I learned a great many new words that day. I do not remember what they all were; but I do know that "mother," "father," "sister," "teacher" were among them—words that were to make the world blossom for me, "like Aaron's rod with flowers."

Helen Keller
The Story of My Life

As though sending flares into darkness, we use words to find each other, to bridge the distance between us. In this way, we live through the very words we speak. It is through language that we become social beings. Helen Keller's first grasp of *w-a-t-e-r* is so moving not because she recognized and named water but because she recognized herself—a human being living in the world among other human beings.

On the day she connected the word *water* to the cool liquid splashing against her hand, Helen Keller joined the world around her. It was as though a door suddenly sprang open and she walked through, leaving the dark morass she had known and entering a place where she was able to let the elements of life distinguish themselves from each other and touch her, each in its own way. As her grasp of language brought the world to her, so too it enabled her to bring herself to the world—eventually to touch many lives by writing the words that let us know her as she had come to know water.

Helen Keller told the story of a journey from silence to voice, from isolation to relatedness. She vividly evoked the oppressiveness of silence and the freedom language can impart. But just as language has the power to connect us to each other, so too it has the power to separate us. Coming into voice is not simply a matter of finding words; it is a matter of finding the *right* words—words that belong to us. Silence—the absence of words—can be deadening, but so can the imposition of words that are not our own upon our most essential experiences.

It is no accident that liberation struggles of all kinds are inextricably bound up with the effort to find voice. Often this entails rejecting the language of the dominant culture and naming one's experience in one's own terms. Sometimes this literally entails choosing to speak one language over another, as when colonized or otherwise oppressed people choose their own language over that of the dominant culture. At other times, when the clash is between two entities who share the broad strokes of a given language, coming into voice may be a more subtle matter. So it is that finding the words to tell the untold stories and speaking out in rich, strong voices have been central features of the civil rights movements of African Americans, women, and lesbians and gay men.

For lesbians and gay men, the most crucial questions of language—and the lack thereof—concern relationships. Loving in defiance of social norms, lesbians and gay men must name their relationships in a world that does not support their existence. Their relationships are not culturally sanctioned nor are they defined in formal institutional structures such as the legal system. The words *husband* and *wife* have straightforward meanings. In contrast, the forbidden nature of lesbian and gay relationships is expressed in the lack of such public, commonly understood names. Thus lesbians and gay men struggle with the appropriate term for their partners. Is she a lover? Is he a mate?

Similarly, when lesbians and gay men have children they face decisions about language—decisions that reverberate throughout their lives, positioning them in relation to society as well as to each other. What should a child's last name be? What will he call each of his parents? These questions arise partly from silence, from the absence of conventional terminology. But the questions are just as powerfully defined by the presence of names and conventions that don't adequately reflect the relationships in these families. While a lesbian who bears or legally adopts a child will be recognized as a mother, her partner is not likely to be so readily acknowledged. Here, *mother* defines family life through both its presence and its absence.

Last names, like role names such as *mother* and *father*, also reflect and shape family relationships—they publicly announce which clan we belong to. Typically in our culture, a child's last name coincides with the biological or legal father's, though more recently—owing to the feminist movement—some children's names are combinations of their father and mother's last names, or correspond to their mother's. The children of unmarried women typically have their mother's last name. Sometimes people also use children's first and middle names as a way of establishing familial connections.

When they name their children, lesbians and gay men make a statement about what clan the children belong to. Should a child have the last name of the biological or legal parent? Of the donor if known? Of the lesbian or gay co-parent? Or some combination of the above?

Families are constructed through these kinds of decisions: Names both establish relationships within a family and describe those relationships to the rest of the world. The clash between the idealized traditional family and these new families is therefore often evident in linguistic choices. A child cries out in the middle of the night "Daddy," and down the hall come not one but two men. A little girl lost in the aisles of a supermarket tearfully tells a perplexed store manager, "I can't find my Didi." A small boy stares intently at the infant held by a woman sitting next to him on the bus and asks, much to her confusion, "Where is its other mommy—is its other mommy at home?"

As these parents decide what terminology to use, they start with the options available in our culture, bound up in the traditional family. Indeed, lesbians and gay men draw on this language even as they define themselves in distinction to the family structure from which it emanates. These parents sometimes accept traditional definitions despite their inadequacy, sometimes draw on common terms but alter their use and meaning, and sometimes invent altogether new language. Just as they transform society's notions of the family, so too lesbian and gay parents transform our use of words. Thus the intricate patterns language weaves through family life are revealed.

Strategies for Naming Parents

Often, when parents are invested in symmetry in the family and want to emphasize that each is a parent, they settle on a single term, *Mommy* or *Daddy*, that the child can call both parents. These parents point out that alternative names like *Mama* and *Papi* are not on an equal footing with the predominant terminology, and therefore do not accurately reflect their family's reality.

But using a single term to name both parents can be confusing. How do children specify which parent they're referring to? Some parents anticipate this and add on an adjunct—"Daddy Mark" and "Daddy Ted," for example. However, many families report that their children vary the language and work out their own solutions.

Nine-year-old Aija, who calls both Cindy and Maryann "Mom," explains that in her family "I call them all sorts of things ranging from 'Moozie' to 'Moo Moo.' Usually only one of them is at home, but when they're both home you call and whichever one calls back, you say 'come here,' or you say 'other one.' Like you call, 'Mom' but both of them answer 'what?' and you go 'Maryann Mom,' or 'Mom Maryann.' But when I used to get scared in the middle of the night, I'd call 'Mommy' and I didn't care which one came. I was just glad to see one of them!"

Andrea points out that her daughter Kelly uses "Mommy" not so much to denote one parent over the other but to express a particular emotional need. "Kelly calls us both 'Mommy' and both by our first names. We've really allowed her to do what she needs to do. We don't feel she has to call us anything. Mostly she calls us both by our first names. Yet when she needs one of us to really be 'Mommy' in a totally cuddly way, in a 'take care of me' way, she'll use the names in the way she needs to. If she's very focused on me and needs me to be especially comforting, Jane will be in the room, and she'll call me 'Mommy,' and she'll do the same with Jane, if that's what she's needing from her. Sometimes she'll call us both 'Mommy.' "

When parents worry about confusion resulting from the use of a single term, they construct variations, often incorporating terms from their own or other cultural heritages, such as *Ima, Mama, Poppa,* or *Papi.* Lily, an Asian American, describes her nonbiological and biological children's use of language: "Claire is called 'Mom' and I'm 'Mama' because that's the term in my culture. I don't believe a kid could call us both 'Mom.' How could they know which one they're calling? And we didn't like first names. I guess I'm sort of traditional in that way—it seems disrespectful for children to call adults by their first names." In Lily's family the different role names that the children, Robert and Ann, use don't reflect nonbiological versus biological parent-child ties; they simply differentiate the parents from each other. "Sometimes when we say that Robert calls Claire 'Mom' and me 'Mama,' people will ask, 'And what does Ann call you?'—as if Ann would call me 'Mom' and

Claire 'Mama.' It would never occur to me to have one kid call us one way and the other kid do it a different way—as if 'Mom' is the real thing and the other name is something else."

Describing her family's experience, Angie points out how important it is that the surrounding community join in their familial terminology. "Evan calls me 'Mama' and Greta 'Mommy.' We didn't want to use first names and we weren't comfortable making up a name. We wanted something that was recognizable to other people. So this really meant 'mother' to him, yet it was different names for each of us. I've talked to other people who felt that 'Mama' wasn't as legitimate as 'Mommy,' but we haven't thought of it that way. At his day-care center they refer to each of us in this way, so it feels like it's working well at this point."

Sometimes parents and children together make up a pet name—Didi, Peep, Neeny—terms that connote the specialness of a relationship but are neither simply a name nor a role recognizable to others. Jill, the nonbiological mother of seven-year-old Kimberly, says "the question of what Kimberly was going to call me was really hard. I just hated that there was no name for what my relationship to her was going to be. As much as I tried to say it shouldn't be such a big deal, it was a big deal to me. I thought it wasn't realistic to have her call us both 'Mommy'—that wasn't going to happen and it would only confuse her anyway. Though we refer to the fact that she has two mothers at this point, I felt she needed some way to distinguish us. I really didn't want her to call me Jill. Probably someday, ultimately, she will call me Jill and that will be okay; but I also felt like I wanted some name for her to call me. So we played around with it for a while when she was an infant, and at that point came up with 'Maji'—it was an idea that combined Mommy and Jill. Before she started to talk, that's how we referred to me. Then when she was just starting to talk she called me 'Didi.' At first we thought it was just a fluke, but then she repeated it in another context. I don't know where it came from—if it was 'Maji' or just something she created for some reason, but it stuck. Now she refers to me as her 'Didi.' When she plays with her little teddies, sometimes there's a 'Mommy' and a 'Daddy,' sometimes a

'Mommy' and a 'Didi.' She knows that daddies are men and that I'm not. It doesn't mean anything to the world, but at least I have it."

Like many lesbian and gay parents who have neither biological nor legal parental status, Jill cares a great deal about what her child calls her. When the parent-child bond is not recognized by the rest of the world, the name itself seems to have the power to mark the relationship as a special one. In this way, language not only reflects relationships but also partly constructs them. Furthermore, Jill's story points to how the significance of names extends beyond relationships in the family. Names also have the power to join or separate the family from the rest of society. The lack of cultural consensus about a term for lesbian and gay co-parents can be quite painful, as Jill describes. "I remember shortly after coming out to my sister, she remarked to me that it upset her that there wasn't a name for her relationship to Debra—that it felt to her like a sister-in-law relationship but she couldn't really refer to her that way. I think it's a much milder form of what I feel about names. I mean, names are important. If I'm in the supermarket and Kimberly calls 'Didi,' it doesn't mean anything, and that part really upsets me— that there's not some universal way of explaining our relationship to each other. It will always upset me that there isn't a universal name for whom I am to her. It feels like it's important enough that there should be something."

Though many parents think carefully about what terms to use because they see language as shaping relationships, some don't buy into this view. In marked contrast to Jill's thinking, Amy argues that relationships transcend language. Starting from that belief, she is far less concerned about what her children call her. She describes the ways her daughters, who were legally adopted only by her partner, refer to their parents: "It changes day to day—it evolves and it changes. They're just going to figure it out. Once a friend of mine was talking about someone else named Amy, and Sharon was listening and she yelled, 'No, that's my Amy!' I felt like she didn't have to call me 'Mommy.' It was clear she had a relationship to me that was key. I don't feel names are so important." Like Andrea, Amy notes that her children's use of language varies according to their emotional needs: "I'm happy with the way it is now because I feel like the different ways they call us clue us in to different needs, sort of like variations in tones of voice."

The wide variety of naming strategies reflects cultural change—previously fixed, given features of our language take on new twists and turns as lesbians and gay men reconstruct the meaning of family.

The choices people make about names and family terminology are in themselves a stunning testament to human diversity and creativity, but what is far more fascinating is the thinking that underlies each choice. When they talk about names, people analyze the meanings of words like *mother, father,* and *parent*—teasing apart and rearranging their gendered, relational, biological, and legal ramifications. Couples position themselves in relation to each other and to their children through words, wondering, for instance, whether calling one parent "Daddy" and the other "Paul" sets up a power imbalance or skews emotional connections in a family. People struggle with homophobia—both their own and the world's—as they choose how much of their stories to reveal through the shorthand of a child's hyphenated last name, or the delineation of two mommies. They puzzle over the complexities of parent-child negotiations in a homophobic environment, as they decide how much space developing children need to choose their own presentation, and how that space will be determined by the choice of names. In making decisions about names, people explore the philosophy of language itself: Do our words have the power to shape relationships, or do our relationships transcend the labels we apply to them? Is it more important for children to be able to join with mainstream culture through conventional language or more important for children's language to reflect their particular realities, and thereby challenge cultural conventions? Most powerfully, as lesbian and gay parents construct their families through words, they throw into question the seemingly natural derivation of our most common kinship terminology, revealing it to be not God-given but created, not inevitable but one of many possibilities.

As they name their family relationships, lesbian and gay parents use varied terminology, borrowing terms from mainstream culture and expanding their meaning as well as inventing new terms. The variation reflects the fact that we are in the midst of great social flux. Yet we are no longer at the very beginning of this cultural transformation. When I started my research a decade ago, rather matter-of-factly I asked lesbian mothers to tell me what their kids called them; or if their children were infants, what they hoped they would call them. My motive back then was quite literal: I simply wanted to know the answers. "They call us 'Mommy Carol' and 'Mommy Jean.'" "He calls me 'Mommy' and her Denise." Those were the sorts of answers I expected. But instead the question thrust me into far richer territory. I had turned off the main road and stumbled on a landscape I had never before imagined, much less seen.

Lesbians choosing to raise children back then were pioneers. There was little cultural precedent and there were no maps for them to follow. The trails they blazed led them to new dimensions of language. Though they were not completely alone in their efforts to develop a language that fit their relationships, many reported that they felt as if they were. They said they didn't know what was right, but had made choices that made the most sense to them as individuals. The dramatic shift in the whole concept of family was reflected in these women's approaches to language. They were sorting out not only the shape of their families but also how those families would be situated in the world. At the deepest level, they were grappling with the significance of language itself.

The conversations I have now with recent parents are also lively and fascinating, but much has changed. Though there is still no cultural consensus about terminology, and there is much to sort out, now there are dialogues about the issues and models to follow. In just these past few years a subculture has emerged that is beginning to define its own conventions.

A Question of Meaning

At the most obvious level, as people make decisions about names they think about meaning. What is a mother or a father? Are the terms defined by biology, law, the quality of relationship, or some combination of these? Many lesbian and gay parents emphasize the relational component of words like *mother* and *father* over the biological and legal components. Marcia, whose biological daughter calls both her partner and herself "Mommy," sums up her thinking this way: "A real mother isn't who carried you during pregnancy. A real mother is who takes care of you and whom you call 'Mommy,' and who lives in your house and holds you in her lap and does all those things that mothers do. It's a social function, not a biological one." Since Marcia sees "mother" as a relational rather than a biological role, it is logical that insofar as her daughter is "mothered" by both herself and her partner, she refers to them both as "Mommy."

Not all lesbian and gay parents agree with Marcia. Some feel strongly that biological or legal parenthood is a necessary component of terms like *mother* and *father*, or they feel that children can really have only one mother or father. These parents are more likely to encourage children to call one parent "Mommy" or "Daddy" and the other parent by his or her first name. These different approaches reflect semantic disagreements—that is, disagreements about the meaning of the words *mother* and *father*—as well as different family configurations.

Some diversity in terminology corresponds to diversity in family structure. While many couples create two-parent families, others create families that include only one parent and that parent's partner. Each family's way of constructing relationships is reflected through language. Jessie, for instance, explains that her adopted daughter's use of names fits the way she and her partner understand their roles in the family. "Jackie may call Martha 'Mom.' We wouldn't say 'Don't call her Mom,' but in our language we refer to ourselves as 'Mom' and Martha. Martha and I think about ourselves as parents, not two mothers. Partly that's because Martha saw herself as helping me. If she wanted to be called 'Mom,' that's a symbol of something. It's not that I would have opposed it. She was so clear that she saw herself as an adjunct."

Insofar as names correspond to family structure, changes in the ways families define themselves are also reflected in language. Just as one moves from being a fiancé to being a husband after the state sanctions a relationship through marriage, lesbians and gay men express their family transformations through the terms they use, and how those terms evolve over time.

A shift in family terminology can be a profound symbol of developing relationships. For instance, when Josh adopted Raymond, he and Bill had not yet become lovers; and though Bill began parenting Raymond while the boy was still quite young, Raymond has always called Josh "Dad" and Bill by his name. However, Bill and Josh were together when Keith arrived, and they decided to encourage Keith to use the terms "Dad" and "Papa." It is as though this shift in language was part of how the family cemented itself as a unit.

By the same token, the disintegration of relationships may be expressed through changing terminology. Tricia, the biological mother of one-year-old Erin, defines *mother* in relational rather than legal or biological terms. She and her lover Randy split up when Erin was an infant, and they found themselves struggling to define a co-parenting arrangement. As Tricia explains, their struggle partly played out in the realm of language: "Before Erin was born, Randy was resistant to using 'Mommy' and 'Mommy' or 'Mommy Tricia' and 'Mommy Randy.' She felt Erin would develop her own term for Randy, and could call me 'Mommy.' I pushed for something different—for us to have the same status, like using our first names. After Erin was born, we started saying 'Mommy Tricia' and 'Mommy Randy.'

"Now it's an issue. Who gets to be a parent? It's the flip side of the superiority of the biological parent. Just because you squeezed the kid out, does that make you a parent? Well, on the other hand, just because you signed a contract, does that make you a parent? I would say not necessarily. It's about who does the caretaking and worrying.

"We're struggling about whether Randy is Erin's parent. She wants to be called that, but I'm dragging my heels because she was absolutely absent for the first six months and has been around the last four only on her own terms. So we are negotiating around that. I stopped saying 'Mommy Randy' and that bothers Randy. She considers herself Erin's parent. I'm not sure what I think yet. Randy wants to clear it up, since Erin is developing language now.''

Tricia's quandary reflects the fact that families headed by lesbian and gay parents are under construction—in the process of being invented. The link between invention and language is clear, as Tricia tries to figure out on her own what would qualify Randy to be called "Mommy." With no conventions to fall back on, and with relationships that are not developing as she had imagined, her uncertainty about the relationships is reflected in ambivalence about language.

Parents are not the only ones, of course, to decide about terminology. Children have their own ideas—ideas that are initially shaped by life in the family, but that become more influenced by other sources as children develop and move about in the world. Thirteen-year-old Steve was conceived through donor insemination by Charlene, and raised jointly by Charlene and Paula. They split up when Steve was eight and have maintained a joint-custody arrangement since that time, with Charlene maintaining primary responsibility. Steve refers to himself as having lesbian parents, and as having "two moms." But he also points out that his use of language varies and reflects a difference in how he perceives his relationships to Charlene and Paula. "I learned about my mom's being gay at a really young age. And I always knew that Charlene was my biological mother. I feel somehow more comfortable with her—more myself. Sometimes I still call Paula 'Mom,' but since the split it's kind of off-and-on, kind of random when I call her 'Mom' or Paula. I almost always call Charlene 'Mom.' "

Steve, like Tricia, expresses the change in his family through his use of language. He is less certain of Paula's parental role than of Charlene's—a fact that derives from many sources: the lack of cultural recognition of two-mother families, the split between Charlene and Paula, and Steve's differing levels of comfort with each woman.

The Social Dimension of Language—In or
Out of the Closet Through Words

There is a dimension of language beyond the realm of meaning—
one that is so taken for granted that it's almost invisible, like water
to the fish who swim in it. Language is a form of social interaction.
The words we use reflect agreements we tacitly make. For instance, when parents name a child they say, in effect, "We call this
child Susan, and we expect that she will call herself Susan, and that
you in the world will call her Susan." Thus a set of agreements is
proposed. We usually don't notice the complexity of the arrangements; we simply participate in them. But when there are disjunc-
tures between various people's ideas, the process of agreement is
revealed as a complex set of relationships.

This social aspect of language is especially visible in lesbian and
gay lives. Existing on the margins of mainstream culture, lesbians
and gay men must derive words to describe their experience from
an existing language that often doesn't fit. They grapple with terminology taken for granted in mainstream culture. This self-
conscious exploration illuminates the relational aspects of language.
Couples may, for instance, find that they don't agree about what
terms to use. Once they reach consensus, they may find that their
children or extended families have entirely different ideas about
what words to use. And even if there is consensus in their immediate circle, lesbian and gay parents, along with their children,
inevitably bump up against a discrepancy between the way they
name their relationships to each other and the way mainstream
society names (or does not name) those relationships. Deciding
what terminology to use invariably entails much more than sorting
through the meanings of words. Through decisions about terminology lesbian and gay parents begin to shape the relationships
they and their children will have to the surrounding community
and to society.

In the social dimension of language, homophobia can powerfully
influence people's choices. For example, some lesbian and gay
parents argue that names are precisely a way of joining with the

culture, and that it is best for a child to have a way of doing that. These parents may choose to use the most traditional terminology, expecting the child to call only the biological or legal parent "Mommy" or "Daddy" and giving the child that person's last name. They thus attempt to construct a particular relation between the child and the larger culture. On the other hand, some parents feel strongly that names should reflect one's sense of definition, and that the culture should be urged to join with the family in honoring the names they establish. These parents are much more likely to decide that both should be called "Mommy" or "Daddy" by the child, and that society should be educated to do the same. Their child might have a hyphenated last name, which clearly reflects the family structure.

Families may come out or stay closeted through their decisions on names. Often people's responses to a homophobic environment are the foundation of their name choices. Here, for instance, Lila explains the reasoning behind her family's use of role terminology: "The reality for these children is that they do have two moms and their mothers are lesbians, and that's a whole package that they'll have to deal with in the world; but it also seemed to me, in terms of their own development, that it was important for them to feel like they had a mother—you know, just one person who was playing that sort of primary role.

"I think they need that internally and I also think they've got to learn at an early age that you can present yourself to the world in a lot of different ways. There are places you can be totally safe and open and say, 'I have two moms, they're both lesbians. I have a sister and a dog,' and there are other places where you simply say, 'My mom is Lila.' "

Other parents feel quite differently. They believe family terminology should reflect the realities of children's lives, and that those who come into contact with these families must learn to understand and respect them. These parents may teach neighbors, for instance, to ask their children not "How is your daddy?" but "How are your daddies?" Nine-year-old Aija attests to the fact that use of family terminology does indeed become part of children's relations to the larger community. She often finds herself explaining her family to her peers, educating them about the reality of her life: "My friends ask who's my real mom. I say 'What do you mean by real?' If they say 'biological' or 'the one who had you' I say 'Maryann.' But if they say 'Who's your mom, Aija? Not both of them could be your mother,' I say 'They both are my mothers—can't you get that into your little head? You could have two mothers, not just one or none. You could have three, four, five, six—however many as love you. It doesn't matter. You can't only have one mother. You can have as many as who love you.' It's almost like being an orphan 'cause you're different, you're very different. Orphans have to explain when they left their family, did they ever know their family— instead of not having a mother, I've got double."

Like role names, people's decisions about last names have both symbolic and practical implications. Angie and Greta chose to hyphenate their son's name because it reflected their sense of their family. "Though neither of us was crazy about hyphenated names, at some point we realized that his name was not Greta's name, it was really our last names. We tend to think of ourselves collectively as the Adler-Browns, but neither of us is interested in hyphenating our last names, so its Angie Brown, Greta Adler, and Evan Adler-Brown."

Names can be a way of constructing not only parent-child relationships but also sibling connections. In Lily's family, both her nonbiological and biological children have her last name. "Claire wanted the kids to have the same last name as each other. I didn't feel strongly about that issue, but when she articulated it, it sounded good to me. It also fit with the fact that I thought the kids should have an Asian last name because they're mixed racially, and in American society there's always a push to act more white. It seemed that since they are already not going to look totally Asian, it would be harder for them to have strong Asian identities unless they had an Asian last name." Here, Lily sees the children's last name as both reflecting their sibling relationship (which is not biologically or legally established) and helping to solidify their ethnic identities.

Often homophobia strongly shapes people's decisions about children's last names. Jenny clearly describes how homophobia played out in her decision about her son Michael's last name. "He has Alma's last name as a middle name. We thought about hyphenating it, but then we thought that satisfies our ego and probably makes his life more difficult. What we've decided is that whatever he wants to tell the world at large is fine. I mean, we don't insist that he be honest, we only insist that we be honest with him. This was my choice, or our choice, to do this. And I don't know what he'll face—I don't know what kids will say to him. Being a kid is hard enough that if he thinks up something that makes his life more comfortable at that moment, then he's got to have his space too. I will give him the space to present it any way that he can."

Jenny and Alma literally constructed a closet out of language, choosing a naming strategy that could obscure their relationship if necessary, precisely to give Michael the space to do that. Such a choice cuts both ways: it can provide the space to choose whom one comes out to; but it also buys into the delegitimizing of the nonbiological, nonlegal parent-child relationship, and this can have unwanted and unforeseen consequences. Marie, who thought similarly to Jenny, disagreed with her partner about what last name to give their son. "Before Toby was born, Jana and I had a big argument about whether we were going to hyphenate his last name. We knew we were going to use my name as either a middle name or part of a hyphenated name. I didn't want the hyphen because I wanted to let him have more of a choice about how public he was. When he gets to be ten or eleven, it will start to matter to him, and I wanted him to have a name he could do what he wants with." As it turned out, Jana prevailed and the couple did hyphenate Toby's last name. After his birth they inadvertently stumbled upon a major practical implication of their decision. Toby, born prematurely, was initially in the ICU and only parents and grandparents were allowed to visit. Though Marie might have been able to explain her position and be granted visitation, his last name rendered explanations unnecessary. "When I arrived at the nurse's station, since we had hyphenated our names for him, they assumed I was his mother."

Both couples—Jenny and Alma, and Marie and Jana—recognized that names can be a shorthand way of marking relationships, and thereby creating the family's relationship to the world around it. Names can create the space for a closet and amplify the delegitimization of lesbian and gay families; or, conversely, loudly declare the family structure to the rest of the world.

Clashes Between Extended Families and Lesbian and Gay Parents

Since language is a social process, naming can be complicated by disagreements within extended families. Homophobia may show itself as an unwillingness to acknowledge in words the parental relationships lesbian and gay couples have created. Children of lesbian and gay parents are often exposed at a very young age to the contested nature of their family structure.

Four-year-old Ian bumped up against differing views of what constitutes his family while visiting his nonbiological mother's parents. Esther, Ian's biological mother, describes her quandary about explaining Leslie's mother's disinterest in being called "Grandma": "We were visiting Leslie's parents and Ian and I were walking around, and he turned to me and said, 'Where's Grandma?' So far, the only 'Grandma' he knew was my mother because Leslie's parents made it clear they didn't want to be called that. I said 'You mean Grandma Pat?' and he said 'Yeah, Grandma Pat.' I was astounded because he in fact got the relationships right. But it concerns me about what will happen when he's old enough to figure out the discrepancy and he wants to know 'Why isn't Pat my grandma?' "

Lois tells the story of how three-year-old Jamie struggled with her grandmother over what to call her nonbiological mother. Grandma said, "Pass the orange juice to Lois." Jamie replied, "You mean my mommy?" Grandma corrected her, "No dear, pass the juice to Lois." Jamie reiterated, "You mean pass the juice to my mommy." Grandma, apparently missing Jamie's point again, said, "No, dear, pass the juice to Lois," at which point the exasperated Jamie cried out, "You mean, pass the juice to my Mommy, Lois!"

With conflicts about the definition of family expressed through these most basic conversations, children of lesbian and gay parents become aware early on of what most people learn much later in life: people have vastly different points of view, and these differences are expressed linguistically. Families process conflicts over terminology in different ways. Jamie's parents, for instance, maintain a hard line that she does indeed have two mommies—it is Grandma who is out of sync with the family definition. But in contrast, Michael's parents, Jenny and Alma, were quite shaken by Jenny's mother's refusal to recognize Alma as Michael's mother. The family dramatically shifted its use of language after Jenny's mother visited and made her opinion clear, as Jenny describes. By the time Michael was two years old, he had begun on his own to call his nonbiological mother Alma "Mommy" and Jenny by her first name. But when Jenny's mother came to visit, "she just put an end to that right then and there," as Jenny recalls. "It was a very painful week because I kept saying 'Mom, he does have two parents, and you need to stay out of this.' He was just learning to talk—he was in his early twos—she would say, 'No, her name is "Mommy"—you call her "Mommy" and this is Alma.' "

As Jenny's mother pursued her mission, emotions ran painfully high between Jenny and Alma. Jenny says, "On one level I was happy because I wanted to be called 'Mommy.' I didn't mind if she was called 'Mommy' but I wanted to be called 'Mommy,' too. On the other hand, it was just brutal torture for Alma to be so shut out because she has always been a parent. She has never said 'he's not mine' or 'I don't want to do this job' or 'you get up.' She has always been there, and it was just so painful."

In the struggle over what Alma would be called, the essence of each family relationship was at stake. What makes a mother—biology or a nurturing, maternal relationship? "My mother does a lot of 'blood is thicker than water' sort of comments. When they come up I say 'Mom, he loves her just the same.' She just says, 'She is not his mother and because of that on some level her feelings for him are not the same as yours.' I don't choose to believe that is true. I'm sure on some level he picks up on all this."

Although Jenny and Alma disagreed with Jenny's mother's thinking, they nonetheless took her words to heart. She made them wonder what it would be like for Michael to name his family in a way that many would not comprehend or accept. "After that visit, Alma and I talked about it, and what we decided was that even though it was hurtful and we wished there would be some kind of generic 'Mommy' name for female caregivers in the household, his life would be made more difficult by there being verbal confusion about who we were. So we decided for his sake, when he goes out in public, it would be better that he refer to me as 'Mommy' and her as Alma.

"When he was littler he looked just like me, so when you would see the three of us together he was clearly my child. So we just decided that we had been a little idealistic and that in order to protect him from the world that this was a distinction that needed to be made. My mother's reaction, while maybe a bit harsh, was a pretty good litmus test of what we might expect out there.

"Since Alma and 'Mama' when said by a child sound a lot alike, we've found that people would hear him and say, 'What did he call her?' and when we said 'He called her Alma,' they became a lot more calm. We decided to go ahead and reinforce that. If he wants to call me Jenny, that's fine. Lots of children prefer to call their parents by their names as compared to their designations, so I don't correct him on that. But we changed it, we changed how we designated ourselves."

By the end of Jenny's mother's visit the painful cycle had reached a conclusion: Jenny and Alma saw their adoption of more traditional terminology as a way to protect Michael. Thus life in their family was reconstructed, first by homophobia in the extended family and then by anticipation of homophobia in the surrounding community. It is hard to know what two-year-old Michael made of his changed world, but it is clear in this family's struggle that lesbian and gay parents do not decide in isolation what language to use. Instead they move in relation to the world around them—a world that often forcefully asserts, through the simplest exchange of words, its refusal to recognize the relationships they've created.

What's In a Name?

"What's in a name?" Lesbian and gay parents grapple with this question in a world that doesn't support the families they have created. As they consider what terminology to use, they contend both with a state of namelessness and with society's imposition of ill-fitting names. In their often painstaking process of finding language through which to create and describe their families, lesbians and gay men are neither free of public convention nor doomed by it. Homophobia pervades the realm of language, showing itself most clearly through silence. Hence, people's efforts to find words to declare their families' existence constitute a crucial form of resistance. As Adrienne Rich wrote:

> Whatever is unnamed, undepicted in images, whatever is omitted from biography, censored in collections of letters, whatever is misnamed as something else, made difficult-to-come-by, whatever is buried in the memory by the collapse of meaning under an inadequate or lying language—this will become not merely unspoken, but *unspeakable*. . . . All silence has a meaning.

· 8 ·

What the Children Must Learn

Facing Homophobia

. . . what the grown-ups can't teach   children must learn
how do you teach a child what you won't believe?
how do you say unfold my flower, shine, my star
and we are hated, being what we are?

Adrienne Rich
"Eastern War Time"

Ten-year-old Sarah hunched over her desk, using her body to shield the note she scribbled to her classmate. "Sky, is your mom a lesbian?" She folded it over itself until it was so small she couldn't fold it anymore and furtively passed it down the row. It came back scrawled with the answer "No—are you a dick?!" Sarah wrote back, "No Sky, my mom is a lesbian and I was just wondering if your mom is also." This time Sky responded, "Megan started that rumor. My mom isn't a lesbian. She has a roommate and they sleep together but they're not lesbians." Sarah considered this carefully before writing her final installment. "Okay, don't tell anyone about my mom." This was fine with Sky and the note made its last journey: "Okay don't tell anyone about mine, either."

Feeling her way around her fifth-grade classroom, Sarah had been hopeful about connecting with Sky, but instead of finding friendship she ran smack into the closet door. Like their parents, the children of lesbians and gay men must sooner or later grapple with homophobia. It makes its first appearance in many ways: an encounter like Sarah's and Sky's, a grandfather who shuns the family, the boy next door who isn't allowed to come over and play, faggot jokes casually tossed about in the schoolyard. Often children first encounter homophobia in a far less tangible form, more an absence than a presence. They see no families like theirs in movies, television, or books on the library shelves. In school they dutifully go through the rituals of Mother's and Father's Day projects, never hearing about families that have more or less than one of each.

Homophobia is all around us. It enters our lives in a multitude of ways, sometimes loudly declaring its presence, like a swastika sprayed on a wall, sometimes quietly seeping under our skin through the slightest of gestures, suddenly downcast eyes, a subtle change in tone. It often wreaks havoc through the most insidious route of all—utter silence. These processes of fear and hatred leave their prints on each and every one of us; they become part of our very being. We are not separable from the worlds we inhabit, nor they from us. Homophobia infiltrates relationships between family members, friends, neighbors, colleagues. It pervades the social institutions in which our lives are embedded—the law, schools, the media. As a culture we have barely begun to recognize its power and are even less far along in grappling with it.

If our society has failed thus far to acknowledge and appreciate lesbian and gay lives, we have failed even more so with respect to families headed by lesbians and gay men. While it is rare enough to find lesbians and gay men in the mainstream media, lesbian and gay parents are essentially nonexistent. The cultural opposition between homosexuals and children is reflected in the absence of images of such family relationships. The world that homosexual parents and their children inhabit is a world that holds a trick mirror to their faces, declaring each invisible.

One of the great paradoxes of lesbian and gay existence is this: as long as there is prejudice against lesbians and gay men there will be closets, and wherever there are closets, that prejudice will be allowed to flourish, unchecked. Unlike many other forms of discrimination, homophobia is directed at a characteristic that is not necessarily readily apparent, so people can to varying degrees avoid its direct slings and arrows by remaining closeted. In fact, one form homophobia takes is the notion that "it's okay to be one but it's not okay to talk about it." Thus people on both sides of the fence contribute to and perpetuate the pervasive silence around homosexuality.

What does all this mean to children? While much has been written about the significance of homophobia and closets in lesbian and gay lives, little attention has been paid to their meaning in families. What are the consequences of homophobia for parents, children, and their surrounding communities? How do families position themselves in an often hostile, fearful, and ignorant social context?

Adrienne Rich, writing about the fate of Jews during the Holocaust, powerfully juxtaposes images of flourishing life—unfolding flowers and shining stars—with the most destructive of human emotions, hatred. How does a child flourish and grow, as children should, amid bigotry? How do parents face the pain of this question and help their children with this task? As a society, how do we dismantle the circumstances that make these questions necessary?

The Parents' Perspectives—Beyond the Closet Door

The first Lesbians Choosing Children Conference I attended back in the early 1980s stands out in my mind, but not for the reasons I expected it would. I, like many others there, was at once nervous and exhilarated—amazed, really, to see so many women assembled to talk about what had seemed to be my most private obsession. And yet it isn't the exhilaration of discovering a community that left its mark. Instead, I remember most vividly the almost overwhelming homophobia that pervaded many of those first conversations.

One after another, women stood up and asked if they had a right as lesbians to bring children into their families. It was one thing, they reasoned, for them to suffer the pain of prejudice for a choice they themselves had made, but it was quite another to involve a child. About halfway through one workshop, an irate woman finally took the floor. She said that as a lesbian mother of two and as a Jew, she was horrified by the discussion. Would any of us, she wanted to know, turning to the mostly white, politically progressive crowd, tolerate this kind of talk about ethnic minorities? Since Jewish children were likely to face discrimination at some point in their lives, should Jewish women consider simply not bringing them into the world? The room fell briefly into an uncomfortable silence. Then they began to take her on. It's not the same, some said, because we've chosen this lifestyle. Thus the tiresome debate about choice or biological imperative threatened to take over the proceedings, as though the pivotal determinant of one's right to live free from bigotry was premised on whether or not one had chosen the despised characteristic. Soon the conversation took other turns: Was the choice to have children a matter really of rights? Was it any more selfish a choice for lesbians than for any others? Was selfishness in this instance really a bad thing—wasn't it better for children to be wanted and chosen than not?

I was grateful to the irate woman for stirring the pot. As the debate whirled around me, I sat lost in memories of my own childhood, thinking about the ways feeling different had shaped me. It had often been painful, but it was also the core of my being, ultimately the richest source of my strength. So I sat there sympathizing with the women who feared the prospect of their children's pain, but I was far more interested in how parents can help kids flourish in the face of life's difficulties, than in the question of whether to throw in the towel before life gets underway.

With that introduction to the choosing children movement, it was not surprising to me to find that homophobia's impact on family life is an often-heated, confusing, and pivotal concern among lesbian and gay parents. How do parents help their children not only thrive but develop strength in response to bigotry? How and when do they try to shield their children from pain, to actively advocate for them, to hold back and let them find their own way of dealing, to be present and bear witness to their suffering? What do the travails that children face stir up for their parents who have gone through, and are most often still in the midst of, their own processes of grappling with homophobia?

While these questions concern the impact of the world's homophobia on children's lives, there is another worry that plagues many lesbian and gay parents: What if a child is the vehicle through which homophobia enters family life? While many lesbians and gay men have faced their parents' homophobia, it is quite another thing—as parents—to face children's homophobia. What if they hide all the gay literature when friends come over, or implore you not to hold hands in public, or say they hate you because you're a lesbian?

Lesbian and gay parents' experiences in a homophobic society are interwoven with responses to questions like these. By the same token, all of these questions have a dimension that is not circumscribed by the vicissitudes of homophobia; instead, they are central to the nature of parenting itself.

One of the first things lesbian and gay parents think about in relation to helping children cope with homophobia is establishing a sense of community. Just as emergence from isolation to comradery often takes lesbians and gay men from shameful despair to a place of pride and hope, an experience of belonging can be crucial to the children of lesbian and gay parents. As Marcy, the mother of two boys, put it, "We have tried to get close to other lesbian families, especially donor-inseminated families, not so much for our support but for the kids. We want them to feel that they're not the only ones, that there are other kids dealing with these issues. It's one thing to say to our children that there are different ways to have a family—that some families have a mommy and a daddy and some families have two mommies—but if all they ever see are families with a mommy and a daddy, it's going to be hard to get across the idea that this is just another way to be." While for some parents the emergence of their children's communities follows naturally from their own lives, many others live in more isolated circumstances, sometimes a result of geography and sometimes because they are in precarious situations, as for example the parent who is closeted out of fear of custody or job loss. A family's vulnerability to homophobia can be shaped, to a large extent, by how free the parents are to establish community ties like the ones Marcy describes.

Of the parents who are able, many are careful not only to provide their children with relationships to families like their own but also to establish an environment rich in diversity. In a culture that often denigrates difference, parents need to work at teaching children to value diversity, and to see their families as one type among many, rather than as deviance from a singular norm. Hannah, the mother of six-year-old Mindy, says, "I think it's important that she know other children of lesbians, but I didn't want her in a day care that was only that because it's not what the world is about. In the real world there are people in all different kinds of situations, different ethnicities, cultures, and sexual preferences. I want Mindy to be where all of that is present and respected. That's not so easy to find."

Beyond thinking about what kinds of families their children will come to know, lesbian and gay parents must think about what values will predominate in children's worlds. Marginalized and often denigrated by mainstream culture, parents are naturally concerned about the attitudes their children will be exposed to. Tricia, the single lesbian mother of three-year-old Erin, says, "Kids need to get socialized, but I'm not sure I want my kid socialized the way this culture does it. There are certain things I don't want transmitted: homophobia, racism, sexism. I want Erin to get exposure to lots of different people, but I want to be able to keep a close eye on what the exposure consists of."

Generally, parents like Tricia find it easier to monitor their young children's environments as compared to later years. For many parents, then, the idea is to establish a strong foundation—one in which kids develop high self-esteem, good family relationships, and an appreciation of diversity. From this base, parents can actively teach children about prejudice even before they encounter it, so they have some framework for recognizing it as a problem in the world, rather than internalizing its destructive messages. Sobered by the thought of how much hatred their children may be exposed to over the years, lesbian and gay parents of young children are nonetheless hopeful about their capacity to cope when the time comes. As Esther, the mother of eight-year-old Ian, put it, "So far he hasn't been thrust into a world where he's very different.

Part of why he's so complacent is that he's not in a world where all he sees are traditional families. He knows he has one kind of family but he also knows people who have similar kinds, as well as many other kinds. I don't know what will happen when his environment changes. I hope he is minimally pained by whatever shit he gets for having lesbian parents. I hope it's not a source of real anguish for him. The plan is that by the time he gets to be a teenager, he'll have enough of a solid foundation and working relationship with Leslie and me that we can help him deal with what's hard, and also that he'll have enough perspective to not internalize what comes at him around that stuff. That, of course, is hard for an adolescent. It's an ideal, but chances are we'll go through a really hard time."

Trying to surround children with an accepting environment rich in diversity is one major task that lesbian and gay parents often set themselves. But regardless of their success in this endeavor, all lesbian and gay parents must eventually face the question of how to deal with bigotry. Here, not surprisingly, the subject of closets quickly emerges. Confronted with the prospect of a child's pain in the face of homophobia, parents not only think about helping their children cope but also about shielding them from the experience.

Jenny and Alma had been out throughout their son Michael's preschool years. But, as for many parents, public school proved to be a different and far more daunting circumstance. Not knowing much about the specific attitudes prevalent in the school, but being well acquainted with the homophobia that pervaded the community, Jenny and Alma made a decision that Alma, Michael's non-biological mother, would retreat from her previously central role as liaison between home and school.

Jenny explains their decision this way: "In preschool, I always had the option of leaving. There I'm a consumer and they have a certain bottom line they have to meet to keep people happy regardless of what they believe. The classes were smaller, the teachers seemed to be a progressive bunch. In the public school, until we have a chance to get in there and see what's going on, we're just going to hang back. We've made a decision that we won't make his life difficult with our choice. I don't know who his teachers will be.

I won't have the same sort of contact with them that I do at his preschool. So I won't have the opportunity to show them that we're just regular people and there's nothing to be afraid of. And I won't allow him to be a victim of their prejudices. So when that starts, Alma will be a less visible person. . . . If there's a parent-teacher conference now, Alma always comes, but she won't come then.

"I don't know what to do other than give him and give us the room to sort it out. I don't want to do anything that can't be undone. And I'm afraid if we march in and announce it like we did at preschool, that it's great gossip—and I won't do that to him. I don't want him ever to be confronted with, 'No, you can't go over to their house.' "

Many lesbian and gay parents strongly disagree with this position, and feel instead that it is crucial to their children's well-being that they are out as a family unit. They see part of their parenting responsibility to be modeling pride for their children, and to confront and eliminate homophobic responses in their children's environments. Diane, the mother of five-year-old Pamela, says, "I feel very strongly about not going into the closet. It may happen that there are people she doesn't want to tell, or kids she feels uncomfortable bringing home because she doesn't trust them enough with that information. I think she would need to think about why she wants to be friends with people like that. I feel very strongly that it's important, for her and for us, that we don't compromise ourselves for her benefit, because I don't think it would be for her benefit in the end.

"I think it's a much better model for her to have us be who we are and be proud of that and comfortable with that, and really up front with that, than it would be for us to be who we are and pretend to be somebody different. That's what I want to help Pamela do—be who she is and proud of it and comfortable with it. The only way I know how to do that is to be who I am."

Here are two very different approaches to helping children cope in a homophobic society. Jenny and Alma emphasize protecting and shielding children from bigotry. Their effort to respect and care for Michael, to appreciate his needs as separate from their own, includes a willingness to create a closet for him and their family as a whole. They distinguish between their choices in structuring the family and his life course—evident in Jenny's comment that "he shouldn't have to suffer for choices we've made."

Diane, on the other hand, emphasizes the development of pride and courage as major coping strategies for children and parents alike. She sees as her bottom line that there will be no closet for her child. Her unwillingness to bow under the pressure of homophobia is her offering to her daughter. It not only sends a message of integrity and pride but also positions her to challenge and confront homophobic responses aimed at the family.

For many, an approach like Diane's draws on the experiences of dealing with prejudice based on ethnic or racial background. Amy, for instance, draws a direct parallel to her own childhood experiences. Speaking of her two daughters growing up in a transracial, lesbian-headed family, she says, "The way I connect with their identity has to do with my growing up as a Jewish minority in a Protestant neighborhood, where we were discriminated against. I was brought up to feel proud of my difference and to feel a sense of pride in who I am. Part of that came from my family and part came from being with other Jewish children and getting a sense of what was special about my Jewish culture. I think that's true for these kids also, both in terms of their ethnicity and as children of lesbians.

"I want them to have a sense of the country they came from, which is as much a part of who they are as the shtetl in Eastern Europe is part of me. Similarly, our being lesbian and their having lesbian parents calls for being able to accept yourself, your difference, and not feeling ashamed but instead feeling proud of being different. I felt proud growing up about not having a Christmas tree, even though there were kids who didn't invite us to their birthday parties. I want these kids to feel proud of having two mommies, and the wonderful things that will be different for them in good, growth-producing ways."

Often parents will draw on their own experiences in overcoming shame in the face of discrimination. Rather than emphasize children's suffering by having gay parents, these parents recognize what is good about their family structure. Elizabeth comments that "It seems to me that where you can turn all of this around to an advantage is that we will be the kind of parents who can start working at an early age with our kids on the fact that there are always going to be certain things that you are going to do or be that some segment of the larger society doesn't approve of, and you have to learn early how to survive in that reality. So we'll share with them the kinds of skills we've developed to do that."

Elizabeth emphasizes her job as a parent to be emotionally present for her children's pain—not to try to keep it from occurring but rather to help them develop strength in the face of it. "We want to help them learn they don't have to be defensive. It will be hard for them. It will be painful. Our position is we will always be there for you to share that pain with. We will not be able to change it, but you will be able to survive and endure it. What you have to be clear about is as long as you feel right about something then you go forward from that position and you learn to deal with the rest of what comes your way."

Many parents choosing an open stance point out that it is not so much their sexuality that is at issue—their relations to their partners—but rather their relations to their children. That is what they are unwilling to hide, not just as a matter of pride but because it would compromise the family structure, skewing all the relationships. The ways parents deal with the surrounding community, and particularly schools, profoundly affect family life. As parental relationships generally involve community contact, if one parent is invisible, the scope of his or her parenting is limited by that. As Mary points out, "It's not a political issue per se that motivates us to go together to meet the day-care people. It's because if we're going to co-parent together, then Deidre's at least as interested in what happens to Sylvia at day care and is just as likely to drop her off or pick her up as I am." This position, in contrast to Jenny's comment about Michael's not needing to suffer from the choice she and Alma made, emphasizes the family structure as one involving all members equally.

The very different positions exemplified by Jenny and Alma on the one hand and Diane on the other do not simply reflect individual disagreement. Though clearly, each position involves a particular way of thinking about one's life, they also reflect different environmental constraints. There is a certain freedom that underlies a position like Diane's. The costs of being out vary tremendously depending on one's community, as well as personal and economic circumstances. It is one thing being out and raising a child in a neighborhood or school where there will be homophobic remarks made by some. It is entirely another matter living in a town where there are frequent gay bashings, worries about losing a job that provides essential income, or threats of custody loss.

While the positions outlined by Jenny and Alma on the one hand and Diane on the other, seem diametrically opposed, a closer look at actual experiences in most families shows a large gray area. Many attentive to their children's needs, including a perceived need for a closet at a particular moment, are drawing on their own experiences of having come to terms with being gay in a homophobic world. Often, making space for a closet is not a final move but rather a temporary step, one accompanied by discussion and scrutiny of the issues. Jenny, for instance, describes the decision that Alma won't attend school meetings as a necessary first move, one that will stand until they feel their way around the school.

Similarly, Jessie links her tendency to hang back initially with regard to her daughter's school to how she navigates her own environment. "I think it's important for kids to have a choice. Some people say they'll come out everywhere, but I don't feel that way. It may be internalized homophobia, but I can't see imposing certain hardships on Jackie out of our own principles, if they don't have to be imposed. I'm an adult and it's my choice. She's a child having to grapple with a lot of nuclear families. There is a parallel to my own handling of this issue. I've been out all my adult life: people at work know that I'm a lesbian, and I'm out to my family, but I didn't walk into day care and say 'I'm a lesbian.' I don't tend to do that right away. I make disclosures that are integrated for me with people I have ongoing relationships with."

One issue parents are grappling with is the distinction between their needs and those of their children. To what extent is being out a matter of family negotiation? Much more than a stance toward homophobia is at stake in these interactions. Parents are often self-consciously working out their family relationships. This is particularly pressing during adolescence, a time of increased differentiation between parents and children—and not coincidentally, a time when children are especially subject to peer-group values and often are concerned about fitting in. Many parents struggle to find a balance between respecting their children's different perspectives and maintaining their own integrity. They want to present children with values that are not compromised, but at the same time, they want to honor their children's growth and differentiation. Anticipating her daughter's adolescence, Mary says, "If Sylvia wants us to be closeted in some way, I'd probably initially go along with what she asked, but then I'd talk about it with her. What I imagine is that she'll take me by surprise the first time, since that's often how kids are. They don't give you a month's notice, but two seconds before their friend walks in the door they might say, 'By the way, don't do any of that weird stuff in front of him.' So my sense is 'Okay, fine, for the moment.' But afterwards I'd want to talk about it and maybe negotiate rules about what would feel comfortable to us as an accommodation and what would feel like a real violation."

Glenda, anticipating her son's adolescence, sees the possibility of his homophobia as a developmental issue. "I think he may go through a phase where he doesn't want to acknowledge anything about me, though I think if we have a decent relationship it won't be that extreme. But adolescents do that sort of thing, and I can be respectful of his need to do that. I suspect that the more respectful I am of his need, the less need he's going to have. If he chooses to hide the issue, I imagine it would come from feeling embarrassed. To me, that would mean there's some work to be done, that we need to at least try to talk about why he feels that way."

The question of how, as a parent, to deal with homophobia in one's own and one's children's lives is very complex. Coming out is rarely an all-or-nothing prospect. Instead, it is an ongoing process, since people find themselves in new situations as well as in evolving emotional territory. Parents have to grapple not only with the consequences their stance toward homophobia has for them but also with the meaning it will have for their children. Many describe parenthood as a trigger for developing a deeper courage to move boldly where they would previously have retreated. Having children necessitates setting an example of openness and of actively challenging homophobia. But others describe an almost opposite development. Having been willing to take risks where their own lives are concerned, they become fearful as protective instincts are triggered by their children's vulnerability. Some parents have to grapple with equally strong pulls in each direction. The wish to respect children and to protect them often underlies the inclination to create a closet, but this carries a danger. It can communicate the idea that closets make sense. Closets are not simply places of refuge and protection. Often they are burdensome, riddled with shame, and of course, isolating. It is this prospect that parents who are adamantly and at all times out so forthrightly reject. To construct closets in response to homophobia is to accept passing as a defense against discrimination. It is striking, but not surprising, that the issue of closets dominates discussions of lesbian and gay parenting. Emerge or retreat? It is a question that lesbians and gay men—and therefore their children—must face.

The Children's Perspectives— Evolving Territory

Childhood is a fleeting and ever-changing landscape. Yet it is easy to lose sight of how much children are constantly developing, continually in process. Remembering this is crucial to understanding children's responses to homophobia.

The children of lesbian and gay parents have much to come to terms with. Often, children whose parents have come out after marriage have grown up with little exposure to lesbians or gay men, and have absorbed some of mainstream culture's homophobia. For these children, the revelation of a parent's homosexuality requires a total shift in perspective. Coming to terms can be complicated if there is an acrimonious divorce, an atmosphere of threat, or homophobic family members. Traversing this territory can take years, and is sometimes never accomplished. But many children—even those steeped in homophobia—are readily moved by love for a parent to reconceptualize their world.

Children raised from the outset by lesbian and gay parents also have to reconcile their family life with the homophobia pervasive in society. Generally, young children have an easier time being unambivalently out and proud of their families. There is perhaps no better way to be reminded that homophobia is learned than to look at how preschoolers handle the issue of two mommies. One of Michael's friends went home after a sleepover at his house and asked her mother, "If Daddy died, could we get another mommy like Michael has?"

Fifteen-year-old Steve, conceived through donor insemination and raised by two mothers, recalls his early years. "I've always been in a community where people are out about being gay and proud of it, so I've never thought that it might be bad. I've never been around adults who ever have said it's a bad thing or it's wrong. I know in kindergarten I was very proud of having two moms—I'd brag about it. I know I wasn't shy about it then." But Steve remembers first or second grade as a time when the tide turned. Commonly, these early elementary school years mark the first exposure to homophobia that sparks doubt and undermines the confidence of children of lesbian and gay parents.

Eight-year-old Danielle notes that teasing first became an issue for her in third grade. "Some kids make fun. They use it as an insult. I just try to defend myself and say there's nothing wrong with that. They say *eeuw*. It annoys me. Sometimes it's to insult another person and sometimes it's when I tell them."

Danielle's parents, Susan and Dana, are out in their community and in her school. Likewise, Danielle proudly talks about her family life, often outdoing her parents in her openness. She drew her family tree on the blackboard for her second-grade class, and one day, to her parents' surprise she chose to wear a Gay Pride shirt to school. "My mom got it when she went to speak at a conference and it said 'Lesbian and Gay' on it. Mostly nobody read it when I wore it to school as far as I know—nobody came up to me. My mother thought maybe I shouldn't wear it, but I wouldn't feel uncomfortable now, either. Some people might see it and tease me more, but it doesn't bother me because I just know they're wrong. In my opinion they're wrong because there are all kinds of people and it doesn't matter if they're black or white, lesbian or straight."

For Danielle, the option of a closet in response to homophobia is not even on the table. She very forthrightly maintains a position that discrimination is wrong, a problem out in the world, not in her. When teased, "I just say there's nothing wrong with it. It hurts, but I can understand why they do it, because they have a mother and a father like most families, so that's probably why they think it's wrong. When I defend myself, they either fight back or just turn their head and ignore me."

Though she takes on the responsibility for fighting her own battles, she turns to her parents for emotional support. "Sometimes I come home and talk to my parents but not my teachers 'cause they'll just say 'Ignore them 'cause you never have to listen if you don't want to.' I know they'll say 'It bothers you but you don't have to listen.' They usually say that sort of thing."

Though Danielle doesn't experience her teachers as actively homophobic, she seems already—at age eight—to expect from her school at best benign neglect of the issue. As she discussed this with her parents, they were surprised and told her that either she or they could ask the teachers to do more. But Danielle said that she is learning to handle it on her own. And, indeed, she seems to be developing significant strength in the process, drawing connections among racism, sexism, and homophobia, and learning to assert herself. Danielle's strength in the face of hurtful comments is something she links to other struggles: "I studied Martin Luther King, and I taught myself that I have to fight for my rights—not punch fight, but defend myself. I taught myself that from now on if I have trouble I'd just defend myself and if that didn't work I'd ignore them. It's also not fair about soccer and girls. Just 'cause I'm a girl doesn't mean I'm bad. Talking to teachers about that doesn't help, either—it wastes time. Unless you plug your ears you always hear it a little bit. Kim used to tease me a lot about my moms being lesbian, and I defended myself so much that one day she helped me defend myself. They know I'll ignore them or fight back."

Like Danielle, nine-year-old Aija views her experience of homophobic teasing as a challenge. Though she is clearly pained by these encounters, she sees herself as in the process of coming to terms with them. "One girl, her mom doesn't let her come over. She goes to my church—actually her mom doesn't really care, but her dad does. I've asked Jodie a lot of times if she could come over and her dad always says no. I don't think there's anything wrong with what my moms are, and I think it's kind of stupid. It made me feel pretty bad 'cause Jodie is really nice but I can't do anything about it."

Like many children of lesbian and gay parents, Aija has developed a watchful style, becoming an acute observer of people's behavior. "With new kids I go along and see if the person is openminded, and if not they just don't come over to my house and I don't tell them. You listen to the way they talk. Like if I don't say anything about gay and lesbian, and I tell my friends to be quiet about it while these people are around, and I listen and if they say something about so-and-so is lesbian and isn't that disgusting, I say I guess I won't tell these people."

At the same time as Aija tries to protect herself through vigilance and cautiousness, she also actively tries to come to terms with homophobia, thinking about her encounters as something to learn from. "I'm learning that people will say anything to make you mad. I'm also learning it's okay to be different; people will tease you but it's okay to be different. Also, the most important lesson and I'm still not very good at this lesson but I'm getting a little better—I'm getting better at being teased. You start to be able to not have it bother you. Let's say someone called me a name and they didn't mean it and I knew they didn't mean it, it would still hurt my feelings and I'd get mad at them. But now if I know someone doesn't mean it I can take it better. Some people say it like if a girl hugs a girl if they haven't seen each other in a while it would be, '*Eeuw*, you're gay'—first of all it would be lesbian. Second of all, what's wrong with it? And third of all, they're just hugging!"

We often mistakenly think in static terms about phenomena that are better understood as processes. The way children grapple with homophobia evolves over time; it changes, not only as they themselves grow and develop but also as their peers do, as their environments shift. There are some who never experience a wish to be closeted, some for whom it is a major concern, and many who pass through different phases. How homophobia is experienced and dealt with cannot be separated from developmental issues. Adolescence generally poses the most significant challenges, for parents and children alike. It is a time of intense focus on personal identity, especially sexuality, and not coincidentally, it is a time when homophobia in the environment can be most intense. Children struggle to differentiate themselves from their families and at the same time to establish themselves in friendships. Often, usually independent, outspoken children become slaves to their peer groups, desperate to fit in and make no waves. It is in this context that the pull to the closet can be most powerful.

Sarah had always been the child in the family who most easily and straightforwardly dealt with her mother's lesbianism. She advised her isolated stepbrother that he'd be happier if he found some kids he could talk to about his family. And she was the only one of the three children who happily agreed to participate in an educational video about lesbian-headed families. Sarah has questioned both herself and the world around her as she's grappled with the ways people approach difference. "It's both good and bad to be different—you're original, some people react like, you're different, it's cool, so why don't you tell people about your difference? But then it's bad 'cause other people react like you're different from them and they don't want any part of that difference. Some people say, 'What do you do at home?'—like it's so different. I eat dinner, do my homework—the same things you do. I don't really care anymore. It used to bother me. I'd think: I'm not different, am I really different? Why am I different? And I didn't know why—what was different. Did I do things differently when I went home? People would say, 'What do you do at home?' and I'd be like, 'I don't know. Do I do something different than you? Should I tell you? Is my life different? Would I be different?' It got me thinking."

When Sarah hit her early teens, she became more cautious. She was reluctant to have kids over and very selective with whom she shared the details of her life. Moving beyond that stage, now fifteen, Sarah has given a lot of thought to the issue of homophobia. She says it's not lesbianism that's the problem; it's some of her peers. She is still cautious in the sense that she feels out situations carefully and takes time to decide whom she'll become intimate enough with to risk disclosure. But she often takes it upon herself to educate her fellow teenagers: "I think growing up in a lesbian household . . . I see nothing wrong with it. We see our parents and they seem okay. The way society acts toward you isn't okay—like saying 'butch, dyke,' like they're bad words. Sometimes people will say that and I'll say 'so what if I was'—people sometimes make fun of me and my friend—if they say a homophobic thing we jump down their throats. . . ."

If her choice about discussing her mother's sexuality is preempted by someone else, she faces the issue head-on: "I haven't told anyone that I didn't think would be okay about it. A few days ago some friends were over and my old boyfriend was here, and he thought they knew but I hadn't told them yet. I tried to tell him to be quiet. They said, 'What, your mom's a dyke?' And I said, 'If that's what you want to call it.' Then they said, 'We'll leave if she comes home.' I said, 'That's so immature.' It's a front, I think— just acting like everyone else, being scared of becoming what a lot of people are. There are so many gay and lesbian people in the world, but people are afraid 'cause society says it's a bad thing. Joe, who I'm not friends with, said, 'That means you could be married and decide you're a lesbian—you could get it.' I told him 'it's not passed that way—but if I was, who cares?' "

Steve, having gotten through elementary school with relatively little angst about having lesbian parents, struggles increasingly in high school. "There's a lot of gay jokes at school. I guess I worry that people would take it out on me—say that I'm strange because of my parents' actions."

Though Steve used to know many children of lesbian and gay parents, he has gravitated toward other friendships, and the shift in peer group presents him with dilemmas. "There's a group of kids that I used to be friends with and all their parents are gay. It helped me just to see what other kids did about their parents, telling their friends and stuff. But I'm not really friends with them anymore. I've just kind of strayed away from them 'cause none of them go to my school. I don't know if anybody in my school has gay parents. I don't feel safe about telling all my friends that my mom is gay. Some kids could probably handle it and still be my friend. And then some kids could just kind of blow up and tell the whole school and I'd just be kind of shoved away."

Steve's fear of ostracism leads him deeper into the closet. Yet it's a move he struggles with—one he's uncomfortable about even as he sees it as vital. "The hardest thing is that I don't really like lying to my friends and sometimes I have to, to keep it a secret. I try to stay away from lying about it as much as I can but sometimes I can't avoid it." Steve and his parents have put a lot of energy into negotiating ways of handling his wish to hide his family structure. "We've always just dealt with making an excuse, not an excuse—it doesn't have to be excused—but just planning ahead what we're gonna say."

For Steve, these negotiations are a two-way street. He feels appreciative of the space Charlene and Paula give him. "Charlene and Paula have always been open to whatever felt most comfortable to me. I can imagine that if they hadn't been willing to do that I'd still be friends with that group of kids who all had lesbian parents, because I would get more embarrassed if I had been forced to tell people—and those kids would have already known. Maybe other kids wouldn't have cared, but it would have made me more anxious if I had to tell." At the same time, Steve has become aware of the impact his retreat to the closet has on his parents, and he in turn tries to respond to this: "I think I might have asked Paula not to come to a couple of things when I was younger, but then I got a little more sensitive to her feelings when I did that when I got older and we just worked it out so that we all had the same stories."

Steve, a once proud and open five-year-old, is now a fifteen-year-old struggling with fears of ostracism and retreating, albeit ambivalently, to the closet. But his story doesn't end there. Even as he grapples with his present fears, Steve looks optimistically to a time when both he and his world will be different. "I have one older friend whose mom is a lesbian. He's in college and he always used to baby-sit me, and I've been kind of close to him for a while. He's been a really big help, because he doesn't really care, and he's kind of shown me that his friends don't care either, who your parents are or what they do. So he's made me a little more open to letting kids come over to my house and stuff. And he's just kind of been a role model. He's just made me realize that once you get into the teenage years kids don't want to meet your parents—you know, if they're straight or—nobody's worried about your parents, nobody cares who your parents are. And he said that once I got into high school and college, that I'd definitely start feeling more open 'cause people have more open minds once they start getting older."

A Question of Responsibility— Homophobia in the Schools

Minnie Bruce Pratt's son, twenty-one-year-old Ben, reflecting on his childhood, says, "Recently I saw for the first time a textbook that had gay parents in it, and I realized how radically it would have changed my life growing up—it would have wiped out the anxiety and suppression if I'd seen this book when I was ten. The fact that I didn't have any friends whose mothers were lesbian didn't mean it didn't exist. I'm sure it did even in Kentucky. You realize the drastic importance of having things public—talked about in school, for instance. It wouldn't just have changed the way I felt, but also the way a lot of other people felt."

Five-year-old Michael has a book Ben would have appreciated. *Heather Has Two Mommies*, published by Alyson Publications, portrays the family life of a child who was conceived through alternative insemination and is being raised by her lesbian parents. She has two cats and a dog, "just like our dog," Michael enthusiastically points out. Michael loves the book—he requests it over and over again at bedtime.

The silence Ben endured is no accident and is, sadly, just about as prevalent now as it was when he grew up. While very few schools even have *Heather Has Two Mommies* in their libraries, the fact that some do has already sparked public outcry and censorship. Though Michael enjoys a preschool environment in which teachers deal matter-of-factly and sensitively with his family structure, *Heather Has Two Mommies* is a book he reads only at home; it is nowhere to be found on his classroom bookshelf.

Jenny, who has been clear that while she has the choice Michael must be in an affirming school environment, is nonetheless hesitant to ask the school to incorporate the book into the curriculum. She worries that it would be a burdensome request, since inevitably some neighborhood parents would take offense. She has never broached the subject, so it's unclear what would actually occur if she did.

This is a common problem between parents and school personnel. Even where blatant homophobia is not an issue, and where schools might be supportive of lesbian and gay parents, there is mutual silence, so the needs never get put on the table. Schools rarely demonstrate to incoming families that they are safe with regard to these issues, and indeed many of them are not. But even those that might be fall short in this regard. Often, neither parents nor school personnel feel comfortable enough to open a dialogue, which if initiated could be quite fruitful.

At Bank Street College of Education, in New York City, a group of researchers and educators looked at how teachers and administrators approached children raised by lesbian and gay parents. Homophobic views were often blatantly evident as professionals discussed their concerns about the children in these families. Assumptions both about what children need in the way of gender role models and what they actually got were clearly operative. When some educators knew a child had lesbian or gay parents, they were likely to attribute any difficulties the child had to the family structure.

Besides these obvious manifestations of homophobia, there were many more subtle ones. Homophobia in the schools was not always evident at first glance. Sometimes people expressed discomfort in oblique, indirect ways while mouthing acceptance of diversity. Many teachers and administrators spoke at length about how much they valued diversity and embraced children from all backgrounds. They said in essence, "It doesn't matter that Peter's parents are gay." These educators made it clear that they would not abide discrimination, and that they wanted to help children to similarly value diversity. Yet when they were asked what exactly they would do to promote that acceptance, they were often at a loss. And even more striking were their responses to the question, Would you, for instance, read *Heather Has Two Mommies* to your kindergarten class? Most said no, they couldn't do that. They saw it as entailing a discussion of sexuality inappropriate to their classrooms, despite the fact that there is no more mention of sex in the book than in books portraying heterosexual parents. They were also reluctant because they worried, as does Jenny, about how they would contend with the homophobic reactions of parents.

The Bank Street study tapped into the fact that many teachers and educational administrators, like everyone else in our culture, harbor subtle or blatant homophobic views—views which are reflected in the classroom in a variety of ways, ranging from a lack of sensitivity to specific children's families, to exclusionary curricula, to rigid ideas about the role of gender in children's lives. It further demonstrated that often even the least homophobic teachers and administrators are ill-prepared to address the issues lesbian and gay families raise.

Yet the urgent need for schools to grapple with these issues is apparent. As Ben grew up feeling isolated, and as Michael faces increasing isolation and vulnerability in elementary school, seven-year-old Raymond has brighter prospects. Raymond attends a school that actively takes responsibility for countering all forms of prejudice, including homophobia. Raymond and his father Bill were riding on the train home from school, discussing the day's activities. Raymond said, "We did homonyms today—Ms. Hooper asked us to say words that have two meanings and she wrote them on the blackboard."

"And what homonym did you think of?"

"I told her *gay*—you know, *gay* like a party and *gay* like you and dad." Years earlier, Raymond had come out to his preschool on behalf of his parents by telling his teacher that he'd had a good weekend because he got to "sleep in the bed with Daddy and Bill."

Sometimes Raymond struggled to communicate about his life with people who had neither the experience nor the imagination to grasp it. Once, at the checkout counter of their local supermarket, Raymond began a discussion with the cashier by saying, "I have two daddies." When she exclaimed, "Oh, aren't you lucky," he continued. "I have a friend who has two mommies." She looked perplexed and then said, "Oh, is one the stepmother?"

"No."

"Oh, is one his real mother?" Raymond just shook his head from side to side and the questions ceased.

Josh and Bill had long ago understood the importance of communicating openly with people in Raymond's world, and they were confident that his teacher handled the issue of Raymond's family structure in a nonjudgmental and supportive way. His casual homonym report came as no surprise.

But several months later, when Bill picked Raymond up at school, a boy asked, "Is that your other daddy?" Raymond, looking stricken, shook his head and mumbled, "No." This unusual behavior was of concern to Bill and Josh. It took some coaxing to find out what had triggered the shame. As it turned out, Raymond at age seven had had his first encounter with homophobia. A group of classmates had teased him about having two dads. Bill and Josh hadn't known when it was going to come or what form it would take, but they'd certainly imagined this moment. In fact, they'd had many discussions about the role of discrimination in Raymond's life. As the African-American adopted child of an interracial couple, and as a child with two fathers, they knew he would be no stranger to bigotry.

That evening Josh called the parents of the children involved, all of whom were supportive and wanted to know how he thought they should handle it. "I told them to talk about different types of families that people live in—you know, a mother and dad, or two daddies, or a grandmother—those kinds of things." Josh also spoke to the principal, Raymond's teacher, and the head of the after-school program where the incident occurred. As a result, the school held a forum on alternative families.

Raymond's experience illustrates the critical importance of an alliance between family and school. Most children of lesbian and gay parents are not fortunate enough to be in an optimal school environment, like Raymond's. Faced with the prospect of outright hostility that might be directed at Michael for years to come, Jenny chose the closet as protection. Bill and Josh, in contrast, not only have different ideas about how to support Raymond but also have the luxury of being in an environment that will help them do that.

As Ben describes, the children of lesbian and gay parents are hungry for public images of their family life—images sorely lacking in the media and our schools. For these children, invisibility is as problematic as denigration. In fact, it sets the stage for denigration to triumph.

Homophobia is rampant in American schools, a fact that has grave consequences not only for the children of lesbian and gay parents but also for the estimated 10 percent of all children who will grow up to be lesbian or gay. Conservative estimates link a third of all teenage suicides to the isolation and despair experienced by lesbian and gay adolescents with few social supports. This estimate does not take into account suicidal behaviors, such as high-risk sex and drug use. Overall, lesbian and gay adolescents are five times more likely than their heterosexual peers to attempt suicide. Gay bashing is a common phenomenon in American high schools. Though schools are supposed to be geared toward children's optimal development, millions of children are left to grapple in isolation with extremely hostile environments.

In an attempt to bridge the gap between what these children need and what the school system provides, some people have proposed curriculum changes. These proposals include sensitivity training for teachers and administrators, availability of books like *Heather Has Two Mommies*, and open acknowledgment of diverse family forms.

The fate of these proposals harkens back to the Anita Bryant and John Briggs campaigns of the 1970s, in which any connection between children and homosexuality is vilified. Though in some schools these proposed curriculum changes are being developed with great success, many other districts have seen heated battles, spurred on by the rhetoric of the religious right. Attempts to eliminate homophobia in the schools are framed as exposing children to obscene sexuality and immoral lifestyles. In New York City, the proposal for a Rainbow Curriculum addressing cultural diversity of all kinds was vehemently attacked for one paragraph of its four hundred–some pages. That paragraph offered a suggested reading list for first-graders that included *Heather Has Two Mommies* and a similar book, *Daddy's Roommate*. Ultimately, schools chancellor Joseph Fernandez was ousted largely as a result of his supporting the proposal, which was shot down.

The lack of social checks on homophobia, exemplified by the situation in schools, means that families are left to struggle alone with its implications for their lives. It is clear that, at this historical moment, children must sort through issues of difference in the context of a world filled with bigotry. Children of lesbian and gay parents are challenged by bigotry at an early age, and parents struggle with the pain this bigotry causes. They are right to worry, since a hostile environment assaults children's self-esteem and general well-being.

But as with much of life, the tasks for children are to find their strength in the face of obstacles and to sort out their own values in the face of opposition. Lesbian and gay parents often struggle with how to best help their children do this. In helping their children, parents inevitably confront issues with which they themselves have struggled—how have they handled homophobia in their own lives? What are their sources of strength and pride, and what are their vulnerabilities and fears? Being a good example is one way parents can help children. It is also crucial that parents be present for their children as they navigate their own worlds, worlds that often pose challenges distinct from parents' familiar experiences. In a homophobic society, how do lesbian and gay parents support their children, teach them pride and values, and simultaneously give them space to work out their own lives? Ultimately, both parents and children need to seize their own power in challenging bigotry. As the poet and lesbian mother Audre Lorde has written in "Good Mirrors Are Not Cheap,"

> It is a waste of time hating a mirror
> or its reflection
> instead of stopping the hand
> that makes glass with distortions . . .

· 9 ·

Children At Risk

The Legal Limbo of the Reinvented Family

One November weekend in 1983, Sharon Kowalski and her partner of four years, Karen Thompson, invited Sharon's niece and nephew to visit them in their new house near St. Cloud, Minnesota. That Sunday afternoon, as Sharon was driving her niece and nephew back to their home, the car was hit by a drunk driver. Sharon's niece was killed and Sharon, initially in a coma, survived with severe brain damage. The tragedy of the accident did not end there. Sharon's fate became the center of a bitter legal struggle that continued for more than eight years.

Karen and Sharon had a clear and deep commitment to each other, but that commitment meant little in the eyes of the law. With Sharon incapacitated, her parents were her legal guardians. Despite Karen's strong commitment to caring for Sharon in the home they'd shared together, Sharon remained in a nursing home; and within two years of the accident, disturbed by the fact of Karen and Sharon's lesbian relationship, the Kowalskis cut off Karen's visitation altogether. Sharon, through the use of a laptop computer and short spoken words, repeatedly communicated her desire to live with Karen, but her competence was questioned by the courts.

Though Karen petitioned for guardianship herself, even when Mr. Kowalski, citing poor health, gave up his guardianship in 1989, guardianship was awarded to a friend of the Kowalskis rather than to Karen. It wasn't until December 1991 that a Minnesota Court of Appeals finally awarded Karen guardianship, noting both that Sharon had expressed a desire to live with her and that Karen was the only person willing and able to care for Sharon outside of an institution.

The story of Sharon Kowalski and Karen Thompson is a grim reminder to all lesbians and gay men of the fragility of bonds that exist in the absence of legal recognition or support. Though partners in lesbian and gay relationships see each other as family, their inability to marry renders their bond invisible in the eyes of the state. As the Kowalski case so painfully demonstrated, this invisibility reaches far beyond the symbolic level. In times of catastrophe it readily translates to a literal and complete dissolution of relationship. Homophobia underlies the lack of legal recognition and, simultaneously, is a key reason why such recognition is critical. Sharon and Karen were unable to formally declare their commitment to each other through marriage. Without that formal commitment, they were later prevented from having contact with each other because of homophobic disapproval of their relationship.

During the past decade the need for legal protection of lesbian and gay relationships has been starkly underscored as AIDS ravages the gay community, yielding a multitude of complications surrounding the process and aftermath of death. State recognition of family bonds—or lack of it—is critical in many situations. As the AIDS crisis and the Kowalski case highlight, the recognition of family bonds is crucial in medical contexts. It is also pivotal to how families function as economic units, with insurance benefits, housing rights, bereavement and child-care leaves, and inheritance rights (particularly in the absence of wills) all hinging on family status.

When children are involved, the ramifications of lack of legally sanctioned family relationships are even more far reaching. When couples split up or the legal parents die, children's relationships with their nonbiological or nonadoptive parents can be completely disrupted, compounding the trauma of these situations.

A Death in the Family

Janine Ratcliffe and Joan Pearlman met in 1970 while walking their dogs near the apartment complex where they both lived in Saint Petersburg, Florida. At twenty-one years old, Janine knew she was a lesbian, though she had never been in a relationship. Joan, a year older, had been out for a while, and was more experienced. Joan's beauty and sense of humor immediately drew Janine in. Janine says she fell in love with Joan almost the minute she first saw her. After that chance encounter, they often found themselves walking their dogs at the same time of day, not entirely by coincidence. Soon the walks became planned occasions through which they shared their visions and hopes for the future.

When Janine moved to Gainesville to pursue her nursing degree, Joan packed her bags and joined her. By then, it was apparent to both that they had much in common and that they wanted to make a life together—to be each other's family. When Janine told her parents about her relationship with Joan, it precipitated years of animosity and near cutoff. To Janine, Joan was family, and she was hurt that her parents didn't embrace her as such. Joan's parents were also not pleased with the arrangement, but they maintained their connection with the couple, despite the strain.

After five years together, Joan and Janine had a commitment ceremony at their church, and shortly after that they moved to Denver, Colorado. Life in Denver was very different from what they were used to. It felt easier to be out, and to establish a strong sense of family with each other. In Florida, they had fantasized about having children together but their relative isolation and the generally conservative climate made it seem an impossibility. What doctor in Florida, they wondered, would even consider inseminating one of them? In Denver, they became close with another lesbian couple, Emmy and Sally—women who, like themselves, wanted to be parents. The couples shared concerns and ideas on how to go about it. Joan very much wanted to bear a child. Janine encouraged this. Her focus on her career fit well with the idea that she would contribute more financial support to the family and would be a second parent to the child. Emmy and Sally located a doctor willing to inseminate unmarried women, and after months of trying Emmy became pregnant. A month later, Joan became pregnant following her first insemination.

At night, Joan and Janine would lie awake for hours contemplating the baby's future. So much was unimaginable to them; they knew no lesbian or gay parents, they had no guidelines to follow. All they knew was that this child was very much wanted and would be dearly loved by both of them.

On January 31, 1979, Joan gave birth through cesarean section to a baby girl. Janine was in the delivery room, and was the second person to hold the infant, the doctor being the first. They had agreed to name a girl Kristen Elizabeth, but Joan surprised Janine with a change of plans: their daughter was named Kristen Janine.

That was the beginning of the most precious time in their lives. They had a sense of just starting out in the world. Their home, already shared with two cats, four dogs, and two birds, finally seemed complete when Kristen arrived. Emmy and Sally also had a baby girl, Charlotte, and the four new parents enjoyed a sense of easy comradery amid the chaos of first babies. Joan's parents, thrilled to be grandparents, came to visit before Kristen's birth and ended up staying in Denver for about a year. Kristen was even-tempered and cheerful. Joan loved being a full-time mother, and Janine enjoyed coming home from work and giving her a break, bathing Kristen and playing with her until she went to sleep. Janine and Joan believed that Kristen had one mother but two parents: "I was her second parent. There was no attempt to say she had two moms or a dad or anything like that—she had her mom and her Neeny. We were a circle and I was a part of that circle. . . . It was a real special time. We'd accomplished something that we'd normally thought would have been very difficult. And she was beautiful. Her Mom would sit in the tub and she'd sit on her belly or she'd sit with me. She was our child. It was just family." For a brief moment they seemed to be leading a charmed life.

But when Kristen was three months old, Joan became ill. On the eve of gall bladder surgery, anticipating the worst, she wrote a letter to Kristen: "To my baby girl, I'm sorry about not supplying you with a father, but as you probably know by now that is not part of my lifestyle. But know that your biological father is a doctor who was very good-looking, popular, and intelligent.

"I am leaving you a wonderful person to love, my daughter, someone who was a part of your making, your birth, and up to now has shared with me all the responsibility of caring for you. You love her face, voice, everything about her now (you are three months old). Please love Neen and respect her. I leave your future and happiness in her hands. Love her as she loves you, love her as she loves me.

"Forgive me, my little one, for leaving you, but know that no matter where I am you will always be with me. You and Neen [are] in my heart and mind always. Make Neen proud of you. Grow to be a proud but sensitive woman. Love life. Make good of yourself."

Joan survived the surgery, but was diagnosed with lupus shortly thereafter. Initially she was not often ill, and the family settled into a comfortable routine. Joan stayed home with Kristen until Kristen went to preschool at two and a half. Janine especially loved her role as second parent. She liked being the parent who "got to play" with Kristen and looked forward each day to taking her for a drive after work, while Joan rested. When Kristen first went to preschool, Joan was able to maintain a part-time job and care for Kristen after school, but within a year she became unable to work. She was often bedridden and frequently hospitalized. As time went on, Janine took on more and more of Kristen's primary care. Despite the strain of Joan's illness, Kristen thrived. She was bright, affectionate, and like her mother, possessed a fine sense of humor. Impressed by Kristen's outgoing nature and ready smile, Joan got her involved in modeling, a task which Kristen approached as she did the rest of life—joyfully.

Since Kristen and Charlotte were best friends and went to pre-school together, Kristen didn't think of her family as particularly unusual. Looking back she says, "I didn't know anything about them being gay or anything—I didn't even know that kids had moms and dads. I just thought every kid had a mom and a Neeny. I just felt like a normal family."

Unfortunately, having lesbian parents was not the main issue in Kristen's life. By this time, Joan was hospitalized for long stretches. Kristen's entire class made get-well cards, which she brought to Joan in the hospital. Every night, Kristen and her parents ate dinner off trays in the hospital room. Joan and Janine tried to make a game of it—to help Kristen feel comfortable in the cold, forbidding atmosphere. Kristen's favorite activity was rubbing lotion on Joan's legs. She slathered it on in great gobs, hoping in this way to make her mother better.

By the time Kristen was five years old, Joan was very weak. She decided she wanted to return to her hometown. The three piled into a camper, along with all their pets, and drove back to Florida. Toward the end of September, Joan was hospitalized in Tampa. It was difficult for Janine to manage working, being with Joan, and caring for Kristen, so Kristen was sent back to Denver to visit Emmy, Sally, and Charlotte. During that time, Joan died suddenly of an apparent heart attack. Janine asked Emmy and Sally to send Kristen home. "When I arrived at the airport, I didn't know that she had died. My Neen took me into this room that she had reserved just for us, and then she told me about it. I just started to cry and all the way home I was just crying on her shoulder."

During the next several months Kristen and Janine were reeling from Joan's death. Despite the years of Joan's illness, her death was shocking. Preparation for the death of a thirty-five-year-old under any circumstances may be a contradiction in terms. The chronic nature of Joan's condition had become a part of life, rather than a specter of death. Looking back, Janine is struck by how much both she and Joan hadn't wanted to see it coming: "I tell myself it was totally unexpected, but you look back on it. I am a nurse. I knew she was sick. I knew she was real sick. I just don't think I wanted to realize how sick she was. And I did a very good job of not seeing it and turning away."

Kristen and Janine carried on their family life amid shared grief. Janine worried that Kristen, having lost her mother so young, would forget her; and she devoted herself to keeping the memories of their good times together alive. She also made a priority of helping Kristen maintain stability in her daily life, keeping a watchful eye on her school progress, making sure she continued her horseback riding, and taking her often on drives together. Joan's parents, Bernard and Rose Pearlman, were deeply grieving as well. Although Joan's loss was felt most acutely by these two pairs of people, they moved in separate orbits, finding few ways to join together in the face of their sorrow.

Immediately following Joan's death, her parents signed a temporary order granting guardianship to Janine. This was necessary because, as Kristen's nearest biological relatives, they had legal authority with respect to her care. The difficulty of confronting the possibility of Joan's death had resulted in an absence of legal documentation of Joan's intentions. Though she and Janine had spoken about making formal provision for Kristen's care in case of her death, no legal document naming a guardian was ever drawn up. It is not clear whether such a document would have held up in court if challenged. As it happens, the letter Joan addressed to Kristen five years earlier was the only written evidence of her wishes.

Gradually, over the course of that first year, life for Kristen and Janine began to approach equilibrium, if not normalcy. As they adjusted to their loss, Janine was more able to look to the future. At that point, she contacted a lawyer to formalize her guardianship of Kristen. She was not worried about losing Kristen; she simply wanted to legally secure the arrangement they had.

Meanwhile, the Pearlmans were also going through changes as they tried to come to terms with Joan's death. They had never been comfortable about their daughter's lesbianism, but as Bernard said, they'd "loved her, whatever she was." When she died, homophobia infused their grief and they made a decision that would irrevocably alter the course of several lives, most notably Kristen's.

Unbeknownst to Janine, Joan's parents hired a lawyer to help them gain permanent custody of Kristen and to prevent her from visiting with Janine. As Rose put it, "I wanted to break off visitation because Janine is not the 'female' gay. She's the 'dyke' gay. And Kristen was getting to that impressionable age."

Janine was caught off guard by the move. From Janine's perspective, when Rose and Bernard had lived in Denver during the first year of Kristen's life, "they never let it be known that it bothered them at all. I mean, we were pretty close, and I never had an inkling there'd be any kind of trouble. I think they blamed me for Joan's death and it was downhill from there on."

The court had to consider several issues. First, it had to determine whether the Pearlmans and Janine were both "fit" to be Kristen's guardians. Second, it had to consider whether either party had a more primary claim to custody. Here, the lack of legal recognition of Janine's parental relation to Kristen was pivotal, since the court did recognize the grandparents' biological connection. The Pearlmans' legal claim to Kristen hinged on their status as blood relatives. Janine, on the other hand, had no recognized relationship to Kristen: she was neither a biological nor an adoptive parent. In the eyes of the law she was a third party, and in that respect had less standing than the grandparents, who were "family." However, as in all custody decisions, the court's mandate was to consider the best interests of the child. It was required to attend to the specifics of Kristen's life, and to base any decision on careful consideration of her present and future well-being.

Though worried, Janine was initially somewhat optimistic about the hearing because there were many supportive witnesses—people who knew the family well. A church minister, Kristen's teacher, and a psychologist went to court on behalf of Janine's maintaining custody of Kristen. On the other hand, Rose and Bernard's only witnesses were friends of theirs who had not known Kristen, Janine, or Joan. Kristen didn't know her grandparents very well, and was quite vocal about her desire to stay with Janine. However, her testimony was not allowed in court and she didn't have representation through either a lawyer or a guardian ad litem.

Kristen remembers the time of the hearing: "Charlotte, Emmy, and Sally were down here and my Neen was going through court—she was wearing all these dresses. It was weird because the first few times we were all happy because my Neen brought back good reports. Then all of a sudden this one day she started saying that it's going down. It went from high spirits to low."

As a result of the hearing, Joan's parents were awarded guardianship of Kristen. In its decision, the court noted that Janine was fit to be Kristen's parent and that the ruling did not hinge on her qualifications, but rather on the fact that the Pearlmans were Kristen's blood relatives. Janine was awarded one weekend a month, as well as some holiday visitation.

Janine came home from court the day the decision was handed down and told Kristen that she was going to live with her grandparents. "I talked about it as much as I could with a kid as young as her. I don't think she really understood all that was going on or why." A few days before Christmas an attorney arrived to pick up Kristen.

Kristen says: "I remember that day. I was real sad. At first I was kind of excited 'cause I thought it would be a big trip and I didn't understand what was really going on. And so I had a little Cabbage Patch kid in her backpack and I was all ready to go. Then the lady pulled up and something hit me—it's like I'm being taken away here and I won't be back for a while. So I started to cry—I got real sad. The lady had to practically almost pry me away from my Neen to get me into the car. Then when we were riding down Thirty-eighth I remember her saying, 'I'm real sorry to do this to you and I bet you're going to hate me if you ever grow to know me.' I remember that real well. Then we went to some building where I met my grandparents."

From the time of Joan's death until that day, Janine, though grief stricken, had devoted all her energy first to caring for Kristen and then to fighting to keep Kristen. Depleted from the battle and overwhelmed by the loss of her family, Janine broke down. She was admitted to a psychiatric hospital with severe depression just hours after Kristen's departure.

Six weeks after she entered the hospital, Janine was released and sought contact with Kristen. The Pearlmans refused to honor the agreement. Citing Janine's hospitalization, they said she was emotionally unstable. A psychiatrist wrote a letter testifying to Janine's psychological stability, and after two months the Pearlmans capitulated. Kristen and Janine began to see each other monthly.

The Pearlmans and Janine lived on opposite coasts of Florida. One Friday each month Janine left work and drove several hundred miles to pick up Kristen. Sometimes they stayed in motels, but most of the time Janine made two round-trips. On Sunday nights after dropping off Kristen, Janine drove home, arriving at two in the morning, just three hours before she had to be at work. "I felt like my limbs had been chopped off from underneath me. I kept on going just because of the two days a month, really." The only occasion on which Janine missed a visit with Kristen was when she broke her arm and couldn't manage the shift on her car.

Kristen, who hadn't been heard in the courtroom, tried to make a space for her voice. In the shaky, uneven print of a hand just discovering letters she wrote to the judge. "Dear Judge McCary, How are you? My name is Kristen Janine Pearlman. I love my Grandma and Grandpa, but my mommy wanted me and my Neeny to always be together. I have lived with my Neeny all my life and I want to please go back with my Neeny. I hope you will help me. Love, Kristen Pearlman." The letter was never answered.

Kristen missed Janine terribly. "She used to call me and write me. I always looked forward to it. But sometimes my Neen said that she had written me and I never got the letter, so we both thought my grandparents were holding back letters. I have a whole big folder full of the cards she sent me. She sent me notepads that had a bunch of frogs on them saying funny stuff."

Kristen saved a stack of letters, each one reflecting Janine's effort to love across the barrier of distance. "Dear Kristen, Hi honey. Hope you are well and over your cold. I am fine. You left your cat hat in the car. I know you missed it and hope you get it back. Maybe you can wear it to school. I sent it back right away so that you will have it for Halloween. You will be so cute in your witch's costume. Send your Neeny your picture if you are able to. Did you do OK with the hurricane? We got a lot of rain and wind but no other problems. Everyone here sends their love. Shadow and Hershel are doing fine. They run all over the house chasing each other. I will write soon. Your Neeny loves and misses you very much. Take care of yourself. All my love, your Neeny.''

In the Pearlman household, Kristen's longing was evident in her constant refrain: "What day is it? What day is it? Is my Neen supposed to call? Where's my letter? Where's my letter?" Somewhat bewildered by the tenacity of Kristen's attachment to Janine, her grandparents shrugged their shoulders and sighed, "She just called yesterday."

The monthly visits, though much cherished by Kristen, were also painful. "I was happy when she came to pick me up but sometimes, when we went to see a movie or something on Saturday, at the end of the movie I'd always get this really harsh feeling inside of me, and it would make me cry because I knew that I would have to leave soon. She never knew it, but I would always cry. I would always go to the bathroom 'cause I would be crying. Even when we left the movie I'd still have the feeling inside of me but I wouldn't cry."

The difficulty of the transitions from visits was heightened by tension in the family. Kristen's grandparents chastised her for crying when Janine left, so she tried to keep a stiff upper lip. They also got embarrassed by Kristen and Janine's hugging in front of their house before Janine's departures, and instructed the two to get their hugging done before entering the gate to the housing development.

After a short time in her grandparents' care, Kristen began to show outward signs of a child in great pain. The Pearlmans were in their seventies and in poor health. Kristen lived with them in a retirement development. There were no children her age to play with. With little to do but watch television, Kristen became lethargic and gained a substantial amount of weight. Formerly an A student, she began to do poorly in school. For the first time in her life she was teased by her peers. Sometimes the children ridiculed her because of her weight. Other times it was her mother's death that was targeted. Kristen vividly remembers the sting of a classmate telling her, "No wonder your mother died—she must have looked at your face."

Within two years the Pearlmans officially adopted Kristen. Whereas the initial judgment had granted them guardianship, the adoption meant they had full parental rights, including the power to prevent visitation with Janine—something they hoped to achieve. Meanwhile, Janine pulled together her resources, sought out a new lawyer, and initiated an appeal to regain custody of Kristen.

From the moment she met Karen Amlong, her new attorney, Janine knew she had made the right choice. Karen's thoughtfulness and forthright style made her a powerful presence. Karen was a veteran of the women's movement, who'd done a lot of work for the National Organization for Women (NOW). Though married herself, she viewed lesbian parenting as a quite viable option. She had also given a great deal of thought to the ways that people's lives increasingly don't resemble *Ozzie and Harriet*. Reflecting on her adult life, she noted that her own family included her ex-husband as well as her current one. Karen not only understood how key relational realities diverge from legal and cultural notions, but also envisioned the possibility and necessity for legal recognition of many such realities. This vision was a pivotal aspect of the challenge she and Janine posed to the Florida courts.

Families were changing, but the law had not begun to incorporate the complexities of those changes. Karen had never encountered a situation like this before. In fact, she was unable to find cases on which to build her argument through the usual route of legal research. Instead, she scoured Nexis, a computerized compilation of news reports, for related cases. Despite the relative novelty of Kristen's situation, Karen believed it could be ethically responded to by carefully building upon existing law. She saw herself as pointing out the connections between traditional and new family forms, rather than breaking new ground.

Janine was not in a strong position as she entered this challenge.

She was, as she had always been, a third party. The Pearlmans, on the other hand, were even more legally solid than before because now they were not only biological relatives but, for all intents and purposes since the adoption, Kristen's parents.

But unlike the previous trial, Kristen had a voice in this one. She was assigned a lawyer of her own—someone to represent her interests as distinct from Janine's and the Pearlmans'. She was also assigned a guardian ad litem—a social worker who had the job of making recommendations based purely on an assessment of Kristen's needs. A court-appointed psychiatrist interviewed Kristen and also made recommendations about her custody.

Karen's objectives were twofold: first, to reunite Kristen and Janine by having Janine reinstated as guardian; and second, to have the Pearlmans' adoption of Kristen overturned. Unless the second objective were accomplished, the arrangement could not be secure. Adoptions are rarely overturned, and in this respect, Karen had a difficult case to argue. She argued it on two grounds, hoping that the judge would find at least one of them persuasive. She challenged the "fitness" of the Pearlmans as Kristen's parents. Their increasing health problems had led them to send Kristen to live with their other daughter. Kristen, meanwhile, continued to exhibit blatant signs of distress. Karen argued that Janine was, in fact, Kristen's "psychological parent" and that it was in Kristen's best interests to be reunited with her. In doing this, Karen had to educate the court about lesbian parenting. She cited the growing body of psychological literature and legal precedent, which argued that the sexual orientation of a parent in and of itself is irrelevant to a child's ultimate well-being. She also relied heavily on the ways Janine's situation was analogous, if not identical, to others that the Florida courts had dealt with. For example, there is legal precedent in Florida for not considering the sexual conduct of a parent to be relevant to custody except insofar as it can be proved to have direct impact on the child.

Karen also challenged the Pearlmans' adoption of Kristen on constitutional grounds. Janine had not been sufficiently notified of their intent to go forward with the adoption. In making the constitutional argument, Karen relied not only on implied federal privacy rights but also on strong privacy rights explicitly guaranteed under Florida's state constitution. Here, the bridge between traditional families and alternative ones was suggested—the notion that Janine's and Kristen's privacy rights had been violated was premised on an implicit recognition of them as having a "familial" association with each other, one which could not be interfered with by the state without due process.

Kristen's lawyer, based on the guardian ad litem's and psychiatrist's recommendations, lined up with Karen. Both argued that Kristen's best interests would be served by her return to Janine's care.

Judge Robert Scott was a Florida Circuit Court judge who'd specialized in family law for over twenty years. In all his time on the bench he had not only never encountered a case like Kristen's, he had never imagined it.

One afternoon Kristen and the judge met in his chambers. Robert Scott shook the hand of the ten-year-old girl, whose very existence pressed up against the limits of his thought, thereby transforming it. As their hands locked together, Kristen looked into the eyes of the man who would determine her fate. They spoke about her life, her wishes. Toward the end of their meeting, the grandfather in him emerged more strongly than the judge. Smiling, he asked her what she wanted for Christmas. Not to be distracted for an instant, she immediately answered, "For Christmas I don't really want a present. All I want is to live with my Neen. That's my Christmas present."

Judge Scott was not particularly interested in advocating for lesbian and gay parents. In fact, he didn't think it was a good idea for lesbians and gays to become parents. It seemed to him the world was a difficult enough place for children, without adding the burden of societal stigma. On the other hand, he was a principled person—one who strove not to let his judgment be clouded by prejudice. He also knew from experience that biological connection in itself does not make a family. He understood the significance of "psychological parents." In thinking about Kristen's

relationships to the Pearlmans and to Janine, he drew on his familiarity with many children whose primary attachments were to someone other than their biological parents: "In many instances a father
is merely a begetter of a child. Their only relationship may be that
he sired the child. Then later, he's suddenly a 'father figure' despite the fact that the child doesn't know him. Sometimes we
become overly concerned about blood relations, and I hope we
don't let that interfere with our better judgment as to what's best
for the kid." Most important, Judge Scott's years on the bench had
honed his ability to appreciate and utilize the most essential guide-
line a family court judge has to follow: the best interests of the
child. He knew what he had to do.

Acknowledging that Janine and Kristen had "in all material re-
spects a family relationship, and in fact, if not in law, the equivalent of a parent-child relationship," Judge Scott found that both
Kristen's and Janine's constitutional rights had been violated by the
adoption. Each had a "fundamental liberty interest in preserving
[their] family relationship" and was therefore entitled to "due process—notice and an opportunity to be heard" prior to termination
of that relationship. He also found the Pearlmans to be unfit as
parents for Kristen. Thus, the adoption was overturned on both
grounds and Janine was awarded legal and physical custody of
Kristen. Under Florida law, since Janine is a lesbian, she was unable to officially adopt Kristen. That is the next challenge.

Kristen explains: "I always thought that one day the judge would
see who I was really right for. One day, I was at baseball practice
and my aunt came to pick me up. She had a frown on her face and
I said 'What's wrong?' She said, 'You're moving back with your
Neen.' That sort of stunned me for a second. I wanted to get out
of the car and run around and scream and everything and jump and
do flips but I couldn't 'cause it would be rude. So I just sat there.
Then when we got home she got really mad. She said, 'Whatever
you said about my parents must have had some really good lies.' So
I started to cry, but I was still happy. I ran outside and I was part
crying and part laughing. I ran down to the end of the block and I
had this little dance I started to do and I started to scream because

I felt so good. After that, my Neen came to pick me up. I'm real happy now."

Five years after she had been whisked away, Kristen came home.

When Lesbian or Gay Parents Separate

Janine's struggle demonstrates the difficulties a lesbian or gay co-parent may face in a contested custody case following the death of the biological or adoptive parent. There have been other cases where, even with a will specifically naming the co-parent as guardian, relatives have challenged custody arrangements. Documents such as wills do not provide the same protection that would exist if the co-parent simply had legal parent status.

The lack of parent status can be even more salient, however, when there is a custody dispute between lesbian or gay parents who are splitting up. Whereas in Kristen's case the courts initially had to consider a custody dispute between two parties who were both nonparents, in lesbian and gay break-ups, the courts generally see a dispute between a nonparent and a parent. As long as lesbian and gay co-parents lack legal parent status, their claims for custody or visitation occur over the objections of a legal parent. Courts are reluctant to grant custody or visitation under these circumstances, because to do so is seen as violating parental rights to autonomy.

The disintegration of a relationship is more often messy and strife-ridden than not. When adults can't resolve differences, and can't dissolve their relationships in mutually agreed-upon ways, children are frequently the casualties. This is true in traditional families: when heterosexual married adults who are the biological or adoptive parents of their children become embroiled in conflict with each other, their children get caught in the crossfire. In fact, even when divorcing parents scrupulously attend to their children's needs, there is much suffering. And when they don't, the results are tragic. By the time such conflicts reach the courts, the children have already sustained massive injury; all too often, the worst is yet to come. Still, there are procedures—basic guidelines that courts can follow—developed with these families in mind.

Lesbian and gay parents can also reach points of irresolvable differences, can also be so consumed by their own conflicts that their children become secondary. Children in these instances, like those involved in brutal divorces, suffer immensely long before anyone reaches the courts. But when these families do enter the courts, they are in radically different territory than their heterosexual counterparts. They enter, as one judge noted, "uncharted legal waters" involving "deep-rooted concepts of human relationships in marriage and parenthood."

For me, this brings to mind the image of a disparate group of people in a life raft with several oars, trying to bring children to safety. They are hampered not only by their lack of familiarity with the ocean but also by a blinding fog. The children are in more desperate need than the others; they aren't as strong or resilient, and their very survival is in question. There are experienced navigators aboard the raft. Of these, some have learned rules they hold dear, but what they haven't yet grasped is that this ocean is unlike any they've ever been on before and the rules may do more harm than good. Others, appreciating this fact, envision new ways to proceed, but have the formidable task of convincing the rest to cooperate. The unknown waters and soupy fog are not the only problems for this crew; there is as much to worry about within the confines of the raft as there is in the world beyond it. People have very different objectives, and cannot trust each other. They have different knowledge bases, different hopes, and different fears. And then there is the key question of who has the oars. At times the boat violently lurches as people battle to gain possession of them; mostly it circles wildly, as each paddles with a different intent.

Michele had always wanted to have children, but when, as an adolescent, she came out in 1964, she thought being lesbian meant giving up the possibility of parenthood. When she first heard about donor insemination for infertile heterosexual couples it occurred to her that lesbians could do the same. She and Nancy got together when they were both in their early twenties. Michele talked a lot about having children, but Nancy, who worked with children, was not keen on the idea. Nonetheless, Michele researched the possibilities for insemination, and over the years she tried to convince Nancy that they should have children together. Then Michele developed gynecological problems, ultimately resulting in a hysterectomy. Around the same time, Nancy was beginning to change her mind about children. By the time she decided she wanted to raise children with Michele, Michele was unable to conceive. So in 1979, Nancy became pregnant through insemination and Amy was born. Michele was listed on the birth certificate in the space provided for "father." On the occasion of Amy's birth, Nancy and Michele changed their surnames to a hyphenated combination of both their names, a name Amy was also given. They were Quakers and had a welcoming ceremony for Amy in which she was named as their daughter. Michele used a Lactaid, a device that simulates nursing, in order to feed Amy. As Amy grew, she called them both "Mommy." They presented themselves to Amy's school as a "two-mom" family. Four years later, Nancy gave birth to a son, Dan, also conceived through insemination. By then, the relationship was rocky, and it became worse despite their efforts to work things out. When Dan was six months old, Nancy moved out, taking him with her but leaving Amy with Michele.

Michele, then a graduate student in biology, moved with Amy to student housing—a difficult accomplishment, given the school's initial reluctance to recognize her need for family housing. The arrangement, which included liberal visitation on the part of both noncustodial parents and shared child support, fit with the primary attachments the children had formed. Over the next four years, though they had their ups and downs, the arrangement continued.

But then Nancy and Michele came upon a conflict that they couldn't work through. Nancy wanted to have both of the children spend half of their time in each household, and Michele didn't want to change the existing arrangement. In the midst of the escalating battle, Nancy picked up Amy from school on her usual visitation day. Then she told her that she would not be going home and would not see Michele again.

Initially, Nancy obtained a restraining order prohibiting Michele from having any contact with both children and herself. Several days later, Michele received a letter from a lawyer stating that the restraining order would be rescinded and Michele could have visitation with the children if she signed the enclosed agreement. The agreement essentially offered visitation in exchange for Michele's written declaration that she was not the children's parent. It also included a clause pointing out that the visitation which it granted could be revoked by Nancy at any time. Michele decided not to sign the agreement, and instead sought a custody and visitation settlement through the courts.

Custody and visitation battles between lesbian or gay parents raise legal questions that are on a continuum with the dilemmas arising in heterosexual custody struggles. Some of the dilemmas are in many ways analogous, but because of the way the legal system is structured, they also diverge in critical ways. For instance, the problem of whether nonbiological parents should have rights and responsibilities with respect to children they've reared is common to both divorcing heterosexual stepparents and lesbian and gay co-parents. In both cases, there may be profound psychological and material relationships in the absence of biological connection. However, because of established law, there are key differences in the way the two may be resolved. Many heterosexual stepparents have the option, prior to divorce, of adopting their spouse's children; this option hinges on marriage. As of this writing, adoption is just beginning to emerge as a possibility for a small percentage of lesbian and gay co-parents. In the absence of adoption, the fact of marriage is incorporated into several legal constructions of nonbiological parent-child relationships, though it does not, in and of itself, protect these relationships upon marital dissolution. Thus, the children of divorcing, nonadoptive stepparents are often in the same boat as those of lesbian and gay co-parents, but sometimes they have a few more protections. In some instances, the differences between heterosexual and lesbian or gay parent positions are absolute. For instance, the female partner of a woman who conceived through donor insemination has the same relation to the child as the infertile husband of a woman who conceived through donor insemination. But the fact that heterosexuals can marry makes all the difference in the world; in the eyes of the law, the man is automatically a "father," whereas the lesbian has no parental status.

In lesbian and gay custody and visitation struggles, different views of reality compete. Not only are the views of individual family members—most notably the embattled partners—vying for recognition but the state's many ways of construing family and parent relationships come into conflict with each other. Choices must be made amid this turmoil. It is all too easy to forget whose lives are at the heart of the struggle, who are the most vulnerable, and who are most significantly affected by both the process and outcome—the children.

The trial court initially awarded Michele temporary visitation. The couple was sent to mediation, and the judgment was not final. By the time mediation failed, a new judge was on the bench, and this time, no visitation was granted. In fact, Michele was not given "standing" to be heard on the issue of visitation because, according to the California Uniform Parentage act, she was not legally a "parent."

Michele had no contact with the children for almost a year. During this time she decided to appeal the decision. Meanwhile, Amy developed serious emotional problems. Approximately nine months after the trial-court decision, Michele got a telephone call from a woman who identified herself as Amy's therapist. She requested a meeting with Michele because she believed that Amy's difficulties were based on Amy's traumatic loss of one of her parents. With the therapist's intervention, Nancy agreed to limited visitation. Michele continued with the appeal effort.

Repeatedly, as cases like Michele's have appeared in court, their disposition has been stymied at a preliminary level. Most nonbiological co-parents who have tried to seek custody or visitation through the courts have been designated as having no standing on which to base their arguments, because in the eyes of the law they are not parents. This means that the merits of custody and visitation questions are not even examined; the women are not granted a right to be heard on the issues. The best interests of the child do not come into play, as they do in typical divorce proceedings, because the conflict is not considered to be occurring between two parents. For the children, this often constitutes a total dismissal of their reality—one that necessarily results in disruption of key attachments, an outcome no court would consider optimal for the children of heterosexual married parents.

The key question, of course, is, What is a parent? In Michele's case, and others like it, the central legal argument advanced by co-parents' advocates is that in order to protect children, a functional definition of parenthood—one that looks primarily at relational considerations—must be utilized by the courts. From a child's perspective, biology and legal sanction pale next to the palpable, deeply felt attachments and dependencies that develop in relation to primary caretakers. Ruptures in these relationships can be extremely damaging. By not recognizing lesbian and gay co-parents as parents, the legal system makes absolutely no space for consideration of this aspect of children's experience.

As lawyers specializing in these cases point out, there is legal precedent for recognizing the functional aspects of parenthood in the absence of either biological or adoptive parent status. Many children have stepparents or are raised by grandparents or other relatives. There are several legal concepts that make room for formal acknowledgment of these nonbiological and nonadoptive parent relationships, all of which were used in Michele's appeal.

The legal construct, *in loco parentis*, recognizes that adults who have taken on the role and responsibilities of parents in the absence of biological or adoptive parent status are "like parents" and have the rights and responsibilities that go along with that. This construct has been used as a basis for stepparents' arguing for visitation upon divorce.

There are other constructs—*de facto* parent, equitable parent, and psychological parent—that similarly attempt to recognize the relational component of parenthood when it exists independently of biological or legal components.

The legal concept of equitable estoppel addresses the issue of inconsistency. Essentially, it prohibits someone from suddenly shifting gears when he or she has previously behaved in a certain role and induced dependency on that role. The argument is most often used to require child support from nonbiological and non-adoptive parents. The reasoning behind it is that if, for example, a man has claimed to be a father and behaved as a father, his children are psychologically and physically dependent on that claim, and therefore he can't turn around in the event of divorce and say that he's not "really" the father. Though most often applied in relation to child support, it has also (but rarely) been used to argue for visitation rights, insofar as it confers not only the responsibilities but also the rights of parental status. Whereas in child-support cases the recalcitrant "father" is most often equitably estopped from denying parenthood, in Michele's case the argument was directed at Nancy, saying that she should be equitably estopped from denying Michele's parent status—a status she had actively participated in creating and maintaining, and which her children were now dependent upon.

In lesbian custody battles such as Michele's these legal arguments have been advanced and the obvious analogies pointed out. However, in most of the cases that have been heard to date, the arguments were rejected and the lesbian co-parent was not given "standing" to have a custody or visitation hearing. That is exactly what happened to Michele on appeal.

The gist of the opposing arguments was that *in loco parentis* has mostly been used in the context of heterosexual marriages; equitable estoppel is mostly applicable to child support as opposed to child custody issues; and *de facto* parents do not have parental status. The most significant objection raised by the courts to attempts to gain recognition of parent status is that if the courts concurred, it would open up a can of worms insofar as anyone— baby-sitters, neighbors, ex-boyfriends—could claim parental status and bring custody or visitation challenges to biological or adoptive parents. In other words it would violate parents' rights to autonomy.

While these concerns have some merit, in fact the arguments put forth in these cases are much more narrowly defined, and would not open the door for just "anyone" to claim parental status. It is not merely emotional closeness, for example, that these arguments are based on; rather, they show a whole constellation of qualities that add up to a parental relationship. For instance, Nancy had her children with the full and active participation of Michele and with a mutual agreement that they would both be parents. Michele was called "Mommy" by her nonbiological children, provided material support and emotional nurturance, and was Amy's primary care-taker until she was eight years old. When Nancy took Amy, she was removing her from her home. The court's refusal to recognize Michele as Amy's parent stems from its blindness to the realities of lesbian and gay family formation. The destructiveness of this over-sight is most evident in the court's failure to appreciate Amy's reality.

In 1984, a court awarded visitation rights to a lesbian co-parent, though it did not grant her parent status. The *Loftin* v. *Flourney* decision reflected the court's recognition of the child's need to maintain a relationship to her "psychological parent." Though there have been similar awards, most decisions don't come close to this recognition of children's needs vis-à-vis their nonbiological parents.

In custody proceedings, courts generally perform a balancing act between adults' rights to parental autonomy and the needs of chil-dren. In a typical proceeding between two legally acknowledged parents, the legal standard is the best interests of the child. Though this is not an easy thing to ascertain, it is a guiding principle that at least has the potential of protecting children's interests. Consider-ing the legally acknowledged parents' rights is not in and of itself problematic. But allowing these rights to supplant consideration of children's needs is an egregious error—one that is not permitted in custody battles between two legally acknowledged parents. None-theless, in lesbian and gay custody battles, where one adult does not have parental status, the court does not operate according to the best-interests-of-the-child standard. Instead, the rights of the le-gally acknowledged parent to "parental autonomy" most saliently inform the court's moves. The other parent is seen as an "outsider," whose intrusion the acknowledged parent has a right to avoid. This is the window through which children's interests are discarded. As more and more lesbian and gay couples who have children are, like their heterosexual peers, breaking up, these cases are cropping up throughout the nation.

Lesbian and gay custody and visitation struggles pose heretofore never-asked questions to a judicial system that has not yet sorted out the dilemmas raised by heterosexual arrangements. The newness of the issues profoundly shapes how they are currently dealt with. But there are forces beyond this unknown territory that influence how these conflicts play out, most notably homophobia. In this context, one cannot ask, What is a family? and, What is a parent? without confronting heterosexist constructions of the family. Thus, the relationships between nonbiological co-parents and their children are, by and large, not legally recognized or protected—partly because they are relatively new and partly because their very existence challenges the sanctity of the traditional family. But as one legal expert has pointed out, the state cannot force families into a particular mold. It can only deal with children's actual lives in ways that either are or are not compassionate and morally sound.

There are several aspects to the courts' refusals to acknowledge these lesbian co-parents as parents. Homophobia certainly plays a role in at least two ways. Individual judges' prejudices can make them reluctant to legitimize lesbian and gay families. In fact, looked at from one perspective, these cases exemplify the clash between how lesbians and gay men view their families and how a homophobic society views them. Here again, the idea that there is an uncrossable line between homosexuals and families crops up. Homophobia is guiding judges' objections to the use of the concepts like *in loco parentis* when those objections are based on the fact that the concepts usually apply in the context of heterosexual marriages. But beyond individual prejudices, homophobia is embedded in the law and, in fact, seems at times to "tie the hands" of judges who would rather make other decisions. Simply the fact that only heterosexual unions can be legally acknowledged, and that within the context of those unions parenting roles can be established (as in the case of donor insemination for infertile couples), skews things against lesbian and gay family formation.

But there is another aspect to these decisions. In several cases judges have expressed great distress about having to conclude that these co-parents have no "standing." Some judges recognize the terrible impact such decisions may have on children, and deplore the lack of legal protection for children of lesbians and gay men. But they see themselves as bound by narrow statutory definitions of parenthood and therefore say in their decisions that these matters should be changed at the legislative level. In other words, though they wish to acknowledge co-parents as parents, they are not free to make new law, only to interpret existing law. One judge summed up the issue this way:

> No matter how this court rules it is absolutely imperative that the Legislature reexamine its laws in order to adequately deal with the increasing numbers of children of homosexual couples. . . . No matter what one's political, social, moral, religious or philosophical bent may be, one may not ignore the fact that children are being born that are products of homosexual unions. We have always sought to protect our children, to recognize and value the importance of family and to create legislative vehicles to continue these relationships and ensure that the best interests of the child are protected. . . . Our laws must clarify the emerging social questions by redefining a family and determining if a nonbiological partner who intends to be a parent of a child, has legal rights to continue custodial responsibilities once the parties have ended their relationship.

There is much debate among legal experts about whether and in what ways the courts are bound by narrow statutory language—in fact, the question of how to interpret the language of relevant statutes is at the heart of many of these cases.

In New York, Alison D. and her partner, Virginia M., co-parented two children, each conceiving one through donor insemination. The children were raised as siblings with two mothers. When the relationship ended, a joint custody and visitation arrangement was agreed upon and carried out by both. But, again, difficulties developed and eventually Virginia cut off all contact between Alison and her nonbiological child. She also cut off contact between the two children.

The New York court ruled that Alison was a "biological and legal stranger" to her nonbiological child, and therefore had no standing on which to base an argument for visitation. This decision said quite simply that Alison D. was not a parent according to Domestic Relations Law #70: "We decline to read the term parent to include categories of nonparents who have developed a relationship with a child or who have had prior relationships with a child's parents and who wish to continue visitation with the child." The ruling, along with others like it, has profoundly negative implications not just for children of lesbians and gay men but also for children of other nonbiological, nonadoptive parents, including heterosexual step-parents.

The most ironic aspect of the judgment was that just a year earlier, in a landmark decision, the very same court had argued for a broader definition of the family—one that does not "rest on fictitious legal distinctions or genetic history, but instead . . . find[s] its foundation in the reality of family life." That was the language of the *Braschi* decision, which concerned the question of whether the male partner of a man who died of AIDS was his "family" for purposes of rent-control law. This speaks strongly to the fact that when children are involved, recognition of lesbian and gay families is difficult to achieve, even among a group willing to acknowledge the family nature of lesbian and gay unions.

There was one dissenting opinion in the Alison D. case. Judge Judith S. Kaye, the only woman on the panel, pointed out the court's self-contradiction given the *Braschi* decision. Acknowledging that there were, at the time, approximately 15.5. million children in the nation who did not live with two biological parents, and an estimated 10 million children living in lesbian or gay households, she went on to say "the impact of today's decision falls hardest on the children of those relationships, limiting their opportunity to maintain bonds that may be crucial to their development. The majority's retreat from the court's proper role—its tightening of rules that should in visitation petitions, above all, retain the capacity to take the children's interests into account—compels this dissent."

Judge Kaye confronted head-on her fellow judges' narrow approach to the question of what makes a parent. She pointed out that "the majority insists . . . that the word 'parent' in this case can only be read to mean biological parent; the response 'one fit parent' now forecloses all inquiry into the child's best interest. . . . We have not previously taken such a hard line in these matters, but in the absence of express legislative direction have attempted to read otherwise undefined words of the statute so as to effectuate the legislative purposes." Judge Kaye was prepared to more boldly interpret the statutes in order to fulfill the spirit of the law; she encouraged her fellow judges to do the same: "It is not my intention to spell out a definition but only to point out that it is surely within our competence to do so. It is indeed regrettable that we decline to exercise that authority in this visitation matter, given the explicit statutory objectives, the courts' power, and the fact that all consideration of the child's interest is, for the future, otherwise absolutely foreclosed."

To date there have been a few cases in which courts granted "standing" to a lesbian co-parent. It is possible that, as courts become more familiar with the needs of children of lesbian and gay parents, more such decisions will follow.

All parents have a responsibility to care for and nurture their children. Likewise society has a responsibility to look out for the needs of children. One thing children need is continuity and stability in their primary attachments. At this point in time, we know a great deal about the damaging effects on children of traumatic losses such as parental abandonment or death. We also know that ongoing bitter family conflict is detrimental. Some traumatic losses are unavoidable, but others are very much within the control of adults.

Lesbians and gay men, like their heterosexual counterparts, take on a long-term commitment when they become parents. That commitment is to ensure their children's emotional and physical well-being. This often means being able to assess a child's needs as separate and distinct from one's own, even when the two are diametrically opposed. It is one of the most difficult aspects of parenthood. When couples split up, it is the key stumbling block for parents and the way they inflict the most damage on their children—embroiling them in parental conflict, playing out their own struggles through their children's lives, failing to appreciate the differences between their relations to each other and their children's relations to each of them.

It is not surprising that these problems arise in lesbian and gay breakups, just as they do among heterosexuals. In this respect, lesbian and gay parents are no different from heterosexual ones. But as a society, in the case of heterosexual divorce, we at least try to ensure that when parents fail to adequately respond to their children's needs, those needs are nonetheless attended to. As flawed as many divorce proceedings may be, there is at least a basic general commitment to view the best interests of the child as primary. When, in splitting up, lesbian and gay parents falter, there is no such societal backup or safety net for the children. Similarly, when biological or adoptive lesbian and gay parents die, there is no societal commitment to ensuring the continuity of children's relationships with their other parents. At these times of transformation, the rift between lesbian or gay families and society's dominant notions of the family is most apparent—and most destructive. The perils of creating families in a social context that, at best, fails to recognize them and, at worst, is actively hostile are clearly evident.

Lesbians and gay men raising children must carry more parental responsibility than their heterosexual peers, or their children will surely suffer. The courts are not a good place to work out any family problem, but they are an even worse place to work out the difficulties arising in families headed by lesbians or gay men.

There is magic involved in saying at one moment that you are creating a family, and at the next, that there is no family there. If a lesbian or gay parent decides to practice this kind of magic, society will be all too eager to help. But for children that is a dangerous sorcery. At this point in time, if a biological or adoptive homosexual parent in the process of a breakup chooses to assert power through a homophobic and inadequate legal system, she or he will most likely succeed. Conversely, if a nonbiological and nonadoptive parent chooses to ignore established parent-child bonds, she or he will also, most likely, not be deterred by the law. But in both cases, this will occur at the expense of the children.

Beyond the individual responsibility that parenting entails, there is a societal responsibility toward children. With all the rhetoric of "family values" that saturates our contemporary consciousness, we continue to fail our children. By clinging to a mythical version of the family, we, as a society, refuse to recognize and help a multitude of children living in actual families.

Donors or Fathers?—What Makes a Parent?

The ideology that construes the family as first and foremost a matter of heterosexual procreative union, when imposed on families that don't fit the mold, often yields tragic consequences. Children whose lesbian and gay parents split up, as with those whose biological parents die, hover in a no-man's-land because our society so strongly frames biological connection as essential to parent-child relationships and, conversely, discounts those parent-child bonds that develop independent of biology. It isn't hard to see how the refusal to recognize nonbiological parent-child relationships can wreak havoc on the lives of children like Kristen. Children of lesbian or gay parents are not the only ones to suffer from this dangerous mistake. The story of Jessica DeBoer, taken at age two from the only home she'd known in order to be returned to her biological parents, pointedly demonstrates that society's stress on biology in family life profoundly affects a multitude of children. There is a point at which the reliance on biology to define the family becomes an act of violence. For the children of lesbian or gay parents, this point is all too often reached. It may be reached not only by failure to acknowledge nonbiological parent-child relationships but also by elevating biological connections to parent-child relationships in circumstances that don't warrant such a move.

As the lesbian baby boom has matured to being almost commonplace, there is increasing urgency to determining what place biology has in defining the family. During the past few years a new kind of battle has emerged. Lesbians who have conceived with known donors without intending to co-parent are finding themselves facing custody and visitation challenges in courtrooms throughout the country. As these battles tear at the lives of children, they force the state to closely scrutinize the meanings of family and parenthood. They also compel all of us, especially lesbians and gay men who are inventing new family forms, to think about how to do so ethically and responsibly.

Whereas the law tends toward a black-and-white vision, the family forms lesbians and gay men create encompass an almost infinite range of grays. Not surprisingly, it is the families in the middle that are most ill-served by the imposition of existing legal definitions of the family. Those lesbians and gay men who, like Barry and Adria, choose to co-parent, essentially form families that, while novel, nonetheless partially fit the state's traditional definitions of family; the biological parents in these families are, by agreement, both functional parents. These families diverge from the state definition only insofar as they often encompass more than two parents and include nonbiological parents in the mix. At the other end of the spectrum, lesbians who conceive through anonymous donors also form families that fit somewhat with the state's view of family; though their partners are not legally recognized as parents, these women choose a mode of conception that both the state and they agree yields a child of a donor, not a father.

But there are many lesbians who form families that fall outside the state's definition, not only because they feature nonbiological lesbian co-parents but also because they include identified donors who have varying degrees of relationship to the children—but are, by agreement, not co-parents. It is these families that so often find themselves caught in the gulf between their self-definition and the state's traditional vision of family.

Just as lesbians have been denied access to anonymous insemination because of an ideology that frowns on women raising children without fathers, so too when donors challenge lesbians for custody or visitation, the courts often support the challenge because of an assumption that all children need fathers. A 1977 New Jersey case involving a single heterosexual woman and a man who had agreed to be a donor resulted in the man's receiving rights and legal father status. The language of the decision clearly reflected bias toward the heterosexual family model: "The courts have consistently shown a policy favoring the requirement that a child be provided with a father as well as a mother. . . . It is in a child's best interests to have two parents whenever possible." This same rationale has guided many courts dealing with custody challenges in families headed by lesbians. Failing to acknowledge nonbiological lesbian mothers as the children's other parents, the courts have gone on to give legal father status to donors despite the fact that these men had neither originally agreed to be fathers nor formed significant parenting relationships with their offspring.

Lesbians have been vulnerable to these challenges for many reasons. Historically excluded from use of anonymous donor insemination, lesbians frequently became pregnant with known donors at the beginning of the lesbian baby boom. As access to sperm banks opened up, many lesbians continued to choose known donors in order to give their children a sense of their biological roots, and often to provide them with a relationship—though not always parental—to their donors. Such a wish is not as preposterous as it may seem from a perspective that automatically pairs biological and functional parenting relationships. In reality, many families thrive with just such an agreement: lesbians take on the responsibilities and rights of parenthood, while donors take on extended-family or friendship roles. In creating families like these, lesbians and gay men have moved beyond what the state recognizes as a family, and these arrangements therefore depend on extraordinary trust and trustworthiness. When people's abilities to work through conflicts falter, some of the most bitter and devastating legal battles can ensue.

That is just what happened to the Russo-Young family of New York City. Before the legal ordeal, they were in many ways a typical family headed by lesbians. Robin Young and Sandy Russo met and fell in love in 1979. Things were clicking into place for them, and having children together was a natural next step. Filled with a sense of possibility and hopefulness, they set about planning their family together. Sandy, approaching forty, had wanted a child for years and knew that time was running out; so she and Robin chose to begin their family with Sandy's attempt to get pregnant.

They thought a great deal about the kind of family they wanted to create. No matter who conceived and bore a child, they would both be mothers. To each of them, motherhood was not a matter of biology but a matter of commitment, responsibility, and love. Along with the wish to co-parent equally came the certainty that they wanted to maintain the integrity of a family consisting of themselves and their children. They rejected the idea of anonymous donor insemination because they worried that a child's inability to know much about half his or her genetic origins would cause pain and psychological damage. Instead they set about finding a donor who would be willing to be identified to the child if the child expressed interest, but who would not be in any way a functional parent. They looked for a gay man whom they could trust to honor the kind of family they were creating, a family consisting of two mothers and their children. They found such a person in California, and Sandy conceived their first child, Cade Russo-Young.

Because they were delighted with Cade, Sandy and Robin quickly decided to have another child, this time one conceived by Robin. They found another donor on the West Coast, Thomas Steel, a gay man who expressed great support for their endeavor. Within two years of Cade's birth, Ry Russo-Young was born. Over the years their family life developed much as Sandy and Robin had envisioned it—they were close-knit and the children thrived. Biology was beside the point in their family: the children called both women "Mommy," and Cade and Ry were sisters, not legally or biologically, but in the way that mattered most—emotionally.

Sooner than Sandy and Robin had anticipated, when Cade was about five, she began to be curious about her origins. Having asked both donors at the outset whether they would meet the children if the children wanted it, Sandy and Robin now called to arrange a trip to the West Coast, during which both girls would meet the donors. The visit went well, and over the next six years, Sandy, Robin, Tom and the first donor developed friendships that resulted in continued contact.

The Russo-Young family fell within the gray area the state had yet to grapple with. The children had two parents, Sandy and Robin, though this was not acknowledged legally. They were sisters, though again, the state failed to recognize this fact. They had relationships to the donors, but these were not parental relationships, a complexity the state had had little experience with. As long as the mutually agreed upon, existing relationships satisfied everyone, the discrepancy between the state's definition of family and this particular family's makeup was barely discernible in daily life. But in the spring of 1991 the discrepancy became painfully vivid as a conflict arose that quickly escalated into a court battle.

Visits had always been at the discretion of Robin and Sandy and had virtually always included all the adults. But that spring, Tom asked that Robin and Sandy send the girls alone to visit him in California. He wanted them to meet his family, something that eleven years earlier, before Ry's conception, all had agreed would not happen. Robin and Sandy were alarmed by the shift in attitude Tom's proposal heralded. Indeed, when they turned down Tom's request to send the children for the visit, their conversations became increasingly heated. Shortly thereafter Tom initiated a paternity suit seeking legal recognition as Ry's father and court ordered visitation with her. The foundation of trust upon which their family had been built collapsed in the blink of an eye. The question became not what could these people work out together but who had the power to define Ry's familial relationships.

The implications of Tom's quest for legal recognition as Ry's father were far reaching, threatening the Russo-Young family on many levels at once. In a context in which Sandy lacked legal recognition as Ry's parent, Tom might gain it. If something were to happen to Robin, would Tom be granted custody of Ry so that she would be separated from her sister and mother because neither of them were acknowledged by the state to be family? Beyond this threat of future loss, the paternity suit had more immediate implications. Sandy and Robin had assiduously avoided making any distinctions in their family based on biology. Each treated both Cade and Ry as their daughters, and they had insisted over the years that the donors treat the children equally. Now Tom was making a distinction between the girls. His claiming Ry as his daughter altered his relations to both girls and their relations to each other. This move not only contradicted the agreements made before Ry's conception but also disrupted relationships that had existed for many years.

Contrasting values and principles were put before the court's consideration. Tom argued that his biological connection to Ry made him her father and Ry needed a father, that Sandy's lack of biological connection made her, according to the Alison D. decision, a "biological and legal stranger" who should therefore not be present at the hearing, and that Sandy had no legal obligation to support Ry financially but he would were he granted father status, which would be in Ry's best interests. Despite his being gay, Tom sometimes presented arguments that took on homophobic tones. He called as an expert witness a psychologist who, never having met the Russo-Youngs, nonetheless argued that their family was an exemplification of lesbian fusion and their resistance to Tom's quest for legal recognition as Ry's parent stemmed from their hostility toward men.

Sandy and Robin put forth a very different set of principles. They argued that their family had been, by mutual agreement and during a decade of action, headed by a lesbian couple; through both their original intentions and their behavior over the years,

Sandy and Robin were Ry's parents, while Tom had functioned as a close family friend.

Most significantly, Ry was profoundly shaken by the lawsuit. The family she loved and depended on was being challenged at its core by someone she'd counted on for support. If Tom won the paternity suit it would mean that in the eyes of the law Robin, Tom, and Ry comprised one family unit while Sandy, Cade, and the other donor comprised another. Ry suffered from anxiety and had nightmares about the court proceedings, and she felt deeply betrayed. As her fate was debated in court, Ry clearly stated that she did not want visitation with Tom.

The court was faced with a complex set of issues. What weight, if any, should be given to Tom and Ry's biological connection? What would his gaining parental status mean in the context of Sandy's lack of such status? And most important, where did Ry's perspective fit into the picture? Were her quite clear feelings of anger and distress about Tom's actions reflective simply of her mothers' influence, as Tom argued, or should the court heed Ry's own words because she was old enough to know both what she felt and what she needed?

Tom's quest for a declaration of paternity fit with the longstanding societal and legal tradition of relying on biological connection to determine parental status. Moreover his arguments tapped into the common assumption that children are always better off with their father than without. But there was a compelling reality on the other side. Ry's family wasn't built on a foundation of biological connections. Ry knew Robin and Sandy to be her parents and Cade to be her sister. She felt deeply threatened by the prospect of a court determining otherwise. Amidst the deeply entrenched legal bias toward recognizing a heterosexual procreative unit as family over other family forms, was there room for the state to honor the family structure Sandy and Robin had created more than a decade ago? Was there room for Ry's own perspective?

Though it was becoming more prevalent, the kind of family Ry and Cade were being raised in was still relatively new and therefore novel in the legal setting. Judge Kaufmann, presiding over the case, recognized the challenge posed by the gap between established law and myriad new family forms, but he was not deterred. Noting that "Ideally, the recognition of new and complex parenting arrangements is addressed by legislation," he went on to say, "There is no legislation, however, that resolves the dispute before me, and I must proceed to resolve it under common law principles."

After reviewing all the facts and arguments, Judge Kaufmann denied both the paternity claim and the request for visitation. He based his decision largely on the doctrine of equitable estoppel, noting that some courts had relied on that doctrine to deny paternity claims when such claims were determined not to be in the best interests of the child. In applying the doctrine of equitable estoppel, Judge Kaufmann argued that to shift the definition of Ry's family when she was at such an advanced age would be damaging to her, and the functional family relationships that had existed from the time of Ry's birth needed to be honored and protected. Describing the paternity suit in his decision, Judge Kaufmann said, "For many years he (Steel) outwardly supported the development of these functional family relationships. When Ry was almost ten years old, he decided, due to changes in his life, to attempt to change the ground rules of her life. This attempt has already caused Ry anxiety, nightmares, and psychological harm. Ry views this proceeding as a threat to her family security. For her, a declaration of paternity would be a statement that her family is other than what she knows it to be and needs it to be. . . . A declaration of paternity naming Thomas S. as Ry's father, under these circumstances, at this late time in her life, would not be in her best interests."

Judge Kaufmann's decision marked a victory, not just for the Russo-Young family, but for the many families headed by lesbians and gay men who suffer from lack of legal recognition. However, the decision has not resolved things either for the Russo-Youngs or for other families that might find themselves in similarly threatening circumstances. As of this writing, Tom Steel is appealing the decision, and the final outcome is still pending. As far as the larger implications of the decision are concerned, it is helpful to many families insofar as it affirms the possibility of state recognition of functional family relationships that don't conform to the heterosexual model. But since the decision relies heavily on both the timing of the paternity suit and on Ry's ability to articulate her point of view, its implications with respect to families with much younger children are limited.

Disputes like these, cropping up more and more frequently, point to the critical need for rethinking the definition of the word *family*. Pat formulas relying on the heterosexual model simply don't apply to large numbers of families today. Not only is the state ill equipped at this point to sort through the complexities of diverse family forms, but we are all compelled to think about how we can behave responsibly toward children as we create these families. The *Steel* vs. *Young* case taps into profound feelings about the significance of biology. It touches on the different ways men and women construe parenting. And perhaps most important, it demonstrates how far we have to go—how much lesbians and gay men have yet to sort out about the meaning of family and what constitutes ethical behavior toward each other and toward children. If we are to invent new family forms, we cannot rely on old definitions to solve our conflicts.

Second-Parent Adoptions

The difficulties faced by the children described in this chapter all stem from the legal limbo that families headed by lesbians and gay men inhabit. Though they function as families, that fact is not legally recognized and key relationships are therefore nonexistent in the eyes of the law. The fact that nonbiological and nonadoptive parents have no legally sanctioned connections to their children leaves these children without the basic economic benefits that parent-child relationships usually entail, such as inheritance rights or inclusion in health-insurance plans. More tragically, it leaves these children vulnerable to the traumas of absolute loss in cases of parental splits or death of legally recognized parents.

As of now, there is little most lesbian and gay parents can do to avoid these difficulties. Wills can specify guardians, but they can also be contested. Parenting contracts are strongly recommended by legal experts, but as custody cases between lesbians have demonstrated, those contracts are often not given much weight in the courts. In other words, there is no adequate substitute for the basic legal recognition of family relationships.

Recently, lesbian and gay parents have begun to make inroads in the struggle for legal recognition. The way adoption law is structured, standard adoptions involve termination of the natural (or legal) parent's rights. Generally, a child cannot have two parents of the same gender. This essentially renders adoption not viable for lesbian and gay parents, since the legal parent would have to give up his or her parental status in order for the co-parent to adopt. But there are variations on that approach that have arisen in response to the changing nature of family life.

Currently, the most prevalent adoptions in the country are stepparent adoptions. In these cases, the natural custodial parent does not give up parental status, though he or she does consent to the adoption. (Generally the noncustodial biological parent does lose parental rights in these cases, but there have been exceptions.) Stepparent adoptions protect the relationships between children and their nonbiological parents in cases of divorce and with respect to inheritance rights, insurance coverage, and parenting responsibilities such as medical and school authorizations. In other words, they address just the issues that arise in families headed by lesbians and gay men. The catch, however, is that stepparent adoptions hinge on marriage—the nonbiological parent can adopt his or her spouse's children.

Second-parent adoptions, like stepparent adoptions, require consent from the legal parent, but do not entail that parent's loss of parental status. Unlike stepparent adoptions, they are not conditioned on marriage. These adoptions have been used by heterosexuals in instances when couples are unable or unwilling to marry, but they are especially crucial to lesbian and gay parents. The first second-parent adoption occurred in Oregon in 1985. Since then, lesbian and gay parents have increasingly made use of it, but its availability is quite limited at this time. As of this writing, eleven jurisdictions—Alaska, California, Oregon, Washington, New York, Washington, D.C., Vermont, Texas, New Jersey, Pennsylvania, and Massachusetts—have all allowed lesbian or gay co-parents to legally adopt their partner's biological or adopted children.

Through second-parent adoptions people like Laura and Victoria of Washington, D.C., are extending their own definitions of their families into one that is culturally recognized. This move not only gives their children much-needed legal protection but also is significant culturally: it redefines the family.

In 1991, Laura Solomon and Victoria Lane lived on a quiet street in Washington, D.C. A tricycle and red wagon adorned their front yard. They belonged to their daughters, six-year-old Tessa Solomon-Lane and two-year-old Maya Solomon-Lane.

Victoria described her childhood in Pleasantville, New York, the home of the *Reader's Digest*, as a "protected, nice suburban life." In the mid-1970s, when Victoria was in her early twenties, she came out as a lesbian. Already a committed feminist who had long ago rejected the Catholicism of her childhood, Victoria thought that choosing to be with a woman didn't seem like a big deal—it felt natural and right. To her, the idea that people "tie themselves to some pre-existing, pre-described role" had never made sense. Victoria worked with children and had always envisioned herself as a parent. Coming out didn't change that.

Laura grew up in Miami, the oldest of three children raised in an observant Jewish home. She watched her mother, like many women of her generation, uncomfortably bend to fit into the narrowly defined roles of wife and mother. Perplexed by the question of how "any woman did anything that was traditional" and remained "able to look at themselves in the mirror every day," Laura also progressed naturally toward coming out, in her mid-twenties.

In 1979, Laura applied for a job at a day-care center where Victoria worked, and not long after she was hired they became involved. About a year later, they began to live with each other. That first year of living together was trial by fire. Laura's father had had a serious stroke the year before, leaving him quite disabled, and her mother was increasingly depressed. Laura moved her father to D.C. and set about getting care for him. Shortly after that, her mother committed suicide. Within a few months Victoria discovered a lump on her neck and was diagnosed with thyroid cancer. The crises pushed their relationship ahead many years; from the outset, there were no facades to get past. Soon after, being strong believers in ritual, they had a commitment ceremony attended by friends and family.

Though they had each thought about children before, they began to seriously discuss the possibility about five years into their relationship. Victoria had always thought of herself as someone who would adopt a child. Her mother is Nicaraguan, and because of this family background, she wanted to look into Latin American adoptions. Laura, on the other hand, was set on becoming pregnant. They had to extend themselves toward each other in order to understand these different desires and to make a joint commitment to each endeavor.

The adoption process was long and drawn out. After several disappointing rounds, they concentrated instead on Laura's becoming pregnant through an anonymous donor. In 1985, Laura gave birth to a girl, Tessa. Laura and Victoria wanted to share parenting as equally as possible, and had to adjust to the asymmetry that began with Laura's nursing Tessa and continued through her toddler years. When Tessa went to preschool, Victoria again pursued adoption. This time her family in Nicaragua helped with the arrangements. Again, there were several disappointing false starts, and they had begun to reconcile themselves to the idea of being a one-kid family when the phone call came saying "the baby's ready." "What baby?" they responded. "What baby" turned out to be Maya, who at four months of age weighed seven and a half pounds, Tessa's birth weight. When they took her to a doctor in the States, they found her low weight was due to an infection that cleared easily with antibiotics.

In preparing Tessa for her baby sister's arrival, Laura and Victoria told stories about how she had been born. Tessa is well-informed about her conception and birth: that a man donated sperm, that she grew in Laura's womb. She knows also that Maya has different birth parents. It has always been clear in the Solomon-Lane household that these two children, however they came to be, are siblings who have two mothers. As Victoria said, "To me it's clear what constitutes a family, and that's the relationships that people create. I think the inherent reality of our family stands for itself."

Laura and Victoria were content with every aspect of the family they created together except one. The fact that to society they were not a family—that each was seen as the mother of only one child and that those children were not in any official sense siblings—did not sit well. So they decided to do something about it. In 1991, Laura adopted Maya and Victoria adopted Tessa. They were the first to successfully complete a second-parent adoption in Washington, D.C. Now, in the eyes of the law, each child had two mothers and a sister. Tessa had a hard time understanding the significance of the event—she, of course, had always known she had two mothers and a sister.

While second-parent adoptions are a bright light on the horizon for lesbian and gay families, they are not a perfect solution to the problem of legal recognition. They are rare at this time, and in many jurisdictions, homophobia along with the built-in heterosexual bias of the law pose substantial barriers. Adoption, like other family law, is governed by local statutes; the question of how narrowly the statutory language is interpreted arises as people attempt to carry out these adoptions. In many instances, the standard route of loss of parental rights—or an exception to that only in the context of marriage—is seen by the courts as binding.

Second-parent adoptions have the effect of giving family status to lesbian and gay parent-child relationships, but nonetheless they do not accurately reflect the reality of lesbians and gay men choosing to parent, and they do have some drawbacks. Second-parent adoptions can be carried out only after the fact, once a child has been in a household, usually for some time. For lesbians and gay men choosing to have children, the planning process is when they begin to form a family. Furthermore, second-parent adoptions entail some level of state scrutiny, such as a home study—which, of course, heterosexuals (unless they are adopting) are not subject to. Homophobic bias can interfere with second-parent adoptions during the home study. To date, the cases that have gone forth have, for the most part, been those with the least number of possible complications. Though in one case a second-parent adoption was granted such that the child ended up with three parents who maintained legal rights, generally they've been carried out only with two parents; thus, lesbians parenting with known donors, for instance, present complications that have not yet been widely dealt with.

Despite these kinks, second-parent adoption is a move that is critical for children of lesbian and gay parents—a point that is unfortunately brought home in times of crisis. Indeed, as of this writing the Solomon-Lane family has changed dramatically. In August 1993, Victoria died as a result of injuries sustained in a car accident. As the judge who had granted the second-parent adoption remarked, "It is tragic that we had to have such obvious and direct evidence of the need [for second-parent adoption]. . . . Maya is not an orphan today because of what we did."

· 10 ·

The Road Ahead

If it were a painting, it might be mistaken for a Norman Rockwell entitled *Grandmother and Baby*. But it is a snapshot—a moment captured on film and tucked away in the family album for Sean perhaps to show his own grandchildren in the year 2050. He is six months old, she is sixty-seven—it is their first meeting. The camera has caught her gently cradling his body, their eyes intensely focused on each other; hers are glistening ever so slightly around the edges, his are wide open and curious. All that is inside the frame.

And all this is outside of it: she is an immigrant from a small town in Germany, a woman to whom family means everything, a woman who has therefore suffered every moment of the distance from her childhood home and loved ones for almost half a century. At the time she met her husband his family had disappeared in the war; he had no one but her. To them America was the proverbial land of promise. He worked in the garment industry—twelve-hour days, low wages, no benefits. She worked in a factory, racing to package the goods as they whizzed by on a conveyer belt. They worked hard because they had a dream they were working for: to make a home with each other, to save enough money to have children and give them a comfortable life. And that is exactly what happened.

She raised two sons—one, a strapping young athlete and serious student who grew to be a lawyer; the other, a quiet boy who spent his childhood drawing and making homes out of any material he could find. It was no surprise that he became an architect. Her sons were her pride and joy. And now, the architect had a baby of his own.

You might infer a story like this if, in seeing the snapshot, you looked into her eyes. But you would probably not infer the rest. You wouldn't guess, for instance, that these are stolen moments. A half-hour ago she told her husband she was going to the grocery store. She went instead to a pay phone down the street and called her son. "I'm coming over," she told him. He looked at his lover in shock. They'd adopted Sean six months ago, and she had never met him—hadn't set foot in the house since his arrival. She burst into tears when she saw him. There was time for one embrace, for one snapshot, but that was all. Her husband would get suspicious if she didn't return quickly.

Craig and Jim had been living together for six years, and during that time Craig stayed close to his family, especially his mother. His parents knew Jim, yet no one ever said the word *gay*. But then Sean was coming, and Craig could no longer wait to speak the truth about his life. So a week before Sean was to arrive he visited his parents and told them that he and Jim had adopted a child. No one could pretend they were anything but lovers once a baby arrived on the scene. There would be a child, they would be a family. His mother cried, his father raged. After that, Craig's father forbade his wife any contact with the son who lit her days, the son who was most like her.

But now she was here. Craig had called her to say they were moving soon. They had to, because ever since Sean arrived, the neighbors in their apartment building had shunned them; and one recently warned them that some might try to stir up trouble about the adoption. Hearing about the move brought her close to panic. She could no longer bear the absence, so she came and cradled her grandson as she'd cradled his father many years before. And that is the moment Jim caught on film.

Minutes after he put the camera down, Jim helped Craig's mother into his car and drove her to a street corner a block away from her house, so as not to raise any suspicions. As Craig warmed Sean's bottle, he agonized about his mother; it seemed to him this might be the death of her.

Like Craig, Jim is a person to whom family is central. When he visited the Italian village of his mother's relatives at age sixteen, he was awed by the villagers who stood below his window serenading him. His heart filled with a sense of belonging as they sang ballads written by his grandfather—songs still used in religious celebrations. Jim's parents were second-generation immigrants who'd grown up amid poverty and hard times. When Jim was a young boy, his paternal grandmother was murdered, and from that time on his father's grief displayed itself as rage. Meanwhile, his mother languished for years suffering mysterious and nameless maladies. Having watched her fade away, Jim felt clearly when she died that what matters most in life is following your heart. Being gay no longer seemed like such a big deal; homophobia was nowhere near as frightening a force as the prospect of a living death. So as a young adult he came out and set about creating his life.

It took many years for Jim and his father and siblings to reach through their pain and find each other after his mother's death. When they finally did, they forged precious bonds. When Jim told his father of Sean's impending arrival, the elder man exclaimed, "You can't be a father. You don't know how to raise a kid." Then he paused, and quizzically peering into his son's face asked, "Do you?"

Craig's father was a stubborn man, but almost a year of witnessing his wife's despair wore him down. When she called to invite Craig and Sean for Thanksgiving dinner, she apologized to Jim for not being able to invite him as well. He and Craig talked it over and decided that Craig would go without Jim this one time—but no more than this one time. It was a painful decision. Thanksgiving was for families, and they were a family, whether or not anyone acknowledged that fact.

When December rolled around, Craig's parents surprised him by accepting an invitation to celebrate Christmas at his house. They brought along his ninety-three-year-old aunt, who greeted Jim with a warm hug and exclaimed, "I'm so glad to meet you. I've heard such wonderful things about you." It was a huge Christmas dinner, with Craig and Jim's families assembled together for the first time. Though Craig's father barely spoke a word throughout the evening, as they were leaving he turned to Jim and struck up a conversation about the new garage; the ice was beginning to thaw.

Now, years later, it has thoroughly melted. Jim and Craig are the center of both their families' lives. That Christmas was the first, but certainly not the last, of their big gatherings. Bringing the love, loss, wounds, anger, and forgiveness that each bears, they come together—a patchwork quilt laden with history. They gather around the dining-room table breaking bread, sharing stories. I imagine the events look just like another Norman Rockwell painting, maybe entitled *Family Values*.

In order for Sean's family to break bread together it had to reinvent itself. Each member had to recognize and assert a broader and deeper meaning of family—one centered on love—over the narrower but more culturally dominant one premised on heterosexuality, biological parent-child connections, and the legal sanction of marriage. Jim and Craig had traversed a difficult path in creating their family—first overcoming shame to embrace their love for each other, then pursuing Sean's adoption despite their fears, and finally steadfastly declaring themselves a family whether or not they were met with acceptance. Sean's grandparents and other relatives had traveled difficult paths of their own, from clinging to deeply ingrained ideas that fostered nonacceptance to choosing the love that made such nonacceptance untenable.

We can all learn from those who have broken free of the narrow constraints of the traditional family, and been able instead to recognize that our essential human bonds transcend any particular family structure and exist in many forms. Those who truly embrace this perspective create the living embodiment of eight-year-old Danielle's view that a family is people who "love each other, understand each other, and help each other out." Like Sean's family, as a society we face a moment when both the opportunity and the necessity to make this move are upon us.

When I first set out to write these closing words, I wanted to tell the story of Sean's family as an analogue to wider societal change. In some ways it is. In recent years some courts have begun to look to the quality of relationships rather than the conventions of heterosexuality to determine what counts as a family. More families, like Sean's, are able to appreciate the diversity both within and beyond their bounds. And many children of lesbians and gay men face the world with pride rather than shame.

But to present the transformation of Sean's family as analogue would be naïve, for it would leave out too much: just recently in Virginia, Sharon Bottoms' mother pursued and won custody of her grandchild on the grounds that Sharon's lesbianism rendered her an unfit parent. In New Hampshire, Jim and Craig, as an openly gay couple, could not have adopted Sean. And in most schools and libraries across the country, the children of lesbians and gay men find no images of themselves and their families. So despite my wish, I must offer the story of Sean's family, not as analogue, but as vision, in a spirit of hope.

As many relegate lesbian and gay struggles to the realm of special-interest advocacy rather than a fight for civil rights, the destructive force of homophobia rages on, unchecked. Perhaps most distressing is the extent to which this occurs in the name of the best interests of the children, with millions of kids thus ravaged by those who claim to be protecting them. The stories of Minnie Bruce Pratt and her sons, Don and David's first foster children, and Kristen and Janine are testament to the destruction that homophobia causes in the lives of children and their families. Yet our society is a long way from acknowledging homophobia as a form of hatred and prejudice as damaging as any other kind of bigotry.

Almost fifteen years ago I was isolated and riddled with conflict, caught between two passions that seemed irreconcilable: my lesbianism and my desire for motherhood. The journey I began from that place took me through rich and varied conversations with others navigating similar territory. Along the way I have been privy to, and tried to document, a few key struggles of our time—some lost, some triumphant, but all still pending. I believe the stories of the New Hampshire gay-adoption ban and Sharon Bottoms' custody loss are not over. By the same token, I believe the five-year struggle over the Massachusetts ban on gay foster parents could easily recur, with less optimal outcome. While there is room for hope, there is no room for complacency in this time of great promise yet equally great danger.

This book is the fruit of my journey, but it is premised on the often painful and courageous journeys of others. If not for the many parents who found the strength to come out, and the lesbians and gay men who set forth to raise children, there would be no story of lesbian and gay parents to tell. Furthermore, without the examples of those who have striven to change themselves and their communities, I would not have had the wherewithal to even try to tell it. At the same time, I am acutely aware that for every story told there is a corresponding silence—a story hidden out of fear and, even worse, a story never brought to fruition. This is what saddens me most as I feel the other fruit of my journey—a life about to begin, kicking inside me. Looking toward her future, I know we have much work to do. Bringing an optimism tempered by realism, I join Minnie Bruce Pratt and countless others on a journey toward an unknown place.

Notes

Chapter 1. Journey

2 *Derived from the Latin* *The American Heritage Dictionary* (Boston: Houghton Mifflin Company, 1982), 674.

5 *Australian Toyota dealers* Tim Redmond, "Gay Car Ads Down Under," *Boston Phoenix*, January 24, 1992, 2.

8 *As this book goes to press* See: Steven Lee Meyers, "Trustees Seize Queens District That Rejected Gay Lessons," *New York Times*, December 3, 1992, p. B1; James Clay, "Working With Lesbian and Gay Parents and Their Children," *Young Children* (March 1990): 31–35.

9 *Researchers found no differences* Susan Golombok et al., "Children in Lesbian and Single-Parent Households: Psychosexual and Psychiatric Appraisal," *Child Psychology and Psychiatry* 24, no. 4 (1983): 551–72; Beverly Hoeffer, "Children's Acquisition of Sex Role Behavior in Lesbian Mother Families," *American Journal of Orthopsychiatry* 51, no. 3 (1981): 536–44; Martha Kilpatrick, et al. "Lesbian Mothers and Their Children: A Com-

parative Survey," *American Journal of Orthopsychiatry* 51, no. 3 (1981): 545–51; Sally Kweskin and Alicia Cook, "Heterosexual and Homosexual Mothers' Self-Described Sex Role Behavior and Ideal Sex Role Behavior in Children," *Sex Roles* 8, no. 9 (1982): 967–75; Ellen Lewin, "Lesbianism and Motherhood: Implications for Child Custody," *Human Organization* 40 (1981): 6–13; Jane Mandel et al., "The Lesbian Parent: Comparison of Heterosexual and Homosexual Mothers and Their Children," paper presented at the American Psychological Association, 1979; Judith Miller et al., "The Child's Home Environment for Lesbian Versus Heterosexual Mothers: A Neglected Area of Research," *Journal of Homosexuality* 7, no. 1 (1981): 49–56; Mildred Pagelow, "Heterosexual and Lesbian Single Mothers: A Comparison of Problems, Coping, and Solutions," *Journal of Homosexuality* 5, no. 3 (1980): 551–72; Catherine Rand et al., "Psychological Health and Factors the Court Seeks to Control in Lesbian Mother Custody Trials," *Journal of Homosexuality* 8, no. 1 (1982): 27–39.

10 *Lesbian and gay parents still* There is a growing body of more diverse research as well. See Charlotte Patterson, "Children of Lesbian and Gay Parents," *Child Development* 63, no. 5 (October 1992): 1025–42.

Chapter 2. Toward an Unknown Place:
Parents Come Out

16 *"I can only pray . . ."* Minnie Bruce Pratt, "Poem For My Sons," in *Crime Against Nature* (Ithaca, N.Y.: Firebrand Books, 1990), 14.

21 *Women like Minnie Bruce were* Adrienne Rich, *Of Woman Born: Motherhood as Experience and Institution* (New York: Norton, 1976), 195.

"We fell into what I felt . . ." Ibid., 194–95.

25 *"While mother's homosexuality may be . . ."* Collins v. Collins, WL 30137 Tenn.App. 1988, cited and quoted in David S. Dooley, "Immoral Because They're Bad, Bad Because They're Wrong: Sexual Orientation and Presumptions of Parental Unfitness in Custody Disputes," *California Western Law Review* 26 (1990): 410.

"I don't say that a mother cannot be fit . . ." Towend v. Towend, 1 Family Law Reporter 2830 (1975), Ohio Ct. C.P., Portage County, March 14, 1975, cited and quoted in Nan Hunter and Nancy Polikoff, "Custody Rights of Lesbian Mothers: Legal

Theory and Litigation Strategy," *Buffalo Law Review* 25 (1976): 697.

32 *Before 1974 there were virtually no* R. A. Basile, "Lesbian Mothers I," *Women's Rights Law Reporter* 2 (1974): 3–18.

33 *Not surprisingly, one researcher* Ellen Lewin, "Lesbianism and Motherhood: Implications for Child Custody," *Human Organization* 40, no. 1 (Spring 1981), 10.

Chapter 3. In The Halls of Justice?
Lesbian and Gay Parents Enter the Courts

34 *"That life is complicated . . ."* Patricia J. Williams, *The Alchemy of Race and Rights* (Cambridge, Mass.: Harvard University Press, 1991): 10–11.

38 *The judge said that this move* In The Matter Of Tammy F., 1 Civil No. 32648, California 1st Appellate District Division 2, August 21, 1973, reported in "Custody and Homosexual Parents," *Women's Rights Law Reporter* 2 (1974): 21; cited and quoted in Nan Hunter and Nancy Polikoff, "Custody Rights of Lesbian Mothers: Legal Theory and Litigation Strategy, *Buffalo Law Review* 25 (1976): 712.

39 *"I would caution Miss Schuster and Miss Isaacson . . . "* Schuster v. *Schuster*, No. 36876, Wash. Superior Court, King County, September 3, 1974, reported in *1 Family Law Reporter* 2004 (1974), cited and quoted in Hunter and Polikoff, pp. 700–701.

In many instances, simply the parent's openness Ashling v. *Ashling*, 42 Or. App. 47, 599 p. 2d 475 (1979), cited and quoted in Annamay T. Sheppard, "Lesbian Mothers II: Long Night's Journey Into Day," *Women's Rights Law Reporter* 8, no. 4 (Fall 1985), 242.

As one judge opined S.E.G. v. R.A.G., 735S.W.2d164 (Mo. Ct. App. 1987), cited and quoted in David S. Dooley, "Immoral Because They're Bad, Bad Because They're Wrong: Sexual Orientation and Presumptions of Parental Unfitness in Custody Disputes," *California Western Law Review* 26 (1990): 410.

40 *In one of the earliest documented* Nadler v. *Nadler*, No. 177331, California Superior Court, Sacramento County, November 1967, cited and discussed in Hunter and Polikoff, pp. 695–96; also cited and discussed in Donna Hitchens and Barbara Price, "Trial Strategy in Lesbian Mother Custody Cases: The Use of Expert Testimony," *Golden Gate University Law Review* 9 (1978–79): 453–54.

40 *However, on appeal a higher court* Nadler v. *Superior Court*, 255Cal.App.2d523, 63 California Reporter 352 (1967), cited in Hunter and Polikoff, p. 695; also cited in Hitchens and Price, p. 453.

41 *"At her second trial . . ."* Hitchens and Price, pp. 453–54, citing Reporter's Transcript, Nadler Rehearing, pp. 6–7.

42 *His closing comments* Basile "Lesbian Mothers I, "*Women's Rights Law Reporter* 2 (1974): 23, citing Reporter's Transcript, Nadler Rehearing, pp. 67–68.

43 *Generally judges consider factors such* Hunter and Polikoff, p. 694.

Sometimes custody disputes Hunter and Polikoff, p. 693.

In 1976, Nan Hunter and Nancy Polikoff Hunter and Polikoff, pp. 691–733.

"From this maze . . ." Hunter and Polikoff, p. 694.

44 *"To deprive a parent of custody . . ."* Hunter and Polikoff, pp. 694–95.

45 *Taken to its logical conclusion* Hunter and Polikoff, p. 732.

Prejudice *means both* *Funk and Wagnalls Standard Dictionary* (New York: Harper Paperbacks, 1980), 626.

46 *"If a man also lie . . ."* Leviticus 20:13.

During the Middle Ages Ronald Bayer, *Homosexuality and American Psychiatry: The Politics of Diagnosis* (New York: Basic Books, Inc., 1981), 17. In this discussion of the religious and moral condemnation of homosexuality Bayer draws on Derrick Sherwin Bailey, *Homosexuality and the Western Christian Tradition* (London: Longmans, Green and Co., 1955), 73.

47 *Such was the fate* Montgomery Brower and Angela Blessing, "His Fundamentalist Mother and His Father's Gay Lover Square Off Over Custody of Young Brian Batey," *People Magazine*, November 1987, 113–14; In The Matter Of The Guardianship of Brian Todd Batey, A Minor, Case No. 134,752, Trial Brief on behalf of Craig Corbett, submitted by Carol Sobel, Gregory Marshall, ACLU Foundation of Southern California, Nov. 3, 1987; personal interview with Craig Corbett.

48 *"Homosexuality has been considered . . ."* Collins v. *Collins*, WL 30173 Tenn.App.1988, cited and quoted in Dooley, pp. 414–15.

"It is not a light thing . . ." Spence v. *Durham*, 283 N.C. at 701, 198 S.E. 2nd at 554, cited and quoted in Basile, p. 7.

49 *In 1553*   Marilyn Riley, "The Avowed Lesbian and Her Right to Child Custody: A Challenge That Can No Longer Be Denied," *San Diego Law Review* 12 (1975): 808, citing F. Pollack and F. Maitland, *The History of English Law*, 2nd ed., 1959; see also *Bowers* v. *Hardwick*, 478 U.S. 186 (1986) dissenting opinion of Justice Blackmun joined by Justice Brennan, Justice Marshall, and Justice Stevens, reprinted in William Rubenstein (ed.), *Lesbians, Gay Men and the Law* (New York: New Press, 1993): 143.

50 *"The commission of certain homosexual acts . . ."*   *Chaffin* v. *Frye*, 45Cal.App.3d39, 119 Cal. Reporter 22 (2d District 1975), cited and quoted in Hitchens and Price, pp. 459–60.

51 *Though some argue*   Dooley, p. 419.

In fact, in many cases   "Custody Denials to Parents in Same-Sex Relationships: An Equal Protection Analysis," *Harvard Law Review* 102 (1989): 635.

52 *At the beginning of the 1960s*   Rubenstein, p. 87, citing "Survey of the Law: Survey of the Constitutional Right to Privacy in the Context of Homosexual Activity," *University of Miami Law Review* 40 (1986), citing "The Constitutionality of Sodomy Statutes," *Fordham Law Review* 45 (1977).

By 1980 only half the states   Rubenstein, p. 87 (same cites as above).

Despite the steadily diminishing number   *Bowers* v. *Hardwick*, 478U.S.186 (1986).

In the nineteenth century   My discussion of the psychological perspective on homosexuality as pathology is drawn from Ronald Bayer, *Homosexuality and American Psychiatry: The Politics of Diagnosis* (New York: Basic Books, Inc., 1981): 18–66, 100–54.

53 *"Homosexuality is assuredly no advantage . . ."*   Sigmund Freud, reprinted in Paul Friedman, "Sexual Deviations," in Silvano Arieti (ed.), *American Handbook of Psychiatry*, Vol. 1 (New York: Basic Books, 1959): 606–607, cited in Bayer, p. 27.

In the 1940s   Bayer, pp. 27–33.

Following this line of thought   Irving Bieber et al., *Homosexuality: A Psychoanalytic Study of Male Homosexuals* (New York: Basic Books, 1962): 18, cited in Bayer, p. 30.

From this work   Bieber, p. 173, cited in Bayer, pp. 30–31.

Notes

54 *"Homosexuality is based . . ."* Charles Socarides, *The Overt Homosexual* (New York: Grune and Stratton, 1968): 8, cited in Bayer, p. 36.

Alfred Kinsey's 1948 study Alfred Kinsey et al., *Sexual Behavior in the Human Male* (Philadelphia: Saunders, 1948), cited and discussed in Bayer, pp. 42–46.

Instead he believed Kinsey, p. 660, cited in Bayer, p. 44.

This perspective was supported Bayer, pp. 46–47. Bayer cites Cleland Ford and Frank Beach, *Patterns Of Sexual Behavior* (New York: Harper and Brothers, 1951).

In 1954, from within the psychiatric profession Evelyn Hooker, "The Adjustment of the Male Overt Homosexual," *Journal of Projective Techniques* 21 (1957), cited and discussed in Bayer, pp. 49–53.

55 *"The psychiatric perspective . . ."* Thomas Szaz, *The Manufacture of Madness* (New York: Delta Books, 1970): 170, cited and discussed in Bayer, p. 59.

"Psychiatric preoccupation . . ." Szaz, p. 168, cited in Bayer, p. 59.

56 *In the first edition* Bayer, pp. 39–40.

In 1968, the revised DSM II Bayer, p. 40.

Finally, in 1973 the American Psychiatric Association Bayer, p. 194.

Eventually, psychiatric discourse American Psychiatric Association, *Diagnostic and Statistical Manual, DSM III-R* (Washington, D.C.: APA, 1987).

57 *For instance, in the Nadler appeal* Hitchens and Price, p. 454, citing Reporter's Transcript, Nadler Rehearing, p. 50.

"Added to the insult . . ." H v. H., N.J. Super. 227, 157 A.2d 72 (1959), cited and quoted in Basile, p. 8.

58 *Hitchens and Price identified* Hitchens and Price, pp. 451–79.

He said that if Smith v. Smith, Civ. No. 125497 (Superior Court of California, County of Stanislaus (1978), cited in Donna Hitchens, "Social Attitudes, Legal Standards and Personal Trauma in Child Custody Cases," *Journal of Homosexuality* 5 (1979–80): 90–91.

"ATTORNEY: Doctor, you . . ." In re Risher, Texas Domestic Relations Court, Dallas County, April 16, 1976, reprinted in

Clifford Gay Gibson, *By Her Own Admission: A Lesbian Mother's Fight to Keep Her Son* (New York: Doubleday, 1977), cited and discussed in Hitchens and Price, pp. 457–58.

60 *The judge reasoned* In re Nicholson (docket number unavailable, case sealed by court), Iowa District Court, Iowa County, November 1974, cited and discussed in Hitchens and Price, pp. 456–57.

61 *In one case a judge* Hitchens and Price, p. 458, citing In re Mathews (docket number unavailable, case sealed by court), California Superior Court, Santa Clara County, 1975.

63 *In the same case* In re Nicholson, Iowa District Court, Iowa County, November 1974, cited and discussed in Hitchens and Price, p. 460.

"The conditions under which . . ." Roe v. Roe, 228Va.722, 728,324, S.E.2d 691,694 (1985), cited and quoted in *Harvard Law Review* 102 (1989): 620.

"Living in the same house . . ." Jacobson, 314 N.W. 2d, cited and quoted in *Harvard Law Review* 102 (1989): 620.

64 *As with the question of sexual orientation* Hitchens and Price, p. 468.

65 *"The father's evident . . ."* Palmore v. Sidoti. This quote is the High Court's recitation of the state proceedings, taken from the state-level App. to Pet for Cert., pp. 26–27. The High Court case is *Palmore v. Sidoti*, 104 S.Ct. (1984), p. 1879, cited and discussed in Annamay T. Sheppard, "Lesbian Mothers II: Long Night's Journey Into Day," *Women's Rights Law Reporter* 8, no. 4 (Fall 1985): 245.

"It would ignore . . ." Palmore v. Sidoti, 104 S.Ct. (1984), p. 1881, cited and discussed in Sheppard, p. 246.

66 *"It is impermissible . . ."* S.N.E. v. R.L.B., 699P.2d876 (Alaska Sup.Ct. 1985), quoted and discussed in Dooley, p. 418.

"Within the context . . ." M.P. v. S.P., 169N.J.Super.425, 404A.2d1256 (App. Div. 1979), quoted and discussed in Sheppard, p. 242.

68 *"Could she harm . . ."* Hitchens and Price, p. 454, citing Reporter's Transcript, Nadler Rehearing, p. 50.

69 *Legal experts suggest* Georgia Dullea, "AIDS and Divorce: A New Legal Arena," *New York Times*, September 21, 1987, p. B17; Roberta Achtenberg, "AIDS and Child Custody: A Guide to Advocacy, "National Center For Lesbian Rights (1989); Michael

T. Isbell, "HIV and Family Law," Lambda Legal Defense and Educational Fund (1992); Nancy Mahon, "Public Hysteria, Private Conflict: Child Custody and Visitation Disputes Involving an H.I.V. Infected Parent," *New York University Law Review* 63 (November 1988): 1092–141; Rhonda Rivera, "Lawyers, Clients, and AIDS: Some Notes from the Trenches," *Ohio State Law Journal* 49 (1989): 883–928; Aline Cole Barrett and Michelle Flint, "The Effect of AIDS on Child Custody Determination, "*Gonzaga Law Review* 23 (1987–88): 167–91.

69 *AIDS and HIV status* See above cites.

In a 1986 Chicago case E. R. Shipp, "AIDS Test at issue in Homosexual's Bid to Have Children Visit," *New York Times*, April 28, 1986. The wife's lawyer eventually dropped the request for HIV testing, as reported in "AIDS Looms as an Issue in Visits by Fathers," *New York Times*, October 5, 1986, p. 33.

Mandatory testing Isbell, pp. 12–13.

More commonly, decisions Doe v. Roe, 526 N.Y.S. 2d 718, cited and discussed in Isbell, p. 13.

That's the situation This account is based on personal interviews; the names have been changed in my account; see also *Doe* v. *Roe*, Civil Action No. 28094, Circuit Ct., Montgomery County, Md. (May 4, 1988).

72 *Numerous studies* A. Lifson, "Do Alternative Modes for Transmission of Human Immunodeficiency Virus Exist?" *Journal of the American Medical Association* 259 (1988); G. Friedland and R. Klein, "Transmission of the Human Immunodeficiency Virus," *New England Journal of Medicine* 317 (1987): 1125, 1132, cited in Achtenberg, p. 8.

Studies of families of AIDS Friedland and Klein, p. 1133, cited and quoted in Achtenberg, p. 9.

He denied the father Stewart v. Stewart, 521 N.E. 2d 956 (Indiana App. 1988), quoted and discussed in Isbell, p. 15.

In fact, an ongoing relationship E. Furman *A Child's Parent Dies: Studies in Childhood Bereavement* 18 (1974), cited and discussed in Achtenberg, p. 20.

73 *She saw Elliot* Doe v. Roe, Civil Action No. 28094, Circuit Ct., Montgomery County, Md. (May 4, 1988), p. 6.

74 *Both* per se *decisions* Riley, pp. 829–38.

75 *Along these lines* Riley, pp. 821–29.

75 *However, several scholars argue* "The Constitutional Status of Sexual Orientation: Homosexuality as a Suspect Classification," *Harvard Law Review* 98 (1985): 1303.

Another potential approach "Custody Denials To Parents in Same-Sex Relationships," pp. 626–29.

76 *In many custody decisions* Riley, pp. 842–48.

"Americans are guaranteed . . ." Riley, p. 856.

While the right to privacy Riley, p. 838.

77 *"Fundamental rights . . ."* In re J., S. and C., 129 N.J. Super. 486, 324 A.2d 90 (Ch. 1974), quoted and discussed in Hunter and Polikoff, pp. 704–705.

However, as Hunter and Polikoff described Hunter and Polikoff, p. 704.

Without explaining what anguish Hunter and Polikoff, p. 705.

78 *"Where neglect, abuse . . ."* Bennett v. Clemens, 230 Ga. 317, 196 S.E.2d (1973) 846, quoted and discussed in Riley, p. 819.

79 *At this writing* As of 1994, information provided by the National Center for Lesbian Rights listed equivalent of *per se* rulings in Arkansas, Kentucky, Missouri, Oklahoma, and Virginia.

80 *As an example, Gil de Lamadrid* Lamberson v. Lamberson, Court of Appeals No. 1202321, Michigan Court of Appeals.

Chapter 4. Save Our Children: Foster Care and Adoption Struggles

83 *In 1977* Dennis Williams, "Homosexuals: Anita Bryant's Crusade," *Newsweek*, April 11, 1977, pp. 39–40.

In 1977, Dade County Ibid.

But within five weeks Tom Mathews, Tony Fuller, and Holly Camp, "Battle Over Gay Rights," *Newsweek*, June 6, 1977, p. 20.

Referring to homosexuals Ibid, p. 22.

84 *On June 7, 1977* Randy Shilts, *The Mayor of Castro Street* (New York: St. Martin's, 1982), 157.

The very next day "More Cities Face Battles Over Homosexual Rights," *New York Times*, May 28, 1978, p. 36.

During the next year Ibid.

84 *"You can act . . ."* John Briggs as quoted in Shilts, pp. 238–41.

85 *On November 8,* Shilts, p. 249.

Just two weeks later Wallace Turner, "San Francisco Mayor is Slain; City Supervisor Also Killed; Ex-Official Gives Up to Police," *New York Times,* November 28, 1978, p. 1.

"If a bullet . . ." Harvey Milk as quoted in Shilts (Epigraph).

86 *In 1985, Dan White* Nancy Skelton and Mark Stein, "Slayer of Moscone and Milk Kills Himself in San Francisco," *Los Angeles Times,* October 22, 1985.

It all began This account of the Massachusetts foster-care debates is based on interviews with Don Babets and David Jean, *Boston Globe* accounts, and interviews with Kevin Cathcart and Gay and Lesbian Defense Committee activists; the names of the foster children involved have been changed.

88 *On Thursday, May 8, 1985* Kenneth Cooper, "Some Oppose Foster Placement with Gay Couple," *Boston Globe,* May 8, 1985, p. 21.

89 *In a statement to the press* Kenneth Cooper, "Policy Sought on Placement in Gay Homes," *Boston Globe,* May 10, 1985, p. 1.

The existing guidelines Kenneth Cooper, "Placement of Foster Children with Gay Couple Is Revoked," *Boston Globe,* May 5, 1985, p. 1.

There was no explicit reference Kenneth Cooper, "Gay Foster Parenting: Debate Grows," *Boston Globe,* May 12, 1985, p. 1.

Caught between the obvious discrimination Cooper, May 10, 1985.

90 *The Gay and Lesbian Advocacy and Defense* Chris Black, "Gay Couple Challenges State's Removal of Foster Children," *Boston Globe,* May 11, 1985, p. 1.

The Unitarian Church Cooper, May 10, 1985.

On the other hand, Archbishop Bernard Law Cooper, May 12, 1985.

91 *Juvenile Court Chief Justice* Cooper, May 12, 1985.

Two state representatives Cooper, May 10, 1985.

"place children in need . . ." Senator David Locke as quoted in Kenneth Cooper, "Officials Check Other States' Policies on Foster Care," *Boston Globe,* May 16, 1985, p. 15.

At the time of the review Kay Longcope, "States' Policies Differ on Issue of Gay Foster Parents," *Boston Globe,* May 12, 1985.

91   *The Massachusetts House*   Kenneth Cooper, "House Votes to Ban Gay Foster Parents," *Boston Globe*, May 24, 1985, p. 1.

92   *"This administration . . ."*   Philip Johnston, as quoted in Kenneth Cooper, "New Policy on Foster Care," *Boston Globe*, May 25, 1985, p. 1.

   Johnston made a point   Andrew Blake, "Foster Placement Policy Inconsistent, Frank Says," *Boston Globe*, July 6, 1985, p. 21.

   At this point, Johnston   Kenneth Cooper, "Policy Debate on Gay Foster Care Is Just Beginning," *Boston Globe*, May 26, 1985, p. 22.

93   *There was a 25-percent shortage*   Cooper, May 10, 1985.

   Immediately following   Interviews with GLDC activists; also Cooper, May 26, 1985.

94   *In the last one*   Interview with Don Babets and David Jean.

   In an unprecedented moment   Kenneth Cooper and Donna Bryson, "Gay Rights Activists Vow to Step up Campaign Against Foster-Care Policy," *Boston Globe*, June 22, 1985, p. 21; Kenneth Cooper, "Gay Foster Care Policy Rapped at Hearing," *Boston Globe*, August 23, 1985, p. 21.

   Nonetheless, Governor Dukakis   Cooper, May 26, 1985.

95   *"We understood that . . ."*   Interview with Marla Erlien, a GLDC member.

96   *It became increasingly clear*   Kirk Sharfenberg, "Foster Care and the 'New' Dukakis," *Boston Globe*, June 2, 1985, p. A2.

   Don and David were joined   My account of the meeting is based on interviews with participants.

98   *It was not until*   Interviews with Kevin Cathcart and Don Babets and David Jean.

99   *The floor debate*   Transcript of proceedings, May 7, 1987.

   On that occasion   John Milne, "Starting Today, N.H. Bars Gay Foster Parents," *Boston Globe*, July 24, 1987, p. 13.

100   *"Now that summer . . ."*   Betsy Janeway, "An Evil Law That Denies Children a Good Home," *Boston Globe*, July 29, 1991, p. 11.

101   *Perhaps less predictable*   This account is based largely on personal interviews with Ed Seebol.

103   *In Florida at the time*   "Kids Need Good Homes; Some Are Gay Homes," *Palm Beach Post*, March 25, 1991, p. 8A.

103 *The ACLU has not always considered* Vern Bullough, "Lesbian-ism, Homosexuality, and the American Civil Liberties Union," *Journal of Homosexuality* 13, no. 1 (Fall 1986): 23–33.

In March 1991 Fran Hathaway, "Can a Home Be Happy, and Gay?" *Palm Beach Post*, March 24, 1991.

Chapter 5. Choosing Children:
Biological Parenting

108 *Underneath the headline* Kris Hundley, "The Lesbian Baby Boom," *Hartford Advocate*, March 7, 1988, p. 16.

111 *In a recent* New York Times Margaret O'Brien Steinfels, "Gay and Conservative," *New York Times*, December 12, 1993, p. 28.

112 *During his 1992 campaign* Michael Kranish, "Swipe at 'Murphy' Snarls White House," *Boston Globe*, May 21, 1992, p. 16.

113 *In 1884, according to* This story of Dr. William Pancoast has been recounted in several sources; its veracity has been questioned by some. See Elizabeth Noble, *Having Your Baby By Donor Insemination* (Boston: Houghton-Mifflin, 1987), 87–88, citing A. D. Hard, "Artificial Impregnation," *Medical World* 27 (1909): 163.

114 *In one major text* Barbara Kritchevsky, "The Unmarried Woman's Right to Artificial Insemination: A Call for an Expanded Definition," *Harvard Women's Law Journal* 4 (1981): 2, citing W. Finegold, *Artificial Insemination*, 2nd ed. 1976, 1st ed 1964.

115 *Among the first legal questions* Kritchevsky, p. 19.

116 *Father status thus* Ibid.

Significantly, in many states Kritchevsky, p. 3; Maria Gil de Lamadrid (ed.), "Lesbians Choosing Motherhood: Legal Implications of Donor Insemination and Co-Parenting" (National Center for Lesbian Rights, (San Francisco, 1991), 8.

117 *A study done in 1979* Kritchevsky, p. 16, citing Curie-Cohen, Luttrell, and Shapiro, "Current Practice of Artificial Insemination by Donor in the United States," *New England Journal of Medicine* 585 (1979).

118 *In practice, the anonymity* Gil de Lamadrid, p. 1.

During the late 1970s Interview with Barbara Raboy, director of the Sperm Bank of California (Oakland).

119 *Despite the fact that* Noble, p. 90.

131 *Surrogacy has been practiced* Martha Field, *Surrogate Motherhood* (Cambridge, Mass.: Harvard University Press, 1988), 5–11.

132 *Mary Beth Whitehead* Field, p. 3,

While there is little legislation Field, p. 157.

133 *The guidelines that minimize* Field, p. 172.

Chapter 7. A Rose by Any Other Name

166 *"We walked down the path . . ."* Helen Keller, *The Story of My Life* (New York: Penguin, 1988), 18.

185 *"Whatever is unnamed . . ."* Adrienne Rich, *On Lies, Secrets, and Silence: Selected Prose 1966–1978* (New York: Norton, 1979), 199, 308.

Chapter 8. What the Children Must Learn:
Facing Homophobia

186 *"What the grown-ups can't teach . . ."* Adrienne Rich, "Eastern War Time," in *An Atlas of the Difficult World* (New York: Norton, 1991) 38.

205 Heather Has Two Mommies Lesléa Newman, *Heather Has Two Mommies* (Boston: Alyson Publications, 1989).

206 *At Bank Street College* Virginia Caspar, Steven Schultz, and Elaine Wickens, "Breaking the Silences: Lesbian and Gay Parents and the Schools," *Teachers College Record*, 94, no. 1 (Fall 1992): 109–37.

210 *That paragraph offered* Michael Willhoite, *Daddy's Roommate* (Boston: Alyson Publications, 1991); Lesléa Newman, *Heather Has Two Mommies* (Boston: Alyson Publications, 1989).

211 *"It is a waste of time . . ."* Audre Lorde, "Good Mirrors Are Not Cheap," in *Chosen Poems: Old and New* (New York: Norton, 1982), 43.

Chapter 9. Children At Risk: The Legal
Limbo of the Reinvented Family

212 *One November weekend* Karen Thompson and Julie Andrzekewski, *Why Can't Sharon Kowalski Come Home?* (San Francisco: Spinsters, 1988).

214 *Janine and Joan* This account is based on interviews with Janine Ratcliffe, Kristen Pearlman, Karen Amlong, and Judge

Robert Scott, as well as letters, newspaper accounts, and court documents.

226 *Judge Scott found that* In re the Interest of Kristen Janine Pearlman, Case No. 87-24926 DA, Circuit Court of 17th Judicial Circuit, Broward County, Fla., March 31, 1989.

228 *"Uncharted legal waters"* Sabol v. Bowling, No.CF27,024 (Cal. Super.Ct., Los Angeles Cty, January 1990), Memorandum of Intended Decision, p. 8.

Michele had always wanted This account is based on interviews with Michele Graham as well as documented accounts: *Nancy S. v. Michele G.*, 279 California Reporter 212 (Ct. App. 1991), reprinted in Rubenstein (ed.), p. 554. The names of the children have been changed.

231 *Repeatedly, as cases like Michele's* Nancy Polikoff, "This Child Does Have Two Mothers: Redefining Parenthood to Meet the Needs of Children in Lesbian-Mother and Other Nontraditional Families," *Georgetown Law Journal* 78 (1990): 459–575. This article deals extensively with the issues discussed in this chapter.

234 *The* Loftin *v.* Flourney *decision* Loftin v. Flourney, No. 569630-7 (California Super. Court. Alameda County, January 2, 1985).

235 *But as one legal expert* Nancy Polikoff, "This Child Does Have Two Mothers," *Georgetown Law Journal* 78 (1990): 572.

236 *"No matter how this court . . ."* Sabol v. Bowling, No. CF27024 (Cal.Super.Ct., Los Angeles Cty., January 1990), Memorandum of Intended Decision, p. 8.

237 *The New York court ruled* Kevin Sack, "Lesbian Loses a Ruling on Parent's Rights," *New York Times*, May 3, 1991, p. B1.

"We decline to read . . ." Matter of Alison D., Court of Appeals, New York State, May 2, 1991.

The most ironic aspect Braschi v. Stahl Assocs., 74 NY2d 201, 211–213.

238 *"The impact of today's decision . . ."* Judge Judith S. Kaye, dissenting in the Matter of Alison D., Court of Appeals, New York State, May 2, 1991.

To date there have been David Margolick, "Lesbian Child-Custody Cases Test Frontiers of Family Law," *New York Times*, July 4, 1990, p. 1.

242 *The language of the decision*   C.M. v. C.C., 152 N.J. Super. 160, 377 A.2d 821 (Cumberland County Court, 1977), quoted and discussed in Barbara Kritchevsky, "The Unmarried Woman's Right to Artificial Insemination: A Call for an Expanded Definition," *Harvard Women's Law Journal* 4 (1981): 13–16.

243 *That is just what happened*   This account is based on interviews with Robin Young, Sandy Russo, and legal proceedings from *Thomas* v. *Robin Y.*, P3884/91, Family Court of New York State, County of New York; and newspaper accounts including Victoria Brownworth, "Family Intervention," *Village Voice*, December 15, 1992, p. 28; Dennis Hevesi, "Court Rejects Sperm Donor in a Bid for Parental Rights," *New York Times*, April 16, 1993, p. B3.

249 *Recently, lesbian and gay parents*   My discussion of second-parent adoptions is drawn from interviews with Laura Solomon and Victoria Lane, as well as the following articles: Emily Patt, "Second Parent Adoption: When Crossing the Marital Barrier Is in a Child's Best Interests," *Berkeley Women's Law Journal* 95 (1988); Carrie Bashaw, "Protecting Children in Nontraditional Families: Second Parent Adoptions in Washington," *University of Puget Sound Law Review* 13 (1990): 321–47; Elizabeth Zuckerman, "Second Parent Adoption for Lesbian-Parented Families: Legal Recognition of the Other Mother," *University of California, Davis Law Review* 19 (1986): 729–59.

253 *As the judge who had granted*   Deb Price, "For Once, the Law Offers a Safety Net to a Gay Family," *Detroit News*, December 30, 1993.

Bibliography

Achtenberg, Roberta. *AIDS and Child Custody: A Guide to Advocacy.* San Francisco: National Center for Lesbian Rights, 1989.

Alpert, Harriet, ed. *We Are Everywhere: Writings By and About Lesbian Parents.* Freedom: The Crossing Press, 1988.

Barret, Robert, and Bryan Robinson. *Gay Fathers.* Lexington: Lexington Books, 1990.

Barrett, Aline Cole, and Michelle Flint. "The Effect of AIDS on Child Custody Determination." *Gonzaga Law Review*, Vol. 23, 1987–88.

Bartholet, Elizabeth. *Family Bonds: Adoption and the Politics of Parenting.* Boston: Houghton Mifflin Company, 1993.

Bashaw, Carrie. "Protecting Children in Nontraditional Families: Second Parent Adoptions in Washington." *University of Puget Sound Law Review*, Vol. 13, 1990.

Basile, R.A. "Lesbian Mothers I." *Women's Rights Law Reporter*, Vol. 2, 1974.

Bayer, Ronald. *Homosexuality and American Psychiatry.* New York: Basic Books, 1981.

Beam, Joseph, ed. *In the Life: A Black Gay Anthology.* Boston: Alyson Publications, 1986.

Bosche, Susanne. *Jenny Lives with Eric and Martin.* London: Gay Men's Press, 1981.

Bozett, Frederick W., ed. *Gay and Lesbian Parents.* New York: Praeger, 1987.

———. *Homosexuality and the Family.* New York: Harrington Park Press, 1989.

Bullough, Vern. "Lesbianism, Homosexuality, and the American Civil Liberties Union." *Journal of Homosexuality* 13 (Fall 1981).

Burke, Phyllis. *Family Values: Two Moms and Their Son.* New York: Random House, 1993.

Caspar, Virginia, Steven Schultz, and Elaine Wickens. "Breaking The Silences: Lesbian and Gay Parents and the Schools." *Teachers College Record*, Fall 1992.

Coontz, Stephanie. *The Way We Never Were: American Families and the Nostalgia Trap.* New York: Basic Books, 1992.

Dooley, David S. "Immoral Because They're Bad, Bad Because They're Wrong: Sexual Orientation and Presumptions of Parental Unfitness in Custody Disputes." *California Western Law Review*, Vol. 26, 1990.

Field, Martha A. *Surrogate Motherhood: The Legal and Human Issues.* Cambridge: Harvard University Press, 1988.

Gibson, Clifford Gay. *By Her Own Admission: A Lesbian Mother's Fight to Keep Her Son.* New York: Doubleday, 1977.

Gil de Lamadrid, Maria, ed. *Lesbians Choosing Motherhood: Legal Implications of Donor Insemination and Co-Parenting.* San Francisco: National Center for Lesbian Rights, 1991.

Golombok, Susan, Ann Spencer, and Michael Rutter. "Children in Lesbian and Single-Parent Households: Psychosexual and Psychiatric Appraisal." *Child Psychology and Psychiatry* 24 (1983): 551–72.

Hanscombe, Gillian E., and Jackie Forster. *Rocking the Cradle: Lesbian Mothers, A Challenge in Family Living.* Boston: Alyson Publications, 1981.

Harbeck, Karen M., ed. *Coming Out of the Classroom Closet: Gay and Lesbian Students, Teachers, and Curricula.* New York: Harrington Park Press, 1992.

Harvard Law Review. "Custody Denials to Parents in Same-Sex Relationships: An Equal Protection Analysis." Vol. 102, 1989.

Harvard Law Review. "The Constitutional Status of Sexual Orientation: Homosexuality as a Suspect Classification." Vol. 98, 1985.

Hemphill, Essex, and Joseph Beam, eds. *Brother to Brother: New Writings by Black Gay Men.* Boston: Alyson Publications, 1991.

Hill, Marjorie. "Child-Rearing Attitudes of Black Lesbian Mothers," in the Boston Lesbian Psychologies Collective, eds. *Lesbian Psychologies.* Illinois: University of Illinois Press, 1987.

Hitchens, Donna. "Social Attitudes, Legal Standards and Personal Trauma in Child Custody Cases." *Journal of Homosexuality* 5 (1979–80).

Hitchens, Donna, and Barbara Price. "Trial Strategy in Lesbian Mother

Custody Cases: The Use of Expert Testimony." *Golden Gate University Law Review*, Vol. 9, 1978–79.

Hoeffer, Beverly. "Children's Acquisition of Sex-Role Behavior in Lesbian Mother Families." *American Journal of Orthopsychiatry* 51, no. 3 (July 1981).

Hunter, Nan, and Nancy Polikoff. "Custody Rights of Lesbian Mothers: Legal Theory and Litigation Strategy." *Buffalo Law Review*, Vol. 25, 1976.

Isbell, Michael T. *HIV and Family Law.* New York: Lambda Legal Defense and Education Fund, 1992.

Jullion, Jeanne. *Long Way Home: The Odyssey of a Lesbian Mother and Her Children.* San Francisco: Cleis Press, 1985.

Keller, Helen. *The Story of My Life.* New York: Penguin Books, 1988.

Kirkpatrick, Martha, Catherine Smith, and Ron Roy. "Lesbian Mothers and Their Children: A Comparative Survey." *The American Journal of Orthopsychiatry* 51, No. 3 (1981).

Kritchevsky, Barbara. "The Unmarried Woman's Right to Artificial Insemination: A Call for an Expanded Definition." *Harvard Women's Law Journal*, Vol. 4, 1981.

Kweskin, Sally, and Alicia Cook. "Heterosexual and Homosexual Mothers' Self-Described Sex Role Behavior and Ideal Sex Role Behavior in Children." *Sex Roles* 8, No. 9 (1982).

Lewin, Ellen. "Lesbianism and Motherhood: Implications for Child Custody." *Human Organization* 40 (1981).

Lorde, Audre. *Chosen Poems Old and New.* New York: W.W. Norton and Company, 1982.

Maggiore, Dolores J., ed. *Lesbians and Child Custody: A Casebook.* New York: Garland Publications, 1992.

Mahon, Nancy. "Public Hysteria, Private Conflict: Child Custody and Visitation Disputes Involving an HIV Infected Parent." *New York University Law Review*, Vol. 63, November 1988.

Mandel, Jane, et al. "The Lesbian Parent: Comparison of Heterosexual and Homosexual Mothers and Their Children." Paper presented at the American Psychological Association, 1979.

Martin, April. *The Lesbian and Gay Parenting Handbook: Creating and Raising Our Families.* New York: HarperCollins, 1993.

Merritt, Sharyne, and Linda Steiner. *And Baby Makes Two: Motherhood Without Marriage.* New York: Franklin Watts, 1984.

Miller, Judith, Brook Jacobsen, and Jerry Bigner. "The Child's Home Environment for Lesbian versus Heterosexual Mothers: A Neglected Area of Research." *Journal of Homosexuality* 7, No. 1 (1981).

Newman, Lesléa. *Heather Has Two Mommies.* Boston: Alyson Publications, 1989.

Noble, Elizabeth. *Having Your Baby by Donor Insemination: A Complete Resource Guide.* Boston: Houghton Mifflin, 1987.

Pagelow, Mildred. "Heterosexual and Lesbian Single Mothers: A Comparison of Problems, Coping and Solutions." *Journal of Homosexuality* 5, No. 3 (1980).

Patt, Emily. "Second Parent Adoption: When Crossing the Marital Barrier Is In a Child's Best Interests." *Berkely Women's Law Journal*, Vol. 95, 1988.

Patterson, Charlotte. "Children of Lesbian and Gay Parents." *Child Development* 63, No. 5 (October 1992).

Pies, Cheri. *Considering Parenthood: A Workbook for Lesbians.* San Francisco: Spinsters Ink, 1985.

Polikoff, Nancy. "This Child Does Have Two Mothers: Redefining Parenthood to Meet the Needs of Children in Lesbian-Mother and Other Nontraditional Families." *The Georgetown Law Journal*, Vol. 78, 1990.

Pollack, Sandra, and Jean Vaughn, eds. *Politics of the Heart: A Lesbian Parenting Anthology.* Ithaca, N.Y.: Firebrand Books, 1987.

Pratt, Minnie Bruce. *Crime Against Nature.* Ithaca, N.Y.: Firebrand Books, 1990.

———. *Rebellion: Essays 1980–1991.* Ithaca, N.Y.: Firebrand Books, 1991.

Raboy, Barbara. "Secrecy and Openness in Donor Insemination: A New Paradigm." *Politics and the Life Sciences* (August 1993).

Rafkin, Louise, ed. *Different Mothers: Sons and Daughters of Lesbians Talk About Their Lives.* San Francisco: Cleis Press, 1990.

Rand, Catherine, Dee Graham, and Edna Rawlings. "Psychological Health and Factors the Court Seeks to Control in Lesbian Mother Custody Trials." *Journal of Homosexuality* 8, No. 1 (1982).

Rich, Adrienne. *An Atlas of the Difficult World: Poems 1988–1991.* New York: W.W. Norton and Company, 1991.

———. *Of Woman Born.* New York: W.W. Norton and Company, 1986.

———. *On Lies, Secrets, and Silence: Selected Prose 1966–1978.* New York: W.W. Norton and Company, 1979.

Riley, Marilyn. "The Avowed Lesbian and Her Right to Child Custody: A Challenge That Can No Longer Be Denied." *San Diego Law Review*, Vol. 12, 1975.

Rivera, Rhonda. "Lawyers, Clients, and AIDS: Some Notes from the Trenches." *Ohio State Law Journal*, Vol. 49, 1989.

Rubenstein, William, ed. *Lesbians, Gay Men and the Law.* New York: The New Press, 1993.

Schulenburg, Joy. *Gay Parenting: A Complete Guide for Gay Men and Lesbians with Children.* New York: Anchor Books, 1985.

Sheppard, Annamay T. "Lesbian Mothers II: Long Night's Journey into Day." *Women's Rights Law Reporter*, Vol. 8., No. 4, Fall 1985.

Shilts, Randy. *The Mayor of Castro Street: The Life and Times of Harvey Milk.* New York: St. Martin's Press, 1982.

Stein, Terry. "Homosexuality and New Family Forms: Issues in Psychotherapy." *Psychiatric Annals* 18, No. 1 (January 1988).

Bibliography

Thompson, Karen, and Julie Andrzejewski. *Why Can't Sharon Kowalsky Come Home?* San Francisco: Spinsters/Aunt Lute, 1988.

Weston, Kath. *Families We Choose: Lesbians, Gays, Kinship*. New York: Columbia University Press, 1991.

Willhoite, Michael. *Daddy's Roommate*. Boston: Alyson Publications, 1990.

Williams, Patricia J. *The Alchemy of Race and Rights*. Cambridge: Harvard University Press, 1991.

Zuckerman, Elizabeth. "Second Parent Adoption for Lesbian-Parented Families: Legal Recognition of the Other Mother." *University of California Davis Law Review*, Vol. 19, 1986.

Acknowledgments

It is next to impossible to fully thank all those who have helped bring this book into being not only because so many have contributed but because those who did were so giving of themselves that it is difficult to find adequate words to convey my deep appreciation.

The women, men, and children who shared their family stories with me have been truly inspirational. My life has been enriched by coming to know them, and it saddens me that due to space constraints I have not been able to directly include all those I interviewed. Whether or not they appear in these pages, each contributed immeasurably to the book as a whole, and I am deeply grateful.

Many professionals shared their expertise and provided guidance. For their analyses of the legal ramifications of lesbian and gay parenting I am indebted to Abby Abinante, Karen Amlong, Lee Bantel, Kevin Cathcart, Beatrice Dohrn, Paula Ettelbrick, Maria Gil de Lamadrid, Ellen Muzinsky, Nancy Polikoff, and Susan Silber. I appreciate Liz Hendrickson's review of the manuscript with respect to its accuracy on legal issues. The National Center for

Acknowledgments

Lesbian Rights and Lambda Legal Defense and Education Fund were invaluable resources. For sharing their work in the field of education I am grateful to Virginia Caspar, James Clay, Steven Schultz, and Elaine Wickens. Eli Newberger's comments about his work in the field of psychiatry were extremely helpful. Barbara Raboy and Cynthia Underhill were very informative about current issues in donor insemination practices.

Several people gave generously of their time and resources throughout this endeavor. I owe special thanks to Robert Kay, Joshua Massey, and Brett Silverman.

This work could not have come to fruition without the extraordinary support of my family and friends. Their warm and patient encouragement kept me going at times when it was hard to see my way clear, and their sharp insights contributed greatly to the development of my thinking and writing. I am forever indebted to Beatrice Benkov, Sari Broner, Carol Cohn, Barbara Dean, Graham Dean, Naomi Dean, Rachael Dean, Jordan Dean, Tanya Donovan, Deborah Dormitzer, Paul Dormitzer, Sandy Farber, Susan Fleischmann, Ellen Grabiner, Liz Grabiner, Jill Kessler, Lauren Levine, Koreen McQuilton, Brian Morton, Abigail Norman, Sara Ruddick, Esther Samra, Sarah Schulman, Paul Wachtel, and Kathy Weingarten.

I am grateful to my editor, David Groff, and to my agent, Charlotte Sheedy, for her unstinting support throughout the development of this book.

Index

Index

Index